THE POLITICAL ECON
RELATIONS

The Political Economy of Industrial Relations

Theory and Practice in a Cold Climate

Richard Hyman

Professor of Industrial Relations
University of Warwick

MACMILLAN
PRESS

First published 1989

Published by
THE MACMILLAN PRESS LTD
Houndmills, Basingstoke, Hampshire RG21 2XS
and London
Companies and representatives
throughout the world

Typesetting by Footnote Graphics, Warminster

Printed in Hong Kong

British Library Cataloguing in Publication Data
Hyman, Richard, *1942*–
The political economy of industrial
relations: theory and practice in a cold
climate.
1. Industrial relations. Political aspects—
Great Britain
I. Title
331'.0941
IBSN 0–333–46430–3 (hardcover)
ISBN 0–333–46431–1 (paperback)

For Emma and Oliver, who would like to appear in print

Contents

Preface   ix

Acknowledgements   xvi

PART I   MAKING SENSE OF INDUSTRIAL
         RELATIONS

  1   Why Industrial Relations?   3

  2   Trade Unions, Control and Resistance   20

  3   Pluralism, Procedural Consensus and Collective
      Bargaining   54

  4   Pressure, Protest and Struggle: Some Problems in the
      Concept and Theory of Industrial Conflict   96

  5   Theory in Industrial Relations: Towards a Materialist
      Analysis   120

PART II   PROBLEMS OF CONTEMPORARY TRADE
          UNIONISM

  6   The Politics of Workplace Trade Unionism: Recent
      Tendencies and Some Problems for Theory   149

  7   The Sickness of British Trade Unionism: Is There a
      Cure?   166

  8   Dualism and Division in Labour Strategies   188

  9   Trade Unionism and the State: Some Recent European
      Developments   202

 10   Class Struggle and the Trade Union Movement   224

Index   255

Preface

I began teaching industrial relations, and learning the subject as I taught it, at the end of the 1960s. It was a time of radicalism and innovation in the social sciences, and of turbulence and creativity in the world outside academe – on the streets of Paris, in the jungles of Vietnam, in the escalating combativity of British trade unionists. Yet all this left industrial relations academics strangely unmoved. Across Europe, and in more muted form in North America, established institutions of class compromise were under challenge; yet academic industrial relations seemed caught in the time-warp of the transatlantic conservatism of the 1950s.

For any student of the subject who was involved in the contemporary politics of the left, there was an obvious need to develop an approach to industrial relations which could make sense of the assertiveness and combativity displayed by workers in mine and mill, factory and hospital, school and office. The categories and insights derived from Marxist analysis had a clear relevance to this task. In two works in particular – *Strikes* (1972) and *Industrial Relations: A Marxist Introduction* (1975) – I attempted to synthesise a wide array of issues within a broad interpretative argument in order to make sense of those developments which conventional analyses could scarcely comprehend. Both works appeared when the level of organisation, self-confidence and will to struggle among British trade unionists was the highest in my lifetime. Times have changed. I remain committed to the main thrust of my arguments in the 1970s, though I would qualify some points and express others differently. In the past ten years, however, I have felt the need to move from broad generalisation – which inevitably oversimplifies – to a narrower focus of investigation and analysis; and also to adapt arguments, first presented at a time of advance and confidence, to a very different political and economic context. Much of my recent writing has therefore taken the form of articles and papers rather than full-length books.

In this volume I have compiled ten of these essays, all written at different times and for different purposes, but covering interconnected themes. Several of them have not previously been published, and the rest are relatively inaccessible to the present-day reader. They are grouped into two broad sections. Part I, 'Making Sense of

Industrial Relations', addresses broad general issues concerning work in capitalist society, the role of trade unions, and the academic study of industrial relations.

The opening essay, 'Why Industrial Relations?', was delivered as an inaugural lecture at the University of Warwick in 1987. In it I argue that while early students of the subject were concerned to improve the 'conditions of labour', their recent successors have been preoccupied with the achievement of order in industry. What began as a reformist vision has become increasingly repressive in its implications. Only by revitalising the critical edge of our analyses, I conclude, can the humane aspirations of the best of the early writers be recovered.

'Trade Unions, Control and Resistance' was written in 1975 for an Open University course on the sociology of work. The central theme is the dialectic of acquiescence and resistance in employment relations. The contradictory pressures towards stability and instability in production relations are identified as a major explanation of the ambiguous character of trade unionism, affecting unions' relations with their members and with employers and the state. The detailed evidence discussed in this chapter is now dated, but much of the analysis remains relevant. It is significant that writing a dozen years ago, in the aftermath of the Heath government and its legislative constraints on trade unions, I stressed the importance of the resistance that developed at grassroots level; but also argued that such a response might not occur in the face of a future legislative offensive. Recent events have justified this caution.

'Pluralism, Procedural Consensus and Collective Bargaining' addresses more abstract issues. The dominant approach in post-war British industrial relations (that of my own teachers, indeed) was generally known as the pluralist perspective. Its central themes were the reality of opposing interests in industry; the legitimacy of their organised expression; and the probability that from the organisation of competing interests would develop a stable negotiated order. In the 1970s a former exponent of this approach, Alan Fox, developed a critique which insisted that the coherence of the pluralist model rested on a misleading assumption of a balance of power in industry. This was contested by Hugh Clegg; my own response to this debate appeared in 1978. Here I indicate the diversity of pluralist models of industrial relations, and suggest that ideas of balance are indeed inherent in most versions of pluralism. A key reason why pluralist authors assume that collective bargaining is the best recipe for stable industrial relations, I suggest, is because they give priority to the *procedures* involved rather than the substantive outcomes; and I question whether such consensual roots of liberal collective bargaining can survive the pressures of economic crisis.

The following chapter, Chapter 4, is also concerned with prevailing models of industrial relations analysis. Written for a conference in the Netherlands in 1980, 'Pressure, Protest and Struggle' looks critically at the common academic usage of the notion of industrial conflict. I suggest that by lumping together a diverse variety of types of action, usually within a managerial perspective, the rationality of workers' struggles is devalued. I go on to question the common assumption that strikes can be comprehended simply as incidents in the conduct of collective bargaining, insisting that they can also express important social and political motivations. Nevertheless, recent attempts to interpret conflict in terms of 'political exchange' are flawed. I end by stressing the important links between conflict, collective organisation and collective identity.

The final chapter in Part I, 'Theory in Industrial Relations', was written for the German Sociological Congress in 1979, appeared in French translation in *Sociologie du Travail*, and was subsequently published in Australia. My central concern is how far a distinctively Marxist approach to industrial relations does, or can, exist. The answer proposed is that, from a materialist perspective, the very idea of an industrial relations system lacks theoretical coherence; the task, accordingly, is not to re-interpret but to transcend the very idea of industrial relations. I explore the implications of this argument with reference to three distinct themes: managerial strategies in industrial relations;[1] the structure and composition of the working class; and the role of state intervention in capital–labour relations. I conclude by considering how far Marxism offers a distinctive theory of trade union action.

Part II of this volume, 'Problems of Contemporary Trade Unionism', focuses more directly on immediate issues of class relations and union action. 'The Politics of Workplace Trade Unionism', published in 1979, is an attempt to evaluate the increasing formalisation and consolidation of shop steward organisation in British industry during the 1970s. I argue that most accounts of workplace trade unionism – from both the right and the left – tend to exaggerate its oppositional character; and that institutional 'reforms' have reinforced its role as a force for order and discipline, to the potential advantage of the employer. Subsequent discussion of this essay has largely concentrated on my not-too-serious use of the notion of 'the bureaucratisa-tion of the rank and file'. There has been less attention to my concluding emphasis on the need to strengthen the mechanisms of democratic accountability between shop steward leaderships and the members they represent. The success of some managements in the 1980s in bypassing workplace union organisation and appealing directly to employees suggests that this theme is even more relevant today.

Chapter 7, 'The Sickness of British Trade Unionism', developed out of discussions in Germany in 1984, and was published in translation there in the journal *Prokla*; an Italian version also appeared in *Prospettiva Sindacale*. It examines the impact of the first five years of the Thatcher government, and argues that a hostile economic and political climate had exposed the fragile basis of apparent trade union strength in the two previous decades. In an analysis which parallels that of the previous chapter, I argue that a fundamental problem has been a growing separation between the internal political life of trade union (and Labour Party) activists, and the beliefs and aspirations of those they claim to represent. Behind this, it would appear, lies a bureaucratic conception of socialism which radical conservatism has successfully challenged. The response, I suggest, is not some 'new realism' in which key ideals are abandoned or content gives way to style and packaging, but an *active* engagement with the experiences and initiatives of ordinary women and men, challenging the artificial division between 'work' and 'life', and seeking to rekindle a credible vision of a humane alternative to capitalism.

The next two essays are comparative in focus. 'Dualism and Division in Labour Strategies' was written for a conference in Frankfurt in 1985, at which the central debate was whether those relations between unions and the state often defined as 'corporatist' had been decisively abandoned in the 1980s, or might be restored in a new guise. I suggest that a dichotomy between 'corporatism' and 'labour exclusion' as state or employer strategies is unduly simplistic. A distinctive feature of British industrial relations in the past decade – in marked contrast, say, to the USA – has been that while managements have adopted a tougher stance, they have rarely sought to exclude trade unionism where it is already established. Old institutions persist, even if their practical effect is reduced. I offer a sketch of the way in which segmentation in product and labour markets appears to be associated with these trends. 'Dual labour market' theories commonly identify two ideal types: secure, advantaged employees with strong collective organisation; and the weak, vulnerable and disorganised. In the period of recession and de-industrialisation, however, there has clearly emerged a substantial group of workers who fit neither type: they are not exposed to significant competition from the external labour market, but are collectively vulnerable to redundancy. In a brief consideration of the implications of this trend, I suggest that a key issue is whether such trade unionists pursue narrowly sectional and exclusive strategies of self-defence, or see their vulnerability as part of a broader social crisis which requires common action with other groups.

The chapter on 'Trade Unionism and the State' was presented to a conference of the Association d'Économie Politique in Montreal in 1987. Here my central concern is how far trade unions' economic weakness, particularly at workplace level, may be offset by supportive legislation. In Britain, extensive legal supports for both individual employees and their collective representatives were endorsed by the TUC and the Labour Party in 1986; I examined this programme critically in an article published in *Capital and Class* immediately before the 1987 election.[2] The chapter in this volume looks more generally at the relationship between the state and workplace industrial relations, drawing on evidence from four European countries as well as Britain. I identify the paradox that those trade union movements which might benefit most from legislative support are worst placed to achieve this. Genuinely advantageous legislation, I suggest, normally requires the mobilisation of effective popular pressure; where trade unions are weak, this normally reflects an erosion of their active popular base. In conclusion, I suggest that any effective union strategy must involve the forging of an effective link between workplace organisation and action, and national political programmes.

The theme of Chapter 7 is continued in 'Class Struggle and the Trade Union Movement', published in *A Socialist Anatomy of Britain* in 1985. Its emphasis is on the contradictory character of trade unionism, as a force both for struggle and for order; hence the contradictory responses of employers and governments. I provide a survey of the current state of British unionism (updated for this volume), analysing the losses which have been suffered during the past decade, and seeking their underlying source in the bureaucratic tendencies within the internal social relations of trade unions as collective organisations. These tendencies, I insist, are not irreversible: there are no 'iron laws' of trade union development. Today, as always, trade unions are open to change; for socialists, they constitute both a problem and an opportunity.

*   *   *

The sub-title of this book is 'Theory and Practice in a Cold Climate'. At first sight it might seem that Part I focuses on theory, Part 2 on practice. Such a division, however, would be misleading. Theory unrelated to practical experience is the worst form of academicism. But conversely, as the familiar maxim insists, practice without theory is blind. What differentiates the two parts of this volume is the predominant level of abstraction of the various essays; an attempt to unite theory and practice is present throughout.

That trade unions – in Britain and virtually every other country of the Western world – are operating in a cold climate is scarcely a contentious argument. The economic environment has sharply deteriorated, and political regimes are far more hostile than in previous decades. Membership, and influence, have generally declined, though not always as fast as in Britain. Two responses to this predicament appear to predominate. The first involves a reiteration of trade unions' traditional rhetoric, in the hope that if proclaimed loud enough the members – and those employees outside the ranks of unionism – will begin to hear. This, however, is to misunderstand the changing composition and expectations of the workforce, and to ignore the evidence that the old slogans no longer appeal to more than a dwindling band of enthusiasts. The other response is to accommodate to the privatised, consumer-oriented drift of contemporary society, and to seek recruits on the basis of personal services: to present the union, in effect, as a combination of insurance company and discount store. The danger here is that the individualist orientations which inhibit union membership are reinforced; and that a passive relationship between member and union is accentuated, making effective collective action the more difficult.

There are no easy solutions. The principles of collective protection of common interests, and of striving for a social and economic order in which ordinary people have control of their own destinies, remain worthy and valid. What has been lost is a language through which these principles can be effectively articulated, and a texture of relations through which their collective pursuit can appear credible. In the third term of an aggressive and profoundly anti-social government, theoretical analysis – the search for a deeper and more adequate understanding of the roots of our current predicament – is not a luxury but a necessity.

I hope that this collection, in its attempt to connect the phenomena of industrial relations to the broader political, economic and ideological forces within our society, will aid such an understanding; and that in better comprehending our world we may enlarge our ability to change it.

RICHARD HYMAN

Notes

1. I have recently offered a more elaborate analysis of this theme in 'Strategy or Structure? Capital, Labour and Control', *Work, Employment and Society*, Vol. 1, 1987.
2. 'Trade Unions and the Law: Papering Over the Cracks?', *Capital and Class*, No. 31, Spring 1987.

Acknowledgements

Several of the essays included in this volume have previously been published elsewhere, though in most cases they have been amended for the present collection. The author and publishers are grateful for permission to reprint:

Chapter 2 was originally published in Geoff Esland and Graeme Salaman, *The Politics of Work and Occupations*, Milton Keynes, Open University Press, 1980.

Chapter 3 appeared in the *British Journal of Industrial Relations*, Vol. 16, No. 1, March 1978.

Chapter 4 was first printed in G. B. J. Bomers and R. B. Peterson, *Conflict Management and Industrial Relations*, Kluwer-Nijhoff, 1982.

Chapter 5 originally appeared in Paul Boreham and Geoff Dow, *Work and Inequality: Ideology and Control in the Capitalist Labour Process*, Macmillan Australia, 1980.

Chapter 6 was published in *Capital and Class*, No. 8, Summer 1979.

Chapter 10 was written for David Coates, Gordon Johnston and Ray Bush, *A Socialist Anatomy of Britain*, Cambridge, Polity Press, 1985.

Part I

Making Sense of Industrial Relations

1 Why Industrial Relations?*

I have chosen to begin with a dangerous question. 'Why indeed?' is the predictable response. Teaching and research in industrial relations are widely viewed with disfavour or suspicion. For some of our learned colleagues the subject is not properly academic: an amorphous and eclectic mishmash, without adequate disciplinary foundation. To many practitioners we are *too* academic; often we are also accused of bias, managers seeing us as pro-union, trade unionists as pro-management. Those who endorse the philosophies of the current government tend to despise industrial relations, as an expression of the system of sectional interest representation and compromise which they denounce as a major cause of Britain's economic problems. Even among industrial relations academics themselves one can detect considerable doubt and uncertainty as to the nature and status of our subject in a changing world of work. [1]

Why then industrial relations? My answer will involve all three tenses, considering in turn the origins of academic industrial relations, its modern development, and its future potential. My central theme is the existence of two faces of what was once known as the 'labour question': the problems of social welfare on the one hand, social order on the other. The scholarly study of industrial relations was stimulated by the apparent coincidence of these two faces; but today they are clearly opposed. In consequence we are forced to redefine the nature and purpose of our subject. This involves us in choices which may well prove difficult and uncomfortable.

ORIGINS OF INDUSTRIAL RELATIONS

It is a commonplace that the study of industrial relations is typically descriptive and pragmatic, the analysis unsupported by an explicit theoretical framework. And even the *empirical* focus of the subject is far from clear. The term 'industrial relations' conveys little substantive meaning to the uninitiated, and was itself invented some time

*Inaugural lecture delivered at University of Warwick, 3 February 1987.

after the first studies in the subject area. These originated a century ago in the growing preoccupation of the upper classes with what they identified as the 'labour question' or 'labour problem'. Their concern made its mark on the machinery of government with the appointment of the Royal Commission on Labour in 1891, and the creation within the Board of Trade in 1893 of a Labour Department which in 1917 was to attain the status of a separate Ministry.

The terms of reference of the Royal Commission could have served, until recently at least, as a passable definition of industrial relations: 'questions affecting the relations between employer and employed, the combinations of employer and employed, and the conditions of labour'. Attention to these issues was stimulated by two major developments in the 1880s. The first was the movement popularly known as 'new unionism': the rapid spread of trade union organisation beyond its established strongholds, the apparent growth of political radicalism among workers' organisations, and an upsurge in the level of industrial conflict (dramatically symbolised by the great London dock strike of 1889). In these circumstances, the labour question was perceived as a problem of social order. Simultaneously, however, there was a growing awareness of the depth and extent of poverty and the associated deprivations suffered by a large section of the working class. Social investigators documented workers' circumstances in painstaking and often lurid detail, most notably in the monumental study by Charles Booth and his associates, *Labour and Life of the People in London*, the first volumes of which appeared in the same year, 1889. Thus the labour question was also perceived as a problem of social welfare.[2]

In America, analogous concerns led Congress in 1912 to appoint a Commission on Industrial Relations, with terms of reference more detailed than those of the British Royal Commission but similar in substance. Though not perhaps the first use of the phrase 'industrial relations', this is certainly the first instance of its widespread propagation. In Britain, the innovation was slow to catch on: the title of the Whitley Committee, established in 1916, involved the older and more ponderous phrase 'relations between employers and employed'. The first public document to utilise the modern terminology was the *Survey of Industrial Relations* produced by the Balfour Committee on Industry and Trade in 1926, and described as an 'inquiry into methods of industrial remuneration, the main causes of unrest and disputes, and the methods of avoidance or settlement of disputes'.

Early British interest in industrial relations – before the term itself
was adopted – was marked by what may be called a *reformist
paradigm*. The widespread assumption was that the two faces of the
labour problem were interdependent, and thus could not be resolved
in isolation. This argument was most eloquently expressed in the
Minority Report of the Royal Commission on Labour: 'the fundamental cause of disputes between employers and employed is to be
found, we believe, in the unsatisfactory position occupied by the
wage-earning class'. The dimensions of this position were itemised:
low pay and poverty, unemployment, long hours of work and
systematic overtime, accidents and disease, and the more pervasive
facts of economic inequality. 'With economic conditions such as we
have described,' the authors continued, 'the relations between
employers and employed cannot, in our view, fail to be unsatisfactory. Strikes, and other signs of resistance on the part of the
wage-earners, however inconvenient they may be in themselves, are
only symptomatic of a discontent with existing social conditions,
which we regard as healthful and promising.'[3]

What adds to the significance of these comments is that they were
written, at least in large measure, by Sidney Webb,[4] who with
Beatrice Webb was the pioneer of scholarly analysis of industrial
relations. Beatrice herself had formerly worked as a member of
Booth's research team, and had invented the term 'collective
bargaining' – soon to be made a key concept in industrial relations
analysis by the Webbs' masterpiece *Industrial Democracy*.

Ironically, given subsequent trade union commitment to 'free
collective bargaining' as an almost overriding principle, Sidney Webb
and the trade union signatories of the Minority Report proposed
extensive statutory regulation of employment relations. But the
Majority Report, while agreeing, in effect, that both aspects of the
labour question must be resolved together, prescribed a totally
different solution: one which was to dominate public policy for
almost a century. 'Many of the evils to which our attention has been
called are such as cannot be remedied by any legislation, but we may
look in confidence to their gradual amendment by natural forces.'
Large-scale industry, the Commission argued, had proved a source
of division and conflict; but social relations were becoming self-
regulating through the growth of collective organisation on the part
of capital and labour. 'Powerful trades unions on the one side and
powerful associations of employers on the other have been the means
of bringing together in conference the representatives of both classes

enabling each to appreciate the position of the other, and to understand the conditions subject to which their joint undertaking must be conducted.'[5]

In brief, stable institutions of employer–union relations had developed largely autonomously and spontaneously, at least in the major industries; and they should be left free to continue on the same basis. State intervention was more likely to exacerbate than to ameliorate conflict. Within government, among leading employers and in trade unions themselves, this soon became an established principle. Collective bargaining was the preferred and socially appropriate mechanism for handling employment issues; the role of the state should be primarily supportive and auxiliary. The perceived virtue of this arrangement was indicated by such approving labels as 'voluntarism' and 'industrial self-government'. Industrial relations thus became consolidated as a distinctive, and accepted, sphere of social interaction.

From these institutional developments can be traced the emergence of industrial relations as a distinct area of academic analysis. The pioneering work of the Webbs has already been mentioned; they were followed by G. D. H. Cole, who like them combined scholarly research with practical engagement in contemporary policy debates. The first university professorships in the subject were created in 1930, with an endowment by Montague Burton; their brief was to study 'the conditions of employment and the relations between employers and employed, with special reference to the causes of industrial disputes and the methods of promoting industrial peace.'

The origins of academic industrial relations thus lie in a public policy commitment to collective bargaining as the main vehicle of social welfare and social control in industry. This British development may be contrasted with circumstances in most of Europe, where employment relations were subject to far more pervasive legal regulation, and collective bargaining attained far less significance. In consequence, the notion of industrial relations rarely figures in most European vocabularies (except as a recent and self-conscious translation from the English). The subject entered British universities with an explicitly pragmatic charter, the reflection of a reformist paradigm and a more general belief in the practical relevance of academic enquiry. Uniting all these themes is the pioneering role of the Webbs, with their sustained commitment to an integrated project of empirical research, theoretical analysis and policy formulation.

MODERN INDUSTRIAL RELATIONS

Modern academic industrial relations has maintained some of these
original linkages, though until very recently the Webbs' theoretical
interests had few followers. In a changed environment, however, the
connection between academic study and public policy has acquired
very different implications, with a shift in the relative importance of
social welfare and social control. The meaning of reformism has
altered accordingly.

The most obvious aspect of the recent development of the subject
is quantitative growth, far more rapid than the general expansion of
higher education. Departments, chairs and courses have proliferated.
The British Universities' Industrial Relations Association, established three decades ago, now lists 300 members. Most notable of all
has been the emergence of Warwick University as an international
centre of excellence in teaching and research.

Today, as in the period of its early growth, the development of
academic industrial relations must be seen against the background of
public policy. The now traditional commitment to collective bargaining was reaffirmed and strengthened in the Second World War and
with the post-war establishment of the Keynesian welfare state. With
near-full employment, trade unions expanded their membership and
extended their bargaining relationships. On the employers' side,
industrial relations became incorporated as a distinctive managerial
function with its own staff specialists. Government agencies took a
more active interest – though modest by continental standards – in
the functioning of the labour market. All these developments
encouraged the rise of a substantial corps of industrial relations
professionals.

The requirements of such practitioners helped encourage the
extension of industrial relations teaching from the adult education
courses which had formerly predominated to fully fledged degree
programmes. One consequence was a growing concern with the
academic status of industrial relations. The early students of the
subject had their disciplinary roots in economics, law or (less often)
sociology; many of their successors defined themselves primarily as
industrial relations specialists, and there were calls to establish the
subject's credentials as a discipline in its own right. A positive
outcome was a shift from the overwhelming eclecticism of much
post-war work to a greater intellectual coherence. A key figure in this

process was Allan Flanders, who ended his career at Warwick: he was the first British industrial relations scholar since the Webbs to devote sustained attention to theory. In particular he sought to give rigorous meaning to the familiar notion of an industrial relations system, leading him to define the subject as 'a study of the institutions of job regulation'.[6]

This emphasis on rules and regulation has informed the bulk of recent research and teaching. The outcome was a sharper focus, but in my view the redefinition of industrial relations involved costs as well as benefits. New disciplines are unlikely to gain admittance to Academe unless they display modesty and deference in the face of established subject areas, and due respect for conventional demarcations. In the case of industrial relations, the entry fee appears to have involved the abandonment of the broad social and political concerns of the pioneer studies. The problem of welfare was relegated to the periphery, while the preoccupation with job regulation brought the problem of control to the centre of the agenda.

In this the trends in scholarly analysis meshed with those in public policy, coinciding with a period in which industrial relations was the focus of intense political controversy. At the level of industry-wide relations between employers' organisations and trade unions, experience since the 1930s appeared to validate the predictions of the Royal Commission on Labour: official national strikes had virtually disappeared. But there was widespread criticism of other aspects of British industrial relations: allegedly there existed an intolerable volume of unofficial strikes, an inflationary pattern of competitive decentralised wage bargaining, pervasive restrictive practices, and a deep-rooted resistance to change. Such phenomena were often attributed to excessive trade union power, in turn encouraged by the absence of the discipline of unemployment and the lack of a satisfactory framework of legal control.

Such contentions led to the appointment in 1965 of a Royal Commission on Trade Unions and Employers' Associations under Lord Donovan. Almost all prominent figures in academic industrial relations were involved in its proceedings, either as Commissioners, as contributors to its research programme, or as witnesses. The eventual report was largely the work of Hugh Clegg, newly appointed as the first Professor of Industrial Relations at Warwick.

The central and memorable argument of the Donovan Report was that 'Britain has two systems of industrial relations. The one is the formal system embodied in the official institutions. The other is the informal system created by the actual behaviour of trade unions and employers' associations, of managers, shop stewards and workers.'[7] National collective bargaining no longer functioned, as the 1891 Commission had argued, as a source of industrial peace, because it had become detached from the increasingly important area of workplace industrial relations. National trade unions and employers' associations were largely incompetent to regulate bargaining at this level; formal procedures offered insufficient guidelines; and managers themselves lacked coherent and consistent policies. The inevitable outcome was a state of 'anarchy and disorder' in workplace relations. This could not be blamed on trade union power: the lack of official control over decentralised bargaining was a sign of weakness rather than strength; nor on shop stewards who were so often denounced as trouble-makers. 'For the most part the steward is viewed by others, and views himself, as an acceptable, reasonable and even moderating influence: more of a lubricant than an irritant.'[8]

This analysis reflected, and further encouraged, a shift in the definition of the subject. The study of industrial relations turned increasingly from formal national institutions to patterns of workplace relations; from the perspectives of the economist or lawyer to those of the sociologist; from documentation to field research. And the intimate connection between academic study and public policy which the Donovan Commission exemplified formed part of a more general process in which official bodies with a bewildering succession of acronyms drew extensively on academic research and personnel. In the years of the subject's rapid expansion, analysis overlapped with prescription and administration in the pursuit of industrial relations reform.

This concept of reform requires elaboration. The philosophy embraced by most recent scholars in industrial relations has stressed the existence of real divisions of interest within industry; but has gone on to insist that conflict can be contained by appropriate institutional arrangements. 'Co-operation needs to be engineered', in the words of one influential research paper prepared for the Donovan Commission.[9] The recommendations of the Royal Commission, and the consensus among academics, identified a solution to disorderly industrial relations in more elaborate and systematic procedure agreements, stronger industrial relations management, and greater integration of shop stewards within official union structures. Above all else, bringing on to the agenda of formally sanctioned plant or company bargaining the issues hitherto determined by covert pressure and *ad hoc* trade-offs would enable managements to 'regain control by sharing it'.[10]

What must be emphasised is that the reformist paradigm associated with the emergence of industrial relations scholarship has now been transformed. For the Webbs, collective bargaining was a *vehicle* of reform. It was an instrument for raising workers' material conditions, and would play its part in a broader reconstruction of industry and society. The title of their analysis of trade unionism, *Industrial Democracy*, was carefully chosen. But today the focus is far more introspective: the reform envisaged is primarily that of collective bargaining itself. The Donovan Commission exemplified this restrictive focus. In its terms of reference it was charged 'to consider relations between managements and employees and the role of trade unions and employers' associations in promoting the interests of their members and in accelerating the social and economic advance of the nation'. But it functioned largely as a Commission on collective bargaining. Disorder in bargaining relationships, and the *managerial* problems which result, preoccupied the Commission to the virtual exclusion of all other considerations. The interests of trade union members, the priorities and problems of their working lives, the aspirations *they* identified with the 'social and economic advance of the nation', were simply ignored.

Much the same can be said of modern academic approaches to industrial relations. The focus of analysis is unambiguously the problem of social order, but largely divorced from the problem of social welfare. The 'conditions of labour' to which the 1891 Commission devoted such detailed attention have disappeared from the agenda.

THE FUTURE OF INDUSTRIAL RELATIONS

It is now time to look to the future of industrial relations. My aim is to establish that the reform of collective bargaining cannot remain our central concern, for reasons both of principle and of pragmatism. It will accord with the subject's practical bent to begin with the latter.

What explains the traditional acceptance of the voluntarist framework by all parties to industrial relations? Why was collective bargaining for so long effective in containing and institutionalising industrial conflict? Three factors are of key significance. The first is the early emergence of industrial capitalism in Britain, and its protracted dominance in the world economy. This provided a material basis for peaceable industrial relations: most firms possessed a margin for compromise. Secondly we may note the modesty and self-restraint traditionally displayed by British unions; in the main they have been more concerned to preserve customary standards, and customary relationships between the pay of one group of workers and another, than to pursue radical advances in their members' situation. And for most of their history, the internal disciplines of union organisation have ensured that more assertive sections of the membership have been kept under control; unions have functioned, in the classic phrase, as 'managers of discontent'.[11] A third feature is the pervasive influence of the liberal social order in Britain: a source of deference on the part of subordinate classes, readiness to compromise on the part of their rulers.[12]

There is little need to emphasise that these preconditions of stability have been largely eroded. Economic crisis has consumed the margin for compromise. Not only is wage bargaining more constrained; managements are under pressure to rationalise and restructure production in ways which threaten jobs and overturn the established unwritten agreements – or 'custom and practice' – governing work organisation. Trade unions are still, in the main, modest in their official objectives; indeed, the much-discussed 'new realism' of the 1980s elevates traditional restraint to a point of principle. But their effectiveness as managers of discontent has been undermined by the decentralisation of union activity in the post-war era. The liberal order has also lost its grip. Recent years have seen on the one hand a rise in individual assertiveness, leading some commentators to speak of the ungovernability of Britain; on the other hand there have been growing demands for strong government, reciprocated by increased state authoritarianism. In such a climate, the genteel conventions of liberal industrial relations have proved fragile indeed.

Other material changes may be added to the catalogue. The structure of employment has shifted from aggregations of 'mass workers' in large urban factories to smaller, more dispersed units; from manufacturing and extractive industries to services; from manual to white-collar occupations; from traditional employment contracts to part-time work and self-employment. Work relations no longer seem to generate a natural and spontaneous collectivism.

The political changes just mentioned mark the culmination of a long-term erosion of the foundations of the 'non-interventionist' tradition. In the post-war decades the state has acquired an inescapable role as an economic manager and hence a potent interest in the outcome of collective bargaining; overtly or covertly, wage restraint has been a persistent component of macroeconomic policy. This concern has been reinforced by the substantial post-war growth in public employment, the pressures to curb state expenditure, and the consequential problems of public sector industrial relations. Not surprisingly, politicians have found it attractive to cast trade unions as scapegoats for economic decline.

Finally, employers have posed a major challenge to accommodative traditions. Market stringency and government encouragement (not to mention industrial relations academics) have impelled employers to seize the initiative in industrial relations. In the 1970s their policies appeared to match the Donovan prescriptions: pursuing greater control over labour costs and work organisation through a deepening and broadening of collective bargaining. But employer commitment to pluralist principles would seem to have been transitional and opportunistic. It is true that American-style de-unionisation has not been imitated by most British companies in the 1980s, but there is obvious resistance to unionisation in new sectors of employment. More significant, though, is the evidence of discreet efforts to *marginalise* trade unions even while recognising their continued right to operate. The traditional area of policy autonomy permitted to industrial relations managers has been eliminated in many major firms; they are now subordinated to broader company strategies in product design, production organisation and financial management. The formalities of collective bargaining remain, but its scope and effectiveness are severely restricted. Workers' collective identification with trade unions is challenged by the cultivation of *internal* mechanisms created and controlled by management. [13]

Thus as industrial relations is consolidated within institutions of higher learning, its traditional terrain of study would appear to be crumbling. It can no longer be assumed that collective bargaining is the dominant form of job regulation in Britain. Where, then, do we go from here? One response is to *redefine* industrial relations in terms of the management of the employment relationship. Trade unions and collective bargaining are thus presented as contingent elements rather than essential components of the subject. This ingenious tactic presents two problems. The first is that, far from guaranteeing the continued distinctiveness of industrial relations as a field of study, it threatens to submerge it within the more general analysis of business management and corporate strategy. The second is that it raises in particularly urgent form the issue of the relationship between academic and practical industrial relations. The two faces of the labour question re-appear, and force us to consider fundamental issues of principle.

It has been seen that the emergence of academic industrial relations, and in particular the rapid expansion from the 1960s, was based in large measure on the *relevance* of scholarly analysis to those concerned with the *management* of industrial relations: in government, in private companies, and to a lesser extent in trade union leadership. Modern industrial relations scholars have often embraced the role of change agents in the process of industrial relations reform. Yet what are the implications of this role if the texture of industrial relations has altered substantially and the liberal institutions of interest accommodation are in decline? The job description of the industrial relations scholar-consultant is then unambiguously to aid, advise and reinforce management in exerting unilateral control over the workforce.

Today, as the pressures for 'relevance' intensify, it is well to recall the words spoken forty years ago by C. Wright Mills, the liberal conscience of post-war American sociology and also an inaugural Vice-President of the Industrial Relations Research Association. At its first annual meeting in 1948 Mills identified an emergent trend in American academic life:

a new sort of career, different from that of the old-fashioned professor, has become available: the career of 'the new entrepreneur'. This type of man ... is able to further his career in the university by securing prestige ... outside it. Above all, he is able to set up on campus a respectably-financed institute that brings the academic community into live contact with men of affairs – thus often becoming a leader in university affairs among his more cloistered colleagues. ... The new developments in industrial relations research and administration offer quite gratifying opportunities to become, so to speak, executives without having to become Deans.[14]

The problem, argued Mills, was that the price of external backing was often a commitment to the interests and objectives of managements, even when these conflicted with those of workers. In consequence, academic production could be reduced to advice to the personnel manager to relax his authoritative manner and widen his manipulative grip by understanding employees better and countering their informal solidarities against management by controlling and exploiting these solidarities for smoother and less troublesome managerial efficiency.... To secure the spontaneous, efficient collaboration of his workers the manager must pay attention to their informal relations.... The answer ... is an institutionalization of manipulation.[15]

These comments were, of course, bound by a specific time and place, though some may detect parallels between the 'human relations' analysts against whom Mills directed his critique, and the exponents of what is today termed 'human resource management'. In any event it remains important to remember that certain kinds of 'relevance' can impose too high a price. Robert Merton, a far more respectable sociologist than Wright Mills ever wished to be, made this point somewhat coyly: 'an intelligence staff for one stratum of the business and industrial population may in due course find itself focusing on problems which are not the chief problems confronting other sectors of that population'.[16] To speak more plainly: power corrupts; and in some circumstances a reformist paradigm is corrupted into a *repressive paradigm*. This is particularly likely when, in the cause of relevance, academics seek to foster order and efficiency without recognising that the meaning of these ambiguous notions has been predefined in terms of the interests of the powerful and against those of 'other sectors'. Such scholars address as merely technical problems what are essentially *political* conflicts.

At Warwick the Industrial Relations Research Unit has been conscious of such pressures, but has sought to resist them. The reason is simple: all too often, conceptions of relevance are unacceptably one-sided. As a corrective we may recall the Minority Report of the 1891 Commission and its catalogue of the 'conditions of labour'. Low pay and poverty still disgrace our society; if absolute deprivation is no longer at the depths prevalent in the 1880s, against the higher standards which are justifiably applied a century later we can scarcely claim progress. Unemployment is as severe a blight, despite modern advances in economic understanding. The uneven *distribution* of what work is available (a problem discussed by Sidney Webb in terms of the still widespread practice of systematic overtime) is a vital contemporary issue, raising fundamental questions of the relationship between employment and broader social existence. Industrial accidents and diseases remain extensive: each week there are 400 major reported accidents, and twelve workers are killed. While some ninteenth-century dangers at work have been curbed or eliminated, they have been exchanged for new technological hazards, often introduced in complete disregard of their possible effects on employees. Economic inequality has survived successive reforming governments, and its dimensions have been deliberately accentuated in the 1980s.

All these issues are in my view of essential relevance to the study of industrial relations. The conclusion reached in 1894 still holds: 'with economic conditions such as we have described, the relations between employers and employed cannot fail to be unsatisfactory'. But today it is far clearer than a century ago that, however important it may be to defend collective bargaining against powerful opponents, collective bargaining is not a sufficient solution to these problems. As the Webbs recognised, its achievements are always constrained by the prevailing balance of power between workers, employers and governments. In addition, it tends to reflect and reinforce inequalities among employees themselves; the weak and vulnerable are commonly marginalised or excluded. More fundamentally still, the very agenda of collective bargaining is itself narrowly confined by broader structures of power. Thus these too must come within our field of vision, if industrial relations analysis is not to be confined to the trivial and parochial.

A few such broader themes may be considered by way of illustration: for example, the remarkably pervasive relationship between work and inequality. Bertrand Russell made the point succinctly:

> work is of two kinds: first, altering the position of matter at or near the earth's surface relatively to other such matter; second, telling other people to do so. The first kind is unpleasant and ill paid; the second is pleasant and highly paid. The second kind is capable of indefinite extension: there are not only those who give orders, but those who give advice as to what orders should be given.[17]

It follows that inequality at work has a *political* dimension, which is intimately connected to its economic dimension. Yet *must* work relations be authoritarian and undemocratic? Are aspirations for industrial democracy utopian? Academics whose own work implicates them in authoritarian structures should surely not evade such questions.

Political inequality within work may be viewed as one reflection of the division of labour. At one pole there is a fragmentation of tasks and competences; at the other, a process of strategic conception and direction within the organisational hierarchy. Yet a division of labour exists within management hierarchies also. Is it a measure of technical progress that we *all* seem subordinated to impersonal domination?

At the macro level, we appear the victims of the dynamics of an economic system out of identifiable control, and this reflects a double paradox in the social organisation of our productive system. The first aspect is the *competitive* basis of socio-economic activity, when its increasingly complex interdependence demands co-operation and integration. We are victims, in the words of Fred Hirsch, of the 'tyranny of small decisions':[18] afflicted by the manifestly irrational aggregate effects of a cumulation of discrete strategies and actions, all rational within their own narrow parameters. Thus individual employers reduce labour costs by dismissing workers, only to swell the unemployment totals and impose an unproductive burden on national resources. Is this what is meant by economic realism?

The second component of the paradox, far harder to indicate with brevity, is the dominance of utilitarian principles within economic activity. Here again it is possible to speak of conflicting rationalities: the systematic calculation of costs and benefits can displace the systematic appraisal of ultimate objectives. Thus ends can become subordinated to means. A passage from another American sociologist, Alvin Gouldner, illustrates the implications for work when technique overrides purpose:

> the malaise of modern industrial society . . . derives from the fact that it relates to men and incorporates them primarily as utilities useful for performing functions, that it has no commitment towards the talents or needs of men except as they are useful in the production of marketable objects or services. It pays for a man's skills but everything else he is, or has, or wants, is – within the context of producing objects or services – subordinated to their efficient employment.

These criteria lead to the forced exclusion of many from employment; but even those who pass this test, argues Gouldner, possess an 'unemployed self' which is suppressed or discarded as unproductive to the employer.[19] His argument, of course, applies no less to women than to men: they are increasingly absorbed into the utilitarian sphere of the labour market. But we must also note the profound importance of a sexual division of labour which assigns women primary responsibilities in the supposedly *non*-utilitarian sphere of domestic production and reproduction. The utilitarian criteria which inform social definitions of work and worth, to the systematic exclusion of such domestic activities, are among the components of inequality in gender relations. There is no wealth but life, declared Ruskin. Is it the summit of human achievement to have turned this maxim on its head?

The aggregate outcome of these contextual conditions of work and employment were summarised in the 1960s by Marcuse, in terms which seem even more apt today: 'a comfortable, smooth, reasonable, democratic unfreedom prevails in advanced industrial civilization, a token of technical progress.'[20] Is there indeed no alternative?

No doubt there are many who will demand irritably: what relevance has all of this to industrial relations? My answer is that social scientists are increasingly obliged to choose between repressive and emancipatory paradigms; and students of industrial relations cannot avoid a similar choice. The emancipatory tradition has a long and honourable history, rooted in the conviction that social research and theorising can unravel the unrecognised determinants and consequences of social action, demonstrating the hidden implications of what is customarily taken for granted. As members of a society become aware of hitherto neglected processes which shape their lives, so they are enabled to consider alternatives. Hence social science can contribute to the mutual enlargement of freedom and reason.

This tradition offers a worthy goal for the study of industrial relations: nothing less than the extension of freedom and reason in the world of work. The implication is that both faces of the 'labour problem' must be investigated as the outcome of deeper, structural problems. To comprehend these we must relate the micro to the macro, the national to the international, pursuing what I have elsewhere termed a political economy of industrial relations. And where analysis connects with practice, the emancipatory tradition implies a redefinition of the reformist paradigm: a broader and more critical conception of the problem of social order, a re-forging of the links with the problem of welfare which the pioneers of industrial relations appreciated. Now, as then, the creation of a stable, morally acceptable order in industry requires the resolution of the far wider issue of the conditions of labour.

This diagnosis may not be popular in some quarters. For many who wield economic and political sway, the traditional values of freedom and reason are uncongenial. To defend these values – in industrial relations as in academic life more generally – purely abstract arguments of principle are unlikely to succeed. We must make our analyses relevant – not in the sense often understood by powerful philistines, but by connecting our intellectual work with the predicaments and aspirations of a broader but less privileged constituency.

If knowledge is power, we must demonstrate that it can be a power not only to dominate but also to emancipate. This, in my view, is the only acceptable answer to the question: why industrial relations?

Notes

1. In the USA, such uncertainties have resulted in the virtual disappearance of industrial relations as a separate academic subject.
2. See Roger Davidson, *Whitehall and the Labour Problem in Late-Victorian and Edwardian England*, Croom Helm, 1985.
3. Royal Commission on Labour, *Fifth and Final Report*, C-7421, 1894, pp. 127–9.
4. See Beatrice Webb, *Our Partnership*, Longmans Green, 1948, pp. 41–2.
5. Royal Commission on Labour, p. 112.
6. Allan Flanders, *Industrial Relations: What is Wrong With the System?*, Faber, 1965, p. 10.
7. Royal Commission on Trade Unions and Employers' Associations, *Report*, Cmnd 3623, 1968, p. 12.
8. *Ibid.*, p. 29, quoting a research paper written by the Commission's research director, W. E. J. McCarthy.
9. Alan Fox, *Industrial Sociology and Industrial Relations*, HMSO, 1966, p. 14.
10. Allan Flanders, *Collective Bargaining: Prescription for Change*, Faber, 1967, p. 32.
11. C. Wright Mills, *The New Men of Power*, Harcourt Brace, 1948, p. 9.
12. For a far more extensive, and more nuanced, discussion of these traditional influences see Alan Fox, *History and Heritage*, Allen and Unwin, 1985.
13. See, for example, the symposia in *British Journal of Industrial Relations*, Vol. 22, No. 2, 1986 and *Employee Relations*, Vol. 8, No. 5, 1986.
14. C. Wright Mills, 'The Contribution of Sociology to Studies of Industrial Relations', in *Proceedings of the First Annual Meeting of the Industrial Relations Research Association 1948*, IRRA, 1949, pp. 205–6. Much of this address was adapted and included in Mills' later book, *The Sociological Imagination*.
15. *Ibid.*, pp. 215–18.

16.   Robert K. Merton, *Social Theory and Social Structure*, Free Press, 1957 (originally published 1949), p. 571.
17.   Bertrand Russell, *In Praise of Idleness and Other Essays*, Allen and Unwin, 1960, p. 13.
18.   Fred Hirsch, *Social Limits to Growth*, Harvard University Press, 1977, p. 41.
19.   Alvin W. Gouldner, 'The Unemployed Self', in Ronald Fraser (ed.) *Work 2*, Penguin, 1969, p. 355.
20.   Herbert Marcuse, *One Dimensional Man*, Sphere, 1968, p. 19.

2 Trade Unions, Control and Resistance*

JOB CONTROL AND CAPITALISM

For the great majority of the 'occupied population'[1] (in Britain, over 90 per cent), work equals wage-labour. Labour relations are thus, at the outset, market relations. The prospective worker must find an employer willing to pay a wage or salary in return for the disposal of his/her skill, knowledge or physical capacities; and can expect such employment to last only so long as this willingness continues. Labour thus has the status of a commodity; and as with all market relationships, the interests of buyers and sellers are antagonistic. The wages and conditions sought by the employee as the means to a decent life, both within and outside work, are a *cost* cutting into the employer's profits. In the absence of specific and untypical counter-tendencies (the need to recruit and retain scarce categories of labour, or a belief that improved conditions will generate greater worker commitment and productivity), the employer is naturally motivated to resist worker aspirations which are liable to increase labour costs. Moreover, because labour represents a cost to be minimised, it is in the employer's interest to continue a worker's employment only so long as it remains profitable to do so. A decline in demand for the goods and services produced, or the development of new techniques permitting these to be produced more cheaply and profitably, may at any moment lead to managerial decisions which throw men and women out of employment.

If labour within capitalism is in one sense a commodity like any other, in another sense it is quite unlike all other types of commodity. For while the employment contract may well specify precisely what the worker receives from the employer, what he/she provides in return is rarely defined specifically. The worker does not agree to sell an exact quantity of labour; for neither physical nor intellectual work can normally be quantified precisely, and few employers could in any case predict with certainty their day-to-day labour requirements. The employer wishes rather to be able to make flexible use of the labour

*First published as Chapter 10 of Esland, G. and Salaman, G. (eds) (1980) *The Politics of Work and Occupations*, Open University Press.

force as circumstances dictate; and the employment contract reflects the employer's interest by imposing on workers an open-ended commitment. Rather than agreeing to expend a given amount of effort, the employee surrenders his/her *capacity to work*; and it is the function of management, through its hierarchy of control, to transform this capacity into actual productive activity. Hence Marx's vital distinction between labour and labour power: the wage or salary is not the price of labour as such but of labour power, the ability to work; but the realisation of this potential is by no means a simple economic exchange, it is a process which occurs 'outside the limits of the market' (Marx, 1959, p. 175). The cobbler who sells a pair of boots is separated from the commodity after the moment of sale, and is engaged in no necessary and continuing relationship with the customer; but the worker's labour power cannot be detached from his/her physical presence, and this necessitates an ongoing social relationship with the employer (or the employer's agents) throughout the labour process itself. Issues of control inevitably pervade this relationship: the conflictual character of job control and the commodity status of labour are reciprocally dependent aspects of social relations of production within capitalism.

The interdependence of the two elements of the employment relationship – the sale of labour power and the control of the labour process – is apparent in the detail of industrial relations. The worker's standards of acceptable payment are influenced by the nature of the work tasks and the pressure under which they are to be performed: witness the popular slogan 'a fair day's work for a fair day's pay'.[2] An increased workload or speed-up which might otherwise be resisted may be accepted if higher payment is received as compensation (either through a scheme linking earnings directly to output – 'payment by results' – through promotion, regrading, a special bonus or a simple wage increase). Conversely, relatively low pay may be tolerated by some workers if the pressure of work or the exercise of managerial authority is comparatively relaxed. For the employer, this interrelationship is also of crucial importance: the three parameters of level of pay, length of working time and labour productivity together determine the possibility and rate of profit. The drive for profitability will in different contexts focus primarily on one factor rather than another; and historically, improvements won by workers in increasing pay and reducing working hours have been compensated by the employer through more *intensive* exploitation of labour.[3]

This interdependence does not, however, vitiate the analytical utility of the distinction between sale of labour power and control over the labour process. And indeed, there is a further aspect of the work relationship which requires to be distinguished: workers' subordination within capitalist production to an alien *structure* of priorities and decision-making. 'Accumulation for accumulation's sake, production for production's sake: by this formula classical economy expressed the historical mission of the bourgeoisie' (Marx, 1959, p. 595). The capitalist mode of production involves a built-in compulsion, remote from deliberate human control, to extract profit from workers' labour and to devote this to the accumulation of capital (or in more modern terminology, 'economic growth') – a compulsion sustained by the competitive struggle between productive units, national and international.[4] Workers *have* to be treated as 'factors of production' rather than as men and women with distinctive needs and aspirations. Their upbringing and 'education' often derive from the need to make them in some narrow respect useful to an employer; it is this utility which determines whether they will obtain and retain employment, and which dominates their actual work experience. Utilitarian criteria may prescribe that they perform tasks which are excessively strenuous or degrading – or so monotonously repetitive as to eliminate any scope for creativity. The same principle which justifies the fragmentation of so much work into routine and meaningless tasks also requires that management organise and co-ordinate these fragmented activities into one collective effort on the basis of hierarchy and authority. Sociable relations among workers are normally tolerated only in so far as they do not obstruct the requirements of profitable production; the same is in large measure true of safeguards against accidents and industrial diseases. Or at least, the application of humane priorities in work normally requires the mobilisation of power against the *resistance* of employers who (whatever their personal sympathies) must give primary consideration to the requirements of profitability.

The normal priorities of work in capitalism reflect the internal 'logic' of the capitalist mode of production and are thus experienced at the level of the individual enterprise or establishment as inescapable external constraints. These pressures and constraints are, however, mediated by the policies and decisions of top managerial and directorial strata of both private and 'public' organisations. In much of the following discussion it is necessary to refer simply to 'management' without consideration of the divergent orientations and interests associated with different levels and functions of management. But a brief examination of the role of management is essential for any serious analysis of the problematics of control in industry. The key feature of capitalist management is that it constitutes an *authoritarian hierarchy*. With the subdivision and specialisation of tasks, work is productive only through its *collective* character; but each worker surrenders his or her labour power to the employer, who has to realise the potential of the collectivity.[5] It follows that management has a dual function. On the one hand it contributes to the collective process of production through providing overall co-ordination of the diverse activities of other employees, and also other technically valuable services and facilities.[6] On the other it carries out functions of control and surveillance, acting as mediator of the coercive and exploitative dynamic of capitalism. This distinction is developed by Carchedi (1975). Any sociological analysis of management is complicated by the fact that specific managerial roles often contain a contradictory mix of elements from both functions. Moreover, the size and complexity of many employing organisations necessitate an elaborate managerial structure with many levels between top director and modest charge-hands, gangers or section leaders who derive only the most limited power from their toehold in the managerial hierarchy.

It is obvious, then, that 'management' is not a homogeneous group with identical interests or a uniform class position; and indeed, there are many managers whose role includes such contradictory functions that meaningful specification of their class position is in principle impossible. Thus, 'personnel management' serves the ends of coercing and manipulating wage-labour, but is not unambiguously repressive. Its 'welfare' functions, designed within capitalism to achieve a tractable labour force, might in a different social context lose their manipulative character. One of the tasks of any effective workplace trade union organisation is to identify and exploit the internal divisions within management – the conflicts between staff and line, the disenchantment of junior managers with their superiors, the pressure on particular supervisors to achieve production targets regardless of cost. Yet despite these crucial differentiating processes, all members of management act within the constraints of the overall policy decisions taken by the top strata within the hierarchy; divergence beyond narrow limits invites retaliation. The class position of these top strata is scarcely disputable: they receive rewards far in excess of any identifiable productive contribution; they embrace their role as coercive agent of capital; and they represent, to the ordinary employee, the manifestation of an alien power.[7] The struggle for job control by ordinary workers – analysed in *general* terms rather than through a detailed examination of the strategies pursued in the individual workplace – involves a confrontation with a managerial hierarchy which, itself controlled from above, constitutes a hostile totality.

THE SALE OF LABOUR POWER

The terms on which labour power is sold are usually set in a highly discontinuous process. In unionised sectors of employment, intermittent negotiations (in Britain, in recent years, typically annually) set the basic rates of wages or salaries for the various grades of labour covered by the resulting collective agreement; and these rates stand until renegotiated. (Historically in Britain, and more notably still in such countries as the United States, such agreements have often run for several years.) Employers of non-union labour often follow wage movements negotiated elsewhere (sometimes as part of a deliberate policy of discouraging unionisation); otherwise the pay of unorganised workers is set unilaterally by the employer and altered infrequently, usually in response to labour market pressures or (exceptionally) the individual bargaining of a particularly valuable employee.

By virtue of the character of the collective bargaining process, the opportunities to exert collective control over the price of labour power thus arise only sporadically. Admittedly, this is not without qualification the case. Particular groups with strategic skills or disruptive potential may press 'irregularly' and achieve pay improvements. Others can boost their pay packets through overtime working or piecework earnings. In both instances, higher wages are in theory a compensation for extra labour, on a formula directly related to basic pay. But it is possible for workers (particularly when faced by unsophisticated management information and control procedures) to exert pressure on both the level and the rate of payment for overtime, and to seize the opportunity of changes in piecework tasks to negotiate job times or prices which permit regularly enhanced earnings. (Some managers have referred to piecework bargaining, particularly in certain sectors of engineering, as a 'Persian market'. (Brown (1973) analyses the operation of piecework bargaining in such a context.) Hence a substantial gap can exist between formally negotiated wage-rates and actual earnings, particularly in the case of male manual workers; in some cases workers may receive double the basic rate. And movements in pay can involve an inconspicuous process of 'drift' supplementing official bargaining.

Despite the importance of this phenomenon, it remains the case that most collectively organised workers (the large majority of public sector employees and of white-collar staff in private companies, for example) depend on formal and infrequently negotiated agreements for the bulk of their earnings increases. 'Wage drift' in Britain was at its most extensive in the early 1960s; since then, employers have made strenuous efforts to reduce or eliminate the scope for fragmented bargaining over pay on the shop floor,[8] while the size of nationally negotiated increases has risen sharply. Even in those sectors of employment where workplace-generated pay increases are still of substantial importance, the process is nevertheless one of intermittent pressure rather than continuous movement: the concept of 'drift' is misleading both in neglecting the active role of workers in pushing up their earnings, and in failing to indicate that this pressure has its outcome in a series of discrete understandings and agreements between workers and managerial representatives.

The setting of wages and salaries necessarily involves relations of control. The superficial equality of buyer and seller in *any* market transaction conceals inequalities of economic power which often permit certain parties in large measure to dominate the terms of exchange; markets are media of control just as much as they are media of exchange. This is particularly true of the labour market, where the concentrated economic power of capital confronts the far more vulnerable sellers of labour power, and where the most orthodox economic theorists are obliged to recognise a multiplicity of 'imperfections' which represent the impact of institutional and ideological pressures on the interaction of supply and demand. In organising collectively, workers do not disturb an otherwise evenly balanced labour market; normally they do no more than partially counterbalance the dominance which the employer can exercise over employees as individuals, and the impact of ideologies of occupational worth which reflect the interests of privileged social groups. (The significance of such ideologies is examined in detail in Hyman and Brough, 1975.) Control relations also pervade the detail of workplace bargaining on rates of pay, especially under payment by results systems. Historically, many employers introduced such systems in order to divide the labour force, believing correctly that the individual operator faced by the rate-fixer would be in a weak bargaining position. But the growth of shop steward organisation allowed in many workplaces a considerable degree of collective control over the rate-setting process. In some cases, rules and practices became established which considerably altered the balance of power in piece rate bargaining: for example, a worker who found the price or time offered for a new job insufficient could reject the company offer and receive payment related to previous average earnings until agreement was reached. Not surprisingly, where workers could establish such controls the rate of wage drift was often particularly high (see Brown, 1973); and it was just in such circumstances that employers were often particularly keen to introduce different payment systems.

The discussion of payment questions accounts for the bulk of formal collective bargaining between unions and employer representatives. This same preponderance is reflected in the demands pressed during strikes: in virtually every Western country, statistics of strike issues show that well over half concern wages and salaries. (Some of the problems involved in interpreting these statistics are discussed in Hyman, 1972, chapter 5.) Not surprisingly, then, trade unions are commonly viewed as institutions exclusively concerned with a struggle for pay increases. This is scarcely remarkable. We live in a society in which the importance of money is pervasively emphasised; in which vast resources are devoted to encouraging new and more sophisticated material aspirations among consumers; but in which workers receive far lower income to satisfy these aspirations than the more privileged social strata. Moreover, the *legitimacy* of wage bargaining as a focus of trade union action is widely accepted, whereas the propriety of demands which challenge managerial authority is more commonly disputed. Hence bargaining over pay is often the line of least resistance for union representatives (a point which is considered further in a later section).

The notion that trade unionism is *exclusively* concerned with wages and salaries would, however, be highly misleading; and the main focus of this chapter is on the less obvious but sociologically particularly interesting aspects of job control not directly related to payment. But one particular feature of the sale of labour power does deserve further consideration, because of its profound implications for the character of the whole trade union movement: the problem of relativities and differentials.

It is clear that workers do not enter the labour market as an undifferentiated mass. Through education and training (access to which is strongly influenced by class-based advantages), a minority acquire skills, qualifications and knowledge which permit entry to the most privileged occupations. Others acquire through particular on-the-job experience the aptitudes which represent less substantial but, nevertheless, significant advantages in the pursuit of relatively favoured employment. Conversely, those who lack such attributes are virtually disqualified from all but the most undesirable areas of work.

The segmentation of the labour market is reflected in the structure of the labour movement. Trade unions are not cohesive class organisations, uniting all who work for a living behind one common purpose. While class opposition forms the basis of work relations in capitalist society, this is overlaid and often concealed by the immense variety of specific work contexts and distinctive group interests. Hence men and women normally identify themselves first and foremost as members of a specific occupational group, employees of a given firm, or workers in a particular industry. It is within such limited milieux that spontaneous collective organisation typically develops. And just as individuals are often most conscious of the narrow area of interests and loyalties lying closest to hand (and hence commonly of what *divides* them from other workers rather than of what unites them), so the policies and priorities of unions often reflect narrow sectional concerns rather than broader class solidarity. (This tendency, it must be noted, is not merely spontaneous in origin; a whole battery of ideological pressures discourages workers from defining their interests in class terms.)

Sectional tendencies are particularly apparent in the operation of wage bargaining. One of the most common notions employed in this context is the concept of 'fair comparisons': the pay aspirations of a particular union or group of workers are characteristically framed and justified by reference to the level or movement of earnings among other employee groups. There is considerable sociological evidence that workers commonly assess their economic situation through restricted 'reference groups': limited inequities close to hand appear to generate greater spontaneous discontent than far more substantial but more distant inequalities of class; and collective bargaining often institutionalises and reinforces this narrow focus.

The main basis of contention is typically whether the relative position traditionally occupied by one group – and justified or criticised in the light of its particular skills, expertise, conditions of work or social and economic contribution – shall be sustained or improved in the context of the gains achieved by other groups. Hence wage bargaining typically involves the contestation of the relative economic advantages of different sections of the working class, rather than the *general* process of exploitation affecting all trade unionists. This necessarily obstructs the possibility of workers' self-conception as a class, or of concerted action challenging their subordination to capital.[9]

It can, therefore, be argued that the conventional processes of wage negotiation have a conservative tendency, in that the emphasis on parochial relativities serves to legitimise – if only by default – the broader inegalitarian structure of the overall incomes hierarchy. Yet this is not to suggest that the pursuit of pay improvements by trade unions cannot have disruptive consequences. In Britain since the end of the 1960s (and there have been similar tendencies in other countries), there has been a tendency for trade unionists to frame more ambitious aspirations, and to utilise broader orbits of comparison; and this has been reflected in an unprecedented level of pay demands and pay settlements.[10] Yet this has occurred when the margin for concession – in terms both of the distribution of the total national income, and the rate of profit in individual firms – has been constrained by an economic crisis international in effect but particularly severe in the context of British capitalism. It is this which has made the control of wages and salaries a particularly contentious issue in Britain (and most other countries) in recent years; and it is against this background that the growing interventions of governments in industrial relations and the growing interpenetration of economic and political elements in trade union policy (both discussed in later sections) must be assessed.

THE CONTROL OF THE LABOUR PROCESS

The previous section has considered one aspect of the employment relationship: the economic exchange through which the worker receives wages as payment for his/her labour power. 'What the capitalist obtains from this simple exchange is a use value: disposition over alien labour' (Marx, 1973, p. 282). The realisation of the

productive potential inherent in employees' labour power necessitates
an elaborate network of roles and institutions ensuring the control of
the employer over the labour process. Marx insisted that this control
was not merely a *technical* requirement of complex modern industry,
but was rather a *social* consequence of capitalist relations of
production:

> the labourer works under the control of the capitalist to whom his
> labour belongs; the capitalist taking good care that the work is
> done in the proper manner. . . . The directing motive, the end aim of
> capitalist production, is to extract the greatest possible amount of
> surplus-value and consequently to exploit labour-power to the
> greatest possible extent. . . . The control exercised by the capitalist
> is not only a special function, due to the nature of a social
> labour-process, but it is . . . rooted in the unavoidable antagonism
> between the exploiter and the living and labouring raw material
> that he exploits. . . . An industrial army of workmen, under the
> command of a capitalist, requires, like a real army, officers
> (managers), and sergeants (foremen, overlookers), who, while the
> work is being done, command in the name of the capitalist.[11]

Why do workers obey such commands? In a real army, a soldier who
disobeys an order may be court-martialled and, in extreme situations,
shot. Such sanctions are not normally available to employers in
modern industry; but what takes their place? Fox indicates a range of
both positive and negative sanctions:

> Financial rewards, promotion prospects, praise and approval,
> transfer to more desired work, and any other form of gratification
> are positive but also have a negative aspect in that they embody a
> conditional clause threatening their withdrawal or withholding if
> the required behaviour is not forthcoming. Conversely, negative
> sanctions such as reprimands, fines, suspension, dismissal, demo-
> tion, or any other form of deprivation all have a positive aspect
> embodied in a conditional guarantee that they will be lifted or not
> be imposed if the desired behaviour is followed. (Fox, 1971, pp.
> 30–1)

The ability to manipulate such sanctions is, of course, a reflection of
the economic (and legal) power on which managements can draw as
representatives of capital. Controlling access to the means of
production, the employer can ultimately determine whether a worker
shall obtain and retain a job and a pay-packet or salary cheque.[12]

This dependence on the part of the workers – the need to obtain a buyer for their labour power in order to earn a living – provides the employer with a potent sanction: behind the detail of the control relationship at the point of production stands the threat of the sack. But the force of this sanction may be attenuated. Where unemployment is low, the threat of dismissal is a lesser deterrent than where jobs are scarce. Its impact is also weakened where workers counterpose the principle of 'one out, all out'. An employer, faced by collective solidarity, is unable to coerce employees simply as individuals: any open conflict must needs involve the labour force as a whole. There is a further reason why managements may be reluctant to rely too overtly on the simple threat of the sack. Employers require not merely the passive compliance of their workers with specific managerial orders but their active co-operation, ingenuity and initiative. Within any complex labour process, it is quite impossible to exercise detailed supervision of the performance of every worker every minute of the working day; nor is it possible to provide instruction on how to deal with every conceivable contingency. Bendix cites 'the case of inmates of Nazi concentration camps, who were employed in factories during the war and who sabotaged the production effort by consistently asking for detailed instructions on what to do next' (Bendix, 1956, p. 204). Without some measure of 'workers' control', industrial and commercial life could scarcely function; hence the chaos when employees withdraw their initiative and 'work to rule'. This becomes increasingly important when workers possess special expertise or skills, or are responsible for sophisticated and costly productive equipment. Yet managerial control based on the blatant exercise of the economic power of capital is necessarily corrosive of employee co-operation, and invites active or passive sabotage when opportunities arise. Significantly, Bendix opens his study with a well-known quotation from Rousseau: 'the strongest is never strong enough to be always master, unless he transforms his strength into right, and obedience into duty'.[13]

Thus the 'problem of order', which has so exercised sociologists in their general analyses of society, is replicated at the level of the workplace; and in both cases, the existence of some form of normative agreement is commonly identified as a necessary basis for stable social relationships. Capitalism is dependent on at least a measure of *self*-discipline, the consciousness of a work obligation which requires the performance of a 'fair day's work' – defined in terms acceptable to the employer. It is clear that powerful social mechanisms exist within our society to encourage such normative commitment on the part of employees. Socialisation within the family and the educational system tend to inculcate an assumption that obedience to those in positions of authority is natural and morally proper; and the legitimacy of industrial management is routinely insisted on by religious dignitaries, politicians, judges, editors of newspapers and others with the ability to exert ideological influence. Hence, as Baldamus indicates, workers typically experience feelings of work obligation which provide important social support for the exercise of managerial control (Baldamus, 1961, chapter 8).

Yet the acceptance of a generalised obligation to follow managerial instruction does not entail that a worker will accept without question every specific order which any manager may issue. There is a logical gap between generalised social values and specific rules in concrete situations. 'We find it difficult to relate the generalities of a value statement to the complex and specific details of everyday situations' (Becker, 1963, p. 130). Skilled toolmakers are normally conservative and stolid members of an engineering labour force, unlikely to contest in general terms the right of management to manage; but a supervisor who instructed a toolmaker to sweep the floor would be likely to be told to fuck off. The possibility of resistance to orders which are viewed as unreasonable is increased by the fact that 'legitimacy' is too strong a concept to apply to most workers' conceptions of management. 'Insofar as authority relations do prevail in the industrial organizations of the West,' Fox suggests, 'they are probably most widely characterized, so far as subordinates are concerned, by a low-key acquiescence' (Fox, 1971, p. 45). The execution of managerial instructions is rarely a matter of conscious choice; the hierarchy of authoritarian control – simply because it exists as a virtually universal feature of employment relationships – is typically regarded as natural and inevitable. Hence only when a worker is asked to perform a task which is out of the ordinary does the possibility of disobedience and resistance normally arise. The rare dissident who explicitly denies the authority of the employer to command is confronted not only by the coercive power of the latter but also by the routinised obedience of the mass of his/her fellows; in the normal situation the only choice for such a worker is between isolated and ineffectual protest or prudent acquiescence. Yet precisely because most workers' customary obedience reflects no more than 'low-key acquiescence', the limits of obedience are easily tested. As Fox puts it, there tends to exist a 'zone of acceptance': workers will, for example, normally perform without question tasks which are clearly technically necessary and which come within the customary range of their functions; but as soon as these limits are exceeded their conformity becomes problematic.

Capitalism is inherently dynamic: it exhibits phases of gradual and rapid technological change; markets expand or contract; the whole system of economic relations is subject to recurrent crises. In consequence, the patterns of managerial control are necessarily unstable; and the legitimacy of this control is to this extent exposed to question. In practice, in the typical work situation, managerial control depends on a complex interplay of power, ideology, and the routine of customary forms of interaction. Legitimacy, in other words, should not be regarded simply as the opposite of coercive power: it is socially created from the dialectical interplay of material resources and ideology. This entails that the *processes* through which managers seek to avoid or contain the possibility and reality of worker resistance – while at the same time realising the goals of profitability which they themselves are required to achieve – demand extremely sensitive sociological analysis.

One concept which is useful for this purpose is that of 'negotiation of order'. Originally developed in a study of social relations in a hospital (Strauss *et al.*, 1971), the term is intended to indicate that where activities within an organisation require the co-operation of individuals and groups with divergent attitudes and interests, there is a natural tendency for understandings, agreements and rules to emerge from processes of formal and informal negotiation. In effect, subordinate employees can make their obedience – or more crucially, the intelligent observance of the spirit rather than the mere letter of managerial instructions – a basis for tacit or even overt bargaining. The 'custom and practice' which is of such importance in British industrial relations indicates the significance of precisely this type of relationship. Its origins characteristically lie in recurrent trade-offs between first-line supervisors, themselves under pressure to achieve production targets, and workers conscious of their own ability to frustrate managerial objectives in the day-to-day work process on the shop floor. Thus foremen will purchase their subordinates' goodwill by conceding such demands as special bonus payments, or by showing restraint in enforcing company disciplinary rules.

Through the process of negotiation of order the 'frontier of control' in each workplace is set. It is a fluid and shifting frontier: the limits of management authority and employee obedience are imprecise and always open to renegotiation. In some situations this instability may take the form of recurrent overt conflict, as either party takes advantage of temporary shifts in the balance of workplace power to alter the basis of the control relationship. Beynon's study is a case in point: the situation he presents as typical is one of 'naked aggression being met by violent defiance' (Beynon, 1973, p. 139). Such overt and recurrent conflictuality is not, however, the universal pattern: in many work situations, managements interact with subordinates through a relatively accommodative process of give-and-take. In such contexts, temporary changes in the balance of power are less likely to be exploited, precisely because it is recognised that such changes *are* temporary. A relatively stable pattern of reciprocity may thus develop: workers obey orders because managers only *issue* orders which workers find reasonable; and such a relationship may persist at least until an exogenous disturbance (changing demands on management, new aspirations by workers) puts it at risk.

What shapes the detailed power balance through which relations at the point of production are negotiated? Occupational groups clearly vary considerably in respect of the sanctions and resources at their disposal, and also in terms of their readiness to mobilise these in opposition to the power of management.[14] Variations in the sources and exercise of control by manual work groups are discussed systematically in a valuable article by Hill (1974).

Skilled workers possess labour power of a specialised character, thus rendering the employer more than ordinarily dependent on their co-operation; often in addition they have a pride in their trade, a sense of community and commitment to common craft principles, which support powerful resistance to forms of managerial control which challenge their autonomy in the detailed performance of their work. (Goodrich, 1975, discusses in detail the forms of workers' control commonly associated with traditional craft principles. For a recent analysis of craft cohesion in the printing industry, see Sykes, 1967.) Other manual workers who, though not craftsmen, fulfil a strategic function in the production process and can easily cause disruption – the Halewood wet-deck team, for instance – also possess sanctions which assist them to negotiate the frontier of control in their favour. The generality of lower-skilled workers are less well placed; though groups like Sykes's navvies, through their manifest refusal to develop a dependent relationship in respect of any single employer, may well fare better than most in asserting an area of control over the labour process (Sykes, 1973).[15]

White-collar employees constitute a heterogeneous stratum (ranging from routine clerical and technical to top managerial and professional occupations) and it is difficult to present meaningful generalisations. It is, however, normally the case that lower-level non-manual workers have little ability to cause immediate disruption to production and at the same time – given that literacy alone no longer holds great scarcity value – are comparatively easily replaceable by the employer. Traditionally, such employees have tended to identify more closely than manual workers with managerial values and hence have displayed less will to resist. Yet conversely, employers have often controlled such staff in a less overtly authoritarian manner than in the case of manual workers; much white-collar work cannot be readily characterised as obeying orders. Their subordination, though still real, is often more diffuse. This relationship carries overtones of what Fox terms 'trust': a reliance by the employer less on close supervision than on the employee's own discretion (Fox, 1974).[16] Such a relationship is itself in a sense 'negotiated': discretion is conditional on performance at some point judged satisfactory by the employer and will otherwise be eventually circumscribed. Autonomy is particularly high in the case of the most elevated occupational groups. Professional competence may make 'correct' performance extremely difficult for the employer to assess; more crucially, perhaps, the occupational solidarity of the most privileged white-collar groups, reinforced by their dominant class position, typically protects even incompetent individuals from the type of controls to which ordinary employees would be subject.

In other respects, the negotiation of order in the workplace is subject to broader social influences. It is often suggested, for example, that women workers are more submissive to managerial authority than most men. If this is so – and the evidence of many active and militant female trade unionists shows that it can be no more than a crude generalisation – it reflects the subordination imposed on women outside as well as inside work. The material dominance of men, in family and other social relationships, and the ideological pervasiveness of sexist stereotypes necessarily influence the relationship between women as workers and their (usually male) supervisors. Black workers, too, are commonly affected in their work relations by the fact that they are black as well as workers. Racist stereotypes often shape managerial strategies in dealing with black subordinates. The latter may on occasion tolerate unusually authoritarian treatment precisely because the same is customary outside work; others by contrast, having learned to resist the racism of authority figures in the wider society, may similarly react against managerial control – even when, exceptionally, this is not influenced by racism. Racism creates divisions within the working class which can be viewed as conducive to the stability of capitalism in that concerted working class action is inhibited. Sexism can have similar consequences. Some writers would argue that both racism and sexism are at times deliberately cultivated for this very reason.

With varying degrees of success, then – reflecting both the material and ideological resources at the disposal of managements and workers respectively – employees can establish an area of control over the work process. This autonomy is, however, always conditional. One condition is that they will continue to contribute to, and certainly not seriously obstruct, managerial goals of productivity and profitability. Hence groups enjoying significant discretion in the performance of work tasks must exercise self-discipline in its application; work groups with the power to obstruct specific managerial decisions cannot go 'too far' without inviting serious retaliation. To this extent, 'workers' control' within capitalism is necessarily partial and reactive: a means of moderating the effects of subordination to the abstract dictates of capital and the specific domination of hierarchical management, not a means of enforcing different priorities. Hence Beynon's conclusion that 'essentially the controls obtained over the job by shop floor union activities involved little more than a different form of accommodation to the more general controls imposed by management' (Beynon, 1973, p. 149).

Employee autonomy is doubly conditional in that it operates within an economic, technical and organisational context which can be expected to persist only so long as the employer is able to derive an acceptable level of profits. The availability of new technology, a shift in market conditions, or even a top-level company decision which has no obvious rationale, can totally disrupt the detailed process of negotiation of order within the workplace. A particular set of work tasks may be displaced or a whole establishment closed down – sometimes through a deliberate policy decision that this is the most effective means of bypassing the controls established by a powerful employee group. Or economic stringency may lead to the intensification of work pressure on production workers or the elimination of the elements of latitude traditionally permitted to white-collar staff.

This helps to underline the fact that control over higher-level policies and decisions – which set rigorous limits to the workplace negotiation of order – is remote from the spontaneous processes of workgroup action and resistance. For this reason, the very notion of 'negotiation of order' can be misleading: for exclusive attention to the disposition of power at the point of employment involves the neglect of *broader* structures of power in the economy and society. Workers who establish the most impressive range of controls in their dealings with junior management are nevertheless unlikely to play any positive part in determining what they will produce and in what quality and quantity; which consumers will be catered for, and through which mechanisms (market or otherwise); what establishments will be opened or closed, expanded or contracted; how the collective labour of the totality of employees will be co-ordinated; how profits will be distributed between reinvestment and dividends. (The absence of positive workers' control over such issues is stressed by Goodrich, 1975.) Influence at this level would be in principle possible only through a different level of collective employee action: a broader, co-ordinated, consciously formulated strategy to counterpose the interests of workers against the priorities of capitalism, positively and aggressively rather than negatively and defensively. Arguably, it is precisely this function which trade unionism is intended to fulfil. To consider further the possibility of transcending the limitations of the workplace negotiation of order it is therefore necessary to examine explicitly the complex role of trade unionism in the process of job control.

TRADE UNIONISM AND CONTROL

Against the background of the previous discussion, the key significance of trade unionism is that it formalises and generalises the processes of worker resistance to, and negotiation with, the structure of capitalist domination in the employment relationship.

At the end of 1974 there were in the United Kingdom an estimated 491 trade unions with a combined membership of 11.75 million.* The figure of aggregate union membership represents almost exactly half the total labour force. This proportion is high by comparison with most Western nations; though a few countries, such as Sweden or Belgium, can claim unionisation of about three-quarters of the labour force, the position in the United States with only a quarter organised

*See Chapter 10 for more recent figures.

is more typical.* In part the relative strength of British unionism reflects its deep historical roots. Organisation among skilled artisans existed as early as the eighteenth century, surviving and expanding despite severe legal repression. From the 1850s can be traced the consolidation of craft societies into impressive national associations, and the emergence of stable unionisation among workers in the large-scale industries of the industrial revolution such as coal-mining, cotton and iron and steel. The turn of the century saw a further wave of unionisation, covering in particular the bulk of transport and manufacturing. The extension of organisation to white-collar workers – initially primarily in the public sector, but in recent years to a significant extent also in private industry and services – is largely the achievement of the present century.

To a large extent, the current pattern of organisation was estab-lished in Britain by 1920, when 45 per cent of the labour force was unionised. Mass unemployment between the wars caused severe losses, roughly halving total membership. Since the last war these losses have been more than recovered, though recent progress has been relatively slow. One reason has been the changing structure of the labour force: a decline in employment in industries and occupa-tions (such as coal-mining, cotton textiles, docks and railways) which have been union strongholds; and growth in service industries and white-collar occupations which have traditionally been more weakly organised. Unionisation has occurred historically in the face of severe obstacles: forcible opposition by employers, the victimisation and blacklisting of activists, the attack of judges, legislators and other agencies of state. While unions today have won greater acceptance, such forms of resistance remain widespread. Hence it is often extremely difficult to organise in workplaces which are small or isolated, and in industries and occupations with a casual or fluctuating labour force. Conversely, virtual 100 per cent unionisation may be maintained in some establishments and occupations through controls which oblige the employer to recruit only union members, or at least require that new employees must join the relevant union. In this way, collective control may be self-sustaining.

Trade unions represent a focal point in a complex network of power relations. Their basic rationale is as a source and medium of power: providing a means whereby employees, individually without significant defence against the employer, can achieve more effective

*Since this was written, the rate of unionisation in the USA has fallen to roughly one in six.

collective support. Unions reduce competition among workers in the labour market, confronting the concentrated power of employers with an analogous (though usually far less tightly integrated) combination of labour power. Within the labour process, trade unionism sustains a solidarity which reduces the vulnerability of the individual employee in the ongoing negotiation of the frontier of control. In higher-level decision-making – involving top management, collective organisations of employers and also the various institutions of the state – unions seek to represent the collective interests of their members in influencing the policies and priorities adopted.

Yet the role of trade unionism in relation to managerial control and the dynamics of capitalist relations of production is essentially ambivalent: a reflection of the multi-directional interaction of power relationships, both internal and external, in which unions are implicated. Trade unions are the institutional meeting point of the contradictory demands and interests of different sectional groups of workers, of employers and state functionaries. Their key task is to mediate and accommodate these conflicting pressures – a task which is at times virtually impossible. This focal role also explains why trade unions are commonly the target of very powerful *ideological* pressures. The pursuit of humane working conditions, a less inegalitarian distribution of economic rewards, increased security of working class life-chances, or greater scope for individual and collective self-determination by working people, conflicts systematically and radically with the priorities of the capitalist mode of production and the interests of those in positions of social and economic dominance within existing society. Hence, not only are very powerful material pressures exerted on the articulation of trade union goals and the selection of specific demands, strategies and tactics,[17] but material power is closely interlinked with the ability to influence the beliefs and perceptions of trade unionists and the 'vocabularies of motive' through which they appraise the actions of employers and their own potential responses.

One example of the ideological offensive to which trade unionists are subject is the force of contemporary stereotypes of 'overpowerful' unions persistently engaged in 'militant' and 'irresponsible' actions. Notions of union militancy lose their plausibility when the objectives actually pursued are measured against the scale of the deprivations and inequalities generated by capitalist wage-labour, and hence the scope of what might potentially be demanded. In assessing union action it is significant that shop stewards – arch-figures in conventional demonology – are viewed by most managers as no more (and often less) militant than the members they represent; and were evaluated by the Royal Commission on Trade Unions and Employers' Associations as 'an accepted, reasonable and even moderating influence; more of a lubricant than an irritant'. (See Donovan, 1968 and McCarthy and Parker, 1968.) As for the image of 'overmighty' unionism, the comments of Fox are particularly apposite:

> Power and social conditioning cause the employee interests to accept management's shaping of the main structure long before they reach the negotiating table. Thus the discussion may be about marginal adjustments in hierarchical rewards, but not the principle of hierarchical rewards, about certain practical issues connected with the prevailing extreme sub-division of labour, but not the principle of extreme sub-division of labour; about financial (extrinsic) rewards for greater efficiency, but not about the possibility of other types of (intrinsic) reward with some sacrifice of efficiency; about measures which may achieve company expansion and growth, but not about the benefits and costs of company expansion and growth; about how the participant interests can protect and advance themselves within the structure operated by management to pursue its basic objectives, but not about the nature of those basic objectives. (Fox, 1973, p. 219)

While the precise specification of the relative power of trade unions involves immense methodological difficulties, there is no serious basis for the assertion that this power even approaches, in any general and systematic sense, that of the agencies with which unions are engaged in continuous relationships. To come to terms with the colourful characterisations of union action which are currently prevalent, it is necessary to regard them less as intellectual formulations to be appraised by rational criticism than as ideological weapons in a social struggle aimed at containing the *potentially* disruptive impact of collective worker action within capitalist society.

Central to any serious sociological analysis of trade unionism is the area of institutional autonomy available to union representatives in mediating the conflicting pressures and expectations of members on the one hand and external agencies on the other. Workers as individuals can exert little meaningful control over their work environment; only by submitting to collective principles and decisions can they share in more significant influence over the conditions of their working lives. But in subordinating part of their individual autonomy to collective decision-making processes, they create an institution which (through the activities and initiatives of official representatives and spokesmen) can pursue objectives which diverge from their own interests (see Beynon, 1973). If a union is to be effective in wielding power *for* its members and against the employer, the possibility exists that this organisational power will be exerted *over* them, possibly on behalf of external interests. Precisely because the secure existence of unionism appears to require at least the acquiescence of governments and major employers, these 'significant others' can influence union representatives to eschew policies which may invite repression, and even to transmit their own imperatives back down to the membership.

At the very least there exist strong pressures on union officials to act, in Wright Mills's famous phrase, as 'managers of discontent' (Mills, 1948, pp. 8–9). They express, and in some circumstances actually stimulate, their members' consciousness of grievances; yet at the same time they seek to limit the expression of industrial conflict to forms over which they can exert control, and which do not jeopardise the arrangements and understandings developed with employers. Established union–employer relations may serve, indeed, to transmute the very character of employee grievances, by defining issues within a narrow focus which shapes the parameters for potential resolution; for if fundamental questions of principle are suppressed, the task of achieving compromise may be greatly eased. In such circumstances, far-sighted managements have little to fear in coming to terms with unionism, and may indeed find great advantages in terms of the achievement of a more predictable labour force. This, then, is the central paradox of trade unionism. Through co-ordinating workers' collective strength, and at times directing this in militant action, unions win significant improvements in their members' conditions (both in the sale of their labour power and within the labour process itself). Against the arbitrary dominance of the employer, they counterpose an 'industrial legality' which represents 'a great victory for the working class' (Gramsci, 1969, p. 15). Yet in certain forms this 'industrial legality' is acceptable and even advantageous to employers; and trade union representatives are subject to powerful influences to pursue objectives and actions of such character.

It follows that the role of trade unions in relation to job control is inherently ambiguous. As Herding argues, 'job-control rights, and demands for them, may serve the union as an organization, particularly a bureaucratic leadership, or they may be geared to benefit specific strata of workers, or the working class in general. In each case we have to single out how and for whom a job-control measure works' (Herding, 1972, p. 16). In America, he suggests, the growing involvement of trade unions in negotiations on such issues has centred mainly around demands – the rationalisation of personnel administration and the reduction of competition within the labour force – which are not antagonistic to employer interests and may even facilitate managerial objectives. By contrast, unions have achieved few significant concessions on the control of the labour process itself, where the interests of employers and workers are diametrically opposed. Indeed the commitment of unions to the 'peace obligation' inherent in their negotiating procedures has reinforced managerial control of job allocation, production speeds and working conditions by disarming rank-and-file workers; for the only effective response to managerial initiatives which adversely affect the workplace frontier of control is immediate direct action.

In Britain, it is possible to discern some parallels. Many unions have shown a willingness to negotiate over and agree to systems of job evaluation and work measurement; payment by results systems based on work study alone (rather than on 'mutuality' between operator and rate-fixer); and 'productivity' schemes which allocate a range of decisions over the labour process to managerial initiative or formalised collective bargaining. The tendency of all such developments, as Flanders has emphasised, is 'to strengthen managerial control over pay and work through joint regulation' (Flanders, 1970, p. 204).

Such developments are in general less advanced in Britain than in most other countries. A crucial factor has been the importance of shop steward organisation, particularly strong among manual workers in private manufacturing industry, but of growing significance (under a variety of titles) in the public sector and among non-manual employees. The 'challenge from below' discussed by Flanders has created a constant obstacle to the institutionalisation and incorporation of trade union action: workplace organisation has proved highly responsive to the spontaneous demands of the rank and file, articulating members' aspirations and grievances, where necessary, independently and even in defiance of official trade union channels. Union officials in turn have had to take account of challenges deriving from an independent workplace power base. Hence there has been a considerable tendency for the exercise of job control through trade unionism to retain its autonomous and oppositional character. (For further discussion of this point see Hyman, 1971.)

Yet some qualification is necessary. Shop steward organisation has normally been less strong in the public sector than the private, in services than in manufacturing, among white-collar employees than manual workers; and the constraints imposed by unionism on managerial initiative have been correspondingly weaker. And even where independent workplace unionism is most firmly established, it is by no means immune from the incorporating pressures diagnosed at the level of official unionism. Workplace representatives are implicated in a two-way relationship of dependence with the official union hierarchy. The balance of power can vary considerably: reflecting, for example, the strategic position of different occupational and industrial groups, the structure of formal union–employer negotiating arrangements, managerial strategies and preferences, and the constitutional arrangements of union rulebooks; but to a greater or lesser extent all such representatives are necessarily tied into the broader system of union–employer accommodation. This integration is facilitated by the emergent tendencies in most workplace organisations towards an institutional separation of the domestic leadership from the mass of the rank and file, with the development of distinctive perspectives, interests, sanctions and resources; the relationship between members and full-time officials is thus replicated in microcosm. The stability of the domestic collective organisation, like that of the larger union, depends substantially on the preservation of established bargaining relationships with the employer (including the tacit or explicit provision of a range of facilities necessary for effective workplace representation). Even an assertive and combative shop steward body, as at Halewood, is constrained by the awareness that carrying resistance to management 'too far' would invite a concerted counter-attack and jeopardise existing achievements. Hence shop stewards too are 'managers of discontent': sustaining job control within the boundaries of negotiation with managerial authority and capitalist priorities, rather than (apart from the most exceptional circumstances) pursuing frontal opposition.

The thesis of this section may appear profoundly pessimistic: the inevitable institutionalisation and emasculation of collective resistance by workers to exploitative work relations. Does the study of the politics of work suggest no possibility of a more fundamental and concerted challenge to capitalist work organisation? How far trade unionism contains such a potential, and how far the institutionalisation of conflict is itself inherently contradictory and unstable, can be assessed only on the basis of a more explicit consideration of the interrelationship of trade unionism, job control, state power and the dynamics of contemporary capitalism.

THE POLITICS OF JOB CONTROL

For Marx, observing the early collective struggles of the proletariat of the industrial revolution, the formation of trade unions was a crucial stage in the growth of class consciousness among workers and presaged an explicit revolutionary challenge to the political economy of capitalism:

> The real fruit of their battles lies, not in the immediate results, but in the ever-expanding union of the workers. . . . Out of the separate economic movements of the workers there grows up everywhere a *political* movement, that is to say, a movement of the *class*, with the object of enforcing its interests in a general form, in a form possessing general, socially coercive force. (In *Manifesto of the Communist Party* and letter to Bolte, 23 November 1871)

The actual development of trade unionism has clearly diverged from this model. Sectionalism has not been increasingly transcended by broader unification, an expectation of Marx deriving from his prediction of the rapid erosion of skill distinctions; while some old divisions within the working class have disappeared, others have arisen. As suggested earlier, sectional consciousness is clearly apparent in the typical motivation to collective action; and while sectionalism is not at all times incompatible with broader solidarity, it commonly inhibits class consciousness. Sectionalism is, moreover, often reinforced by the organisational distinctiveness of a multiplicity of competing unions.

Nor has trade unionism developed spontaneously into a political movement. In Britain, indeed (and the same has been even more evident in the United States), trade union representatives have normally insisted on a rigid separation of 'industrial' and 'political' activities. Marx noted the vigorous political campaigns mounted by the early textile unions for statutory limitation of hours of work. Miners were concerned with achieving safety legislation and controls on other conditions of their work. The formation of the TUC in 1868 stemmed primarily from a concern to safeguard the legal position of trade unionism in general. But the premise became rapidly accepted that the industrial strength of workers must on no account be mobilised to force the political authorities to concede their demands. Strikes and related forms of action were legitimate only in the context of the 'industrial' issues which were the unions' central focus of interest; 'political' demands could properly be pursued only through due observance of constitutional proprieties.

This commitment is without rational foundation. The distinction between 'industrial' and 'political' issues is at root merely conventional; there is, as Fox insists, nothing intrinsic in a specific demand which requires it to be classified in one category rather than another. Rather, to call a demand 'political' is simply to assert that unions *ought* not to use all their resources to achieve it. Hence the conventional distinction 'bears an ideological connotation in that it underpins a particular interpretation of the proper role of trade unions in our society' (Fox, 1974, p. 150). It is, moreover, only the *overt* use of economic pressure on political decision-making that offends conventional notions of 'the sovereignty of a democratically elected government' (Allen, 1966, p. 35); the power of capital is a permanent constraint on the economic and social objectives which can 'realistically' be pursued. Precisely because a central concern of governments – whatever their political complexion – is to maintain the 'confidence' of those who control industry and to sustain an environment conducive to profitability, the coercive force of those who own and control major economic resources is normally latent rather than overt. (Though on occasion, governments may fail sufficiently to respect capitalist interests and invite the blatant use of economic power: Chile is a case in point.) The traditional self-restraint of British unions has thus seriously inhibited any concerted attempt to counterpose different priorities to those deriving from the pervasive influence of capital.

This ideological segregation of the 'industrial' from the 'political' is reflected in the relationship beween the unions and the political organisation established largely on their initiative, the Labour Party. While insisting on favourable consideration of 'industrial relations' questions, union leaders have normally been happy to abstain from any initiating role in the formulation of general Party policy. The Party has been correspondingly anxious to establish its autonomy from the unions, and to disavow any interest in 'unconstitutional' forms of political pressure. 'Of political parties claiming socialism to be their aim', Miliband has argued, 'the Labour Party has always been one of the most dogmatic – not about socialism, but about the parliamentary system. Empirical and flexible about all else, its leaders have always made devotion to that system their fixed point of reference and the conditioning factor of their political behaviour' (Miliband, 1964, p. 13). Hence the Party leadership has always been concerned to prove its 'fitness to govern' by managing capitalism more efficiently (which often has to mean, in practice, more ruthlessly) than the traditional capitalist parties; while its anxiety to appear as a 'national' rather than class party has limited any special attention to the interests of workers and their families. Certainly Labour leaders have traditionally sought (often quite sincerely) to identify the Party with an idealistic commitment to the development of the welfare state; but their fate has been to achieve office in periods of economic stringency when this goal has proved largely incompatible with the priority of maintaining the viability of capitalism.

This conventional segregation of industrial and political goals and strategies invites attention to the orientation often termed 'economism'. Writing at the turn of the century, Lenin argued that workers' industrial struggles led in themselves to no more than 'trade union consciousness': 'the conviction that it is necessary to combine in unions, fight the employers, and strive to compel the government to pass necessary labour legislation, etc.'[18] Any sustained and comprehensive attack on capitalist relations of production, by contrast, required a fully fledged revolutionary consciousness which could not emerge spontaneously from economic conflicts alone but demanded the intervention of a revolutionary party.

A somewhat different conception of 'economism' has been proposed by Mann, who contrasts wage demands with those which focus on control. The former, he suggests, provide a ready basis for compromise, for 'the economic interests of rival parties can in principle be served by increasing the total reward available for share-out by collective cooperation. By contrast, there tends to be a fixed amount of work control available for distribution, and for one party to increase control the other must necessarily lose some of *its* control.' Mann's argument is that 'as trade unions are organized toward the attainment of economic bargaining gains, they tend in practice to lose sight of control issues, whether these concern the immediate work situation or wider-ranging questions of industrial structure.' In consequence 'they operate to *weaken* workers' class consciousness' and integrate them into the structure of capitalist society (Mann, 1973, pp. 21–3).

While these two interpretations of economism parallel some of the analysis in this chapter, it should be clear from the discussion in the previous sections that any attempt to posit a clear boundary between 'economistic' and 'non-economistic' trade unionism is misleading. Firstly, the *organisational* interests which are particularly salient for union officials necessarily transcend mere economism: they are concerned to establish *procedures* which underwrite union security and status. Even if union members (perhaps encouraged by their leaders) were to see their organisation only as a means of pressing a narrow range of substantive demands, the procedural interests of their representatives would necessarily involve explicit attention to control issues. Operating within an environment of power, the right of unions to exist and to operate effectively is necessarily a political question. Secondly, 'pure' economism is in principle impossible because workers do not *merely* sell their labour power; this economic exchange, as was shown in detail earlier, is merely the preliminary to the control relationship in the workplace which inevitably generates conflict which must be the subject of formal or informal negotiation. Thirdly, it is by no means evident that wage demands always permit ready compromise; this can be achieved only when the size of the demands, the resources and determination used in their support, and the margin for concession available in the economy are in some sort of equilibrium. Otherwise even economistic trade unionism will prove economically – and in consequence also socially and politically – disruptive, a point which scarcely requires emphasis in view of the recent history of Britain as well as other Western economies. Fourthly, a preoccupation with simple wage-bargaining on the part of union officials presupposes a reasonable balance of supply and demand within the labour market; for otherwise, the *control of employment opportunities* becomes an issue of overt concern for trade unionists. Again, it is quite obvious that in recent years union representatives have been obliged to focus their attention on 'wider-ranging questions of industrial structure' as a precondition of successful negotiation on more limited issues.

Drawing all these arguments together, it is possible to appreciate that trade union economism has always rested on certain *historically contingent* preconditions. The readiness to avoid the use of workers' potential industrial strength in the political arena has been the reciprocal of a parallel abstention by the state in the field of industrial relations: the tradition of 'voluntarism'. Since the mid-Victorian era, *direct* intervention by the law and the state machinery has occurred in Britain usually only on the margins of employment relations; in general, unions and employers have been left free to negotiate autonomously on the main substantive issues of terms and conditions of employment. This 'collective *laissez-faire*' has never been absolute, as the most cursory knowledge of labour history will indicate. More crucially, this tradition (like *laissez-faire* in general) has represented not the neutrality of the state but rather its abstention *in favour* of the stronger party in economic relations: those who own and control capital. Voluntarism had its roots in an era when unions were relatively weak (through limited membership and often high unemployment) and willing to exercise considerable self-restraint in the use made of power they did possess. The notions of 'responsibility' embraced by trade union leaders ensured a relatively stable pattern of industrial relations: unions pursued wage objectives sufficiently modest to be accommodated within the general framework of economic development (the significance of the ideology of 'responsibility' is explored by Allen, 1966, chapter 1) and hence problems of *control* both within the labour process and in relations between unions, employers and the state were only intermittently the subject of large-scale conflict.[19]

Over recent years many of the foundations of voluntarism in state policy and economism in trade union action have been eroded. *Laissez-faire* as a general orientation has given way to government intervention to manage the overall level of economic activity, support specific industries and enterprises, finance costly research and development, guarantee markets and influence investment. Attempts to control labour costs, supply and utilisation fit naturally within the logic of this development, and have been apparent in a wide range of government initiatives in Britain in the past decade. The *long-run* trend to interdependence between state and monopoly capitalism is reinforced by more acute economic pressures: after two decades of relatively full employment and sustained expansion, world capitalism – and British capitalism in particular – is beset by an unprecedented combination of recession and rapid inflation. In this unfavourable environment, the economic aspirations of employees appear to have become more ambitious, and union leaders have been forced to sponsor an increased militancy of aims and tactics. *Managerial* attempts to sustain profitability by pushing back the frontier of control on the shop floor ('productivity' bargaining, work measurement, speed-up, new payment systems and work organisation) necessarily turn non-economic issues into a major focus of collective bargaining and industrial conflict. Even if the initial stance of trade unionists in such control conflicts is primarily defensive, the experience can stimulate more aggressive and wide-ranging demands for control as the only effective means of defending the existing limited areas of work autonomy. (Hence it is no accident that the revival of interest among trade unionists in theories of workers' control and the possibility of positive strategies of self-management has coincided with employer and government efforts to alter the previously relatively stable frontier of control within production.)[20] Simultaneously, large-scale unemployment and widespread closures and redundancies have thrown into relief the trade union interest in top-level company decision-making and in overall government economic strategies; the distinction between 'industrial' and 'political' concerns loses all credibility. Government attempts to contain the (usually unintended) disruptive consequences of union action challenge the traditional norms of 'free collective bargaining', making the procedural status of trade unions themselves a focus of explicit contention. The fact that Labour governments have been in office for most of the period of these developments has imposed severe strains on the traditional understandings between party and unions.

The changing material context of trade union action – which ultimately reflects the contradictory basis of the capitalist mode of production itself – creates a volatile and unstable interrelationship between unions, employers and the state. At times, governments see the only solution in explicit attacks on the procedural status of trade unionism (such as the Industrial Relations Act of 1971); but such strategies necessarily provoke official union opposition which in turn legitimises more radical resistance by rank-and-file activists. Collaborative strategies – the cultivation of union acquiescence in government economic priorities, as a trade-off for government abstention from repressive measures (and possibly also certain symbolic concessions to the social objectives of the unions) – almost always receive a favourable response from union leaders; but their own limited control over the rank and file entail that they may be unable to guarantee membership compliance. The response of workers themselves – faced by contradictory material and ideological pressures – becomes a critical but unpredictable factor.

This discussion does not lead to any tidy conclusions: the analysis is necessarily open-ended, for control relations themselves are fluid and dynamic. The sociologist can seek to assign meanings and discover causes, and can attempt to identify the key problems in the control relations between workers, union officials, managers and state functionaries. But the solution to these problems emerges only in the struggle for control itself.

Notes

1. This official category, comprising employers, employees and self-employed, encapsulates an interesting ideological bias. Those whose work is not implicated in commercial exchange relations are simply not classed as productively engaged; hence the great bulk of housework, for example, is excluded.

2. Marx and Engels criticise this popular trade union slogan as a 'conservative motto': for notions of fairness typically reflect the assumptions of capitalist political economy and the interests of employers. For a discussion of the significance of ideas of fairness in modern industrial relations see Hyman and Brough (1975).

3. In Marxian terminology, the interrelationships of these three factors (given a particular exchange value of the commodities produced) sets the ratio of *necessary* to *surplus* labour. Necessary labour represents the proportion of working time in which the market value of what is collectively produced compensates the employer for the workers' wages and other necessary costs of production; surplus labour the proportion of which the employer is able to *appropriate* the value added by the workers. Historically, the profitability of early capitalism depended on the *extensive* exploitation of the labour force: surplus value was obtained through low wages and long working hours. As capitalism developed, the tendency has been towards *intensive* exploitation: the length of necessary labour has been sharply reduced by various strategies to increase labour productivity, allowing the maintenance (or even increase) of the rate of surplus value despite higher wages and shorter hours.

4. The process of concentration and centralisation of capital, creating large and potent monopolies, overturns the assumptions of a perfectly competitive economic system. Nevertheless, no monopoly is so powerful as to be wholly immune from competitive pressures – particularly given the increasingly overt international character of capitalist production.

5. 'The division of labour within the workshop,' wrote Marx (1959, pp. 356–61), 'implies the undisputed authority of the capitalist over men, that are but parts of a mechanism that belongs to him . . . . By nature unfitted to make anything independently, the manufacturing labourer

develops productive activity as a mere appendage of the capitalist's workshop.' It has been argued that historically the development of factory production owed less to the resulting increase in technical efficiency than to the consequential concentration of control in the hands of the employer (Marglin, 1974). It might be added that the degree to which this monopolisation of managerial power is eliminated is one acid test of any society purporting to have established socialist relations of production.

6. While some such services, e.g. research and development, would be of value within any social formation, others derive their function specifically from capitalism. Thus 'marketing' is necessary only where the social distribution of products is abdicated to the blind forces of the market; much financial control is similarly specific to capitalist economic relations.

7. Marx and Engels wrote, in *The Holy Family*, that while the capitalist was alienated – because subject to the determination of externally coercive economic laws – he was 'comfortable and confirmed' in this alienated state. The same is true of top managers and directors today. For an analysis of their beliefs and attitudes, indicating their sense of personal powerlessness and also their commitment to their role, see Nichols (1969).

8. An obvious example is the campaign by Chrysler and British Leyland to replace piecework by measured daywork. This trend reflects a growing determination on the part of employers (strongly encouraged by the government, through such agencies as the National Board for Prices and Incomes in 1965–70) to contain and reduce labour costs by reinforcing managerial control over earnings, movements and labour utilisation. This tendency is discussed in Cliff (1970).

9. A remarkable historical stability in the share of the national income going to wages and salaries has often been asserted; Glyn and Sutcliffe (1972), in an important analysis, challenge this familiar argument. Their own interpretation appears, however, to require some qualification. Firstly, they put excessive weight on short-run trends; the significant gains by British labour in the late 1960s appear to have been more recently reversed. Secondly, they give insufficient attention to the extent to which the rapidly increasing share of *salaries* may represent, in effect, a reward for the exercise of traditional capitalist functions rather than a return to productive labour. Thirdly, they treat somewhat simplisticly the growing interdependence of the state and capitalist industry: a development which arguably renders any simple analysis in terms of factor shares unilluminating.

10. Some of the reasons for this recent 'wage explosion' are discussed in Jackson *et al.* (1972) and also in Hyman and Brough (1975).

11. Marx (1959, pp. 184–5, 331–2). Here again, Marglin's (1974) article is a notable recent elaboration of the thesis that managerial control in capitalist industry is more a reflection of exploitative social relations of production than of technical necessity.

12. This domination has the curious ideological consequence that the employer can appear to perform the worker a favour by exploiting his/

her labour power. In some countries this topsy-turvy viewpoint is built into the language of employment: employers are known as 'work-givers', employees as 'work-takers'.

13. Bendix, p. 1. Nor is it necessarily satisfactory for the employer that the worker should fail to view the employment relationship as a coercive subordination to superior power, if he/she regards it simply as an economic exchange. For a purely instrumental orientation fails to engender a normative acceptance of the employer's standards of work performance. For the sake of wages an employee may accept his/her subordination to managerial authority, and agree to perform boring and routine tasks; but any dissatisfaction with the level of pay will corrode any sense of work obligation. 'The "cash-nexus" may snap just because it is *only* a cash-nexus – because it is single-stranded; and if it does snap, there is nothing else to bind the worker to acceptance of his situation' (Westergaard, 1970, p. 120).

14. For workers whose position is in principle strong may fail to recognise their potential strength, or because of an unusual commitment to managerial norms and objectives may fail to apply it in their own interests.

15. It might be added that the navvies' readiness to 'jack in' their work could have been encouraged by the buoyant labour market for construction workers at the time of Sykes's research: workers were not dependent on any single employer because they could easily find another. In a situation of recession relationships might well alter significantly.

16. This distinction, it must be added, does not simply divide manual from white-collar occupations: some of the former enjoy considerable discretion in work performance, some of the latter very little. But the rough generalisation remains heuristically useful.

17. Such material pressures are a central theme of the present writer's *Industrial Relations: A Marxist Introduction* (1975), and are not discussed further here.

18. *What Is to Be Done?*; for references and discussion see Hyman (1971). It should be noted that 'economism', for Lenin, did not preclude certain forms of political action: he was aware of the practice of Victorian British trade unionism. But he believed (unlike Marx) that such action would not develop spontaneously into a general political challenge to capitalism.

19. This traditional stability should not be exaggerated. The status of trade unions – and hence their legitimate role in control relations involving both individual employers and broader political action – has involved recurrent conflicts with parliament and the courts. 'Public opinion' – the social production of which commonly follows closely the interests of employers – has on many occasions indicated intense hostility to trade union functions. Recognition from employers has more often been the outcome of struggle than of spontaneous acceptance. Control issues at workplace level have not infrequently provoked fierce contention: in engineering, for example, three national lock-outs have arisen from the conflict between managerial control and craft autonomy.

20. One reflection of the growing questioning of traditional authority
    relations both within the workplace and at higher levels of company
    decision-making is the current propagation of notions of 'job enrich-
    ment' and 'participation': concepts denoting strategies to increase
    workers' commitment to managerial objectives by giving the *appear-
    ance* of enhanced self-determination in work. For a critical appraisal
    see Fox (1974).

References

Allen, V. L. (1966) *Militant Trade Unionism*, London, Merlin Press.
Baldamus, W. (1961) *Efficiency and Effort*, London, Tavistock.
Becker, H. S. (1963) *Outsiders*, Glencoe, Free Press.
Bendix, R. (1956) *Work and Authority in Industry*, New York, Harper and
    Row.
Beynon, H. (1973) *Working for Ford*, Harmondsworth, Penguin.
Brown, W. A. (1973) *Piecework Bargaining*, London, Heinemann.
Carchedi, G. (1975) 'On the Economic Identification of the New Middle
    Class', *Economy and Society*, Vol. 4, pp. 1–86.
Cliff, T. (1970) *The Employers' Offensive*, London, Pluto Press.
Donovan, Lord (1968) Royal Commission on Trade Unions and Employers'
    Associations (Chair: Donovan) *Report*, London, HMSO.
Flanders, A. (1970) *Management and Unions*, London, Faber.
Fox, A. (1971) *A Sociology of Work in Industry*, London, Collier-Macmillan.
Fox, A. (1973) 'Industrial Relations: A Social Critique of Pluralist Ideology',
    in Child, J., *Man and Organization*, London, Allen and Unwin.
Fox, A. (1974) *Man Mismanagement*, London, Hutchinson.
Glyn, A. and Sutcliffe, R. (1972) *British Capitalism, Workers and the Profits
    Squeeze*, Harmondsworth, Penguin.
Goodrich, C. L. (1975) *The Frontier of Control: A Study in British Workshop
    Politics*, London, Pluto Press.
Gouldner, A. W. (1954) *Patterns of Industrial Bureaucracy*, New York, Free
    Press.
Gramsci, A. (1969) *Soviets in Italy*, Nottingham, Institute for Workers'
    Control.
Herding, R. G. (1972) *Job Control and Union Structure*, Rotterdam,
    Rotterdam University Press.
Hill, S. (1974) 'Norms, Groups and Power: The Sociology of Workplace
    Industrial Relations', *British Journal of Industrial Relations*, Vol. 12, pp.
    213–35.
Hyman, R. (1971) *Marxism and the Sociology of Trade Unionism*, London,
    Pluto Press.
Hyman, R. (1972) *Strikes*, London, Fontana.
Hyman, R. and Brough, I. (1975) *Social Values and Industrial Relations*,
    Oxford, Blackwell.

Trade Unions, Control and Resistance
53

Jackson, D., Turner, H. A. and Wilkinson, F. (1972) Do Trade Unions Cause Inflation?, Cambridge, Cambridge University Press.
Mann, M. (1973) Consciousness and Action among the Western Working Class, London, Macmillan.
McCarthy, W. E. J. and Parker, S. R. (1968) Shop Stewards and Workshop Relations, London, HMSO.
Marglin, S. (1974) 'What Do Bosses Do?', Review of Radical Political Economics, Vol. 6, pp. 60–112.
Marx, K. (1934) Letter to Bolte, 23 November 1871, in Selected Correspondence of Marx and Engels, London, Lawrence and Wishart.
Marx, K. (1959) Capital, Vol. I, London, Lawrence and Wishart.
Marx, K. (1962) Manifesto of the Communist Party in Marx-Engels' Selected Works, Vol. I, Moscow, Foreign Languages Publishing House.
Marx, K. (1973) Grundrisse: Foundations of the Critique of Political Economy, Harmondsworth, Penguin.
Marx, K. and Engels, F. (1956) The Holy Family, Moscow, Foreign Languages Publishing House.
Miliband, R. (1964) Parliamentary Socialism, London, Merlin Press.
Mills, C. W. (1948) The New Men of Power, New York, Harcourt Brace.
Nichols, T. (1969) Ownership, Control and Ideology, London, Allen and Unwin.
Strauss, A., Schatzman, L., Ehrlich, D., Bucher, R. and Sabshin, M. (1971) 'The Hospital and its Negotiated Order', in Castles, F. G., Murray, D. J. and Potter, D. C. Decisions, Organizations and Society, Harmondsworth, Penguin.
Sykes, A. J. M. (1967) 'The Cohesion of a Trade Union Workshop Organization', Sociology, Vol. 1, pp. 141–63.
Sykes, A. J. M. (1973) 'Work Attitudes of Navvies', in Weir, D., Men and Work in Modern Britain, London, Fontana, pp. 203–20.
Webb, S. and Webb, B. (1920) History of Trade Unionism, London, Longman.
Westergaard, J. H. (1970) 'The Rediscovery of the Cash Nexus', in Miliband, R. and Saville, J., Socialist Register 1970, London, Merlin Press.

3 Pluralism, Procedural Consensus and Collective Bargaining*

It is often a sterile exercise to attach labels to particular theorists in the hope that this will clearly indicate their beliefs and fashions of analysis: this is one of the lessons to be drawn from recent controversy on pluralism in industrial relations. Practical persons are usually unconcerned with the finer points of definitional exactitude, and it is no accident that pluralism was once described as 'just a term for a convenient mode of treating *pragmatism* from a theological point of view'.[1] The links between pluralism and pragmatism in industrial relations are particularly intimate;[2] because of the overriding concern of most adherents with immediate practical problems, pluralism as a theology has been remarkably poorly endowed with explicit dogma (however rich in unstated and implicit presuppositions). There is thus little value in arguments along the lines that a certain author is a pluralist and must therefore be held to endorse a given series of propositions.

The purpose of the discussion that follows is not then to insist on a particular interpretation of what pluralism really means. The aim is rather to examine how far certain affinities in terms of orientations and underlying assumptions (commonly identified as pluralist) have shaped the academic analysis of industrial relations; and how far this has encouraged a conception of the subject and of the dynamics of the industrial relations 'system' which obscures or excludes altogether from consideration what should be an important part of the subject's focus.

The main burden of what follows may be briefly summarised. Pluralism is in no way a homogeneous body of analysis and prescription; its development in philosophy, in sociology and in political theory reflects varied disciplinary roots, diverse conceptual and interpretative problems, and the impact of historically changing ideological forces. The usage of the notion of pluralism in industrial relations is comparatively recent, and the reference made to previous

*First published in *British Journal of Industrial Relations*, Vol. 16, No. 1, March 1978.

meanings of the concept, if explicit at all, has tended to vary according to writer and context. A further complication is that, well before the label pluralism was generally applied to Anglo-American industrial relations orthodoxy, much of the literature appeared to incorporate assumptions reflecting pluralist approaches to other fields of study; and these assumptions have seemingly, though rarely unambiguously and explicitly, been carried over into the mainstream of what became known as industrial relations pluralism. A further perplexity is that few of those British theorists most commonly identified as industrial relations pluralists have offered detailed definitions of the concept, or indeed have even made much use of the term in their own writings; but it is not difficult to detect significant variations in the form and derivation of different pluralists' pluralism. This fact is of key importance for any appraisal of Clegg's critique of Fox in 'Pluralism in Industrial Relations':[3] for while Clegg helpfully clarifies his own previous conception of pluralism, and exposes certain weaknesses in the construction of Fox's critique of 'pluralist ideology', it might be thought that he makes only limited contact with the core of the latter's argument precisely because each employs a conception of pluralism which is in crucial respects distinctive.

This suggests the conclusion that if 'pluralism' is to be a useful component of the vocabulary of British industrial relations, it must be regarded as a loose and incomplete set of ideas, beliefs and values which acquire coherence only when complemented by background assumptions which are rarely articulated explicitly by pluralist writers themselves. This gives rise to problems of interpretation analogous to those discussed by Macpherson in the context of seventeenth-century political philosophy: the presumption that a theorist is 'using some assumptions beyond those he has explicitly formulated . . . cannot be certainly established'.[4] For normal purposes of argument, points taken for granted within a writer's intellectual environment do not require explicit assertion; hence it may be possible to show that their incorporation unifies and integrates the writer's thesis, but not to *prove* that this is definitely intended. Despite this limitation, an attempt to 'complete' the assumptions of industrial relations pluralism can be of value in illuminating a central problem of the most influential current approaches to the subject.

PLURALISM'S PLURALISM

'The concept of pluralism,' according to the recent comment of a political theorist, 'is ambiguous and contentious'.[5] Historically its usage has itself displayed considerable pluralism. The first instance known to the *Oxford English Dictionary* dates from 1818: a denunciation by Bentham of 'obtainment on false pretences, as proved by Non-Residence, Pluralism and Sinecurism'. The term 'pluralist' was used as early as 1626 to denote a religious functionary occupying more than one benefice; by the late nineteenth century the concept of 'pluralism' was applied to multiple office-holding of any kind.

As the characterisation of an intellectual approach or doctrine the term entered the English language comparatively late (if the OED is to be relied on, towards the end of the nineteenth century). The original application was in the field of philosophy, and the antecedents were German. 'Pluralismus' – the conception of reality as constituted on the basis of a number of distinct and autonomous fundamental principles – was expounded in the early nineteenth century by Christian von Wolff. Philosophical pluralism found its most influential populariser at the beginning of the present century in William James, who developed first an epistemological, then an ontological interpretation of the doctrine: from a starting point that reality can only be *known* pluralistically he reached the conclusion that its *existence* is essentially pluralistic. His arguments achieved extensive dissemination with the publication of his 1909 Hibbert lectures under the title *A Pluralistic Universe*.[6]

The concept was rapidly borrowed and adapted to suit the varied analytical controversies of the social sciences. The most extensive application of pluralism in recent years on both sides of the Atlantic has, of course, been in the study of politics. It must be emphasised that, as Nicholls demonstrates in his *Three Varieties of Pluralism*[7] (arguably a considerable understatement), political pluralism in Britain and the United States has differed substantially in orientation and emphasis.

British political pluralism was very much a product of the early twentieth century, developing largely as a reaction to the dominance of neo-Hegelian theories of the supremacy and organic unity of the state. 'The Pluralist movement in England', comments Martin, 'was fed by many streams; it became as curious an amalgam as could be found in the complicated history of political chemistry'.[8] The range of sources was evident in the writings of Harold Laski, perhaps the most prolific exponent of the school. Through Maitland he discovered the theories of the German constitutional and legal historian Gierke, who argued that state sovereignty had traditionally been qualified and conditioned by the legal recognition of the rights and privileges of innumerable semi-autonomous groups and associations.[9] The denial of the idea of state sovereignty was central to the work of the French legal theorist Duguit (whose *Law in the Modern State* the Laskis translated into English):[10] while the *power* of the state had come increasingly to exceed that of the various collectivities which mediated between it and the individual, it possessed no *right* to command obedience. The citizen's loyalty to the state should be considered conditional on its performance of a public service; and the people themselves had the right to judge whether this function was adequately discharged. Laski was in addition profoundly influenced by William James, whose *Pluralistic Universe* he regarded as of 'vital significance for political theory'.[11] James's principle that 'the pluralistic world ... is more like a federal republic than an empire or a kingdom'[12] was presented by Laski as essential for an adequate understanding of the state: 'men belong to it; but, also, they belong to other groups, and a competition for allegiance is continuously possible'.[13] The theologian J. N. Figgis, whose analysis of the respective rights of church and state showed many parallels with the concerns of Gierke and Maitland, was another important originator of British political pluralism; according to Laski his writings had 'done much to dissipate the notion of an omnicompetent state'.[14]

The doctrine constituted from these diverse influences combined aspects of constitutional law, social and historical analysis, and political prescription. Historically and legally, it was insisted, the authority of the state did not override the rights of groups and associations which formed the most immediate contexts of citizens' collective attachments. Such groupings, it was often added, generated a network of social relationships and linkages which sustained individual identity and social integration. British pluralists endorsed Durkheim's dictum that 'a nation can be maintained only if, between the State and the individual, there is intercalated a whole series of secondary groups'.[15]

Beyond agreement on these fundamental points, the approaches of the early political pluralists diverged. Some identified closely with the traditions of liberal individualism (later to exert a dominant influence on the development of American pluralism). Others were socialists who rejected the identification of collectivism with an accumulation of centralised state power: their preferred alternatives took many forms, including the revolutionary programmes of anarcho-syndicalists and the more gradualist blueprints of Guild Socialists.[16] Yet others developed the notion of functional differentiation within society, and the organisation of this differentiation on the basis of corporative groupings, into a theoretical position later susceptible to the appeal of fascism. What united these diverse tendencies within British pluralism was an inclination to discern the pluralist ideal in mediaeval society; a belief that traditional rights and liberties were under threat from increasing state authoritarianism; and an insistence that a resistance to this trend, a reinforcement of the status of intermediate associations, was a precondition of the maintenance of individual freedom as well as a support (though not necessarily a guarantee) for political stability. 'The richness of corporate lives', argued Laski, was an important bulwark against 'simple servility'.[17]

British pluralism was thus self-consciously heterodox, a challenge to what was identified as the dominant material and intellectual tendency of contemporary politics: the theory and practice of the 'servile state'. American pluralism, by contrast, came into its own as an essentially *conservative* doctrine: a legitimation (or often glorification) of socio-political relations in the post-war United States, an elaboration of the orthodoxy of everyday political discussion. While 'pluralist democracy' for the early British theorists was under attack from *within* their societies, most notably from the institutions of state power itself, for Americans the challenge was external: 'pluralism' denoted current political practice in the USA, explicitly counterposed to the 'totalitarianism' of the Soviet Union and its satellites. The sway of American political pluralism was both a product and a justification of the cold war.

Nicholls has traced American pluralism back to the writings of A. F. Bentley at the turn of the century (though he does not explain the gap of fifty years before his ideas achieved a position of intellectual dominance).[18] Far more rapidly influential was Schumpeter's 'new theory of democracy' which appeared mid-way through the Second World War.[19] Adapting classical economic propositions to the analysis of politics, Schumpeter defined democracy as 'that institutional arrangement for arriving at political decisions in which individuals acquire the power to decide by means of a competitive struggle for the people's vote'.[20] His basic purpose was to demolish what he termed the 'classical' theory of democracy, the central principle of which was the need for active popular participation in political decision making.[21] Schumpeter argued that just as in traditional economic theory the interests of consumers were safeguarded by competition among sellers in the marketplace, so the interests of citizens were guaranteed by the electoral competition of rival political parties. Though not *directly* subject to popular control, governments were ultimately accountable since opposing parties would seek to expose and attack unpopular policies with an eye to future elections. Rights of organised opposition were thus the prerequisite of democratic credentials (a principle of obvious attraction for the armoury of anti-Communism). Schumpeter refers, though only in passing, to sectional interest groups and associations as a component of the fabric of democratic society; later writers, often drawing on the acute insights of de Tocqueville, were to pursue a variety of empirical studies of 'pressure group politics' and to combine their conclusions with the more central Schumpeterian arguments to produce the theory of democracy as 'polyarchy'.[22]

American pluralism, like its British predecessor, thus came to assign key significance to intermediate groups between the state and the individual: a protection against the social atomism of the 'mass society' in which citizens were susceptible to totalitarian manipulation. But whereas British pluralism stressed the *functional interdependence* of intermediate groups, the American version emphasised *inter-group competition*. British pluralism idealised a pre-capitalist past; American pluralism idealised the existing political institutions of American capitalism. In the 1950s, comments Nicholls, pluralist theory increasingly

> took on the role of an 'ideology', designed to explain and justify the system of government found in the United States.... A free society, as opposed to totalitarianism, is characterised, and is protected, by the existence of semi-autonomous groups with overlapping membership; there is thus no single centre of power, no monolithic body, attempting to impose upon the country some total way of life, but rather a benevolent empire ensuring that all groups are able to have a foot in the political door. The old ideology of rugged individualism, no longer tenable either in the field of economic organisation or in political theory, was replaced by a conception of 'countervailing power'.[23]

The orthodoxy of American political sociology was buttressed by a series of 'community power' studies which sought and (given their methodological identification of power with decision-making) necessarily discovered a pluralistic diffusion of power. 'Any active and legitimate group', according to Dahl, 'will make itself heard at some stage in the process of decision'.[24] The membership of voluntary social and economic groupings was at one and the same time divergent yet cross-cutting and overlapping; a complex network of interests and affiliations prevented dangerous accumulations of social power or the instability of radical social divisions (an insight attributable to Simmel). In place of class antagonism, pluralism posited the complex interpenetration of sectional interests; in place of class-based political domination, the alternation in government of rival parties each subject to the constraints and influence of organised group pressure.[25] The central theme of the American doctrine was succinctly presented by Dahrendorf: 'pluralism of institutions, conflict patterns, groupings, and interests makes for a lively, colorful and creative scene of political conflict which provides an opportunity for success for every interest that is voiced'.[26]

The assumptions of this (by then) dominant tendency in political theory were explicitly applied to the field of industrial relations by Clark Kerr, in his 1954 presidential address to the Industrial Relations Research Association.[27] Kerr identifies 'the diffusion of power into substantial, or even large, numbers of centers' as the distinctive contribution of the USA to human freedom. His own approach he relates to the theories of inter-war pluralists who 'brought to the forefront the question of what to do with the many organized power centers in modern western society [and who] argued that these centers should have substantial authority over the affairs of men, if not full sovereignty'.[28] Just as pluralism is compatible with stability in political life, so the organised interaction (and opposition) of interest groups in industrial relations need not entail disruption. One reason for the compatibility of pluralism and industrial peace is the historical background of economic expansion, allowing scope for compromise among the contending parties. Another is the fact that 'rules of the game have been developed by government and the parties themselves to keep within generally reasonable bounds their actions towards each other'.[29] This latter proposition was already familiar to students of industrial relations under such labels as the 'institutionalisation of conflict', and was soon to become one of the commonplaces of the literature on the subject.

Before turning to a more detailed examination of pluralism in industrial relations, some problems evident in the more general development of pluralism as a theory of (or approach to) reality and society may be summarised. As Eldridge remarks, 'written into the notion of pluralism in the most formal sense is the idea of competing social forces which constrain and check absolutism'.[30] The form and extent of the necessary competition is unspecified in so general a definition: and the detail is completed by different pluralists in different ways. For some the contrast is with social monism: the 'countervailing power' of two adversaries can constitute pluralism. For others, the emphasis is on competition among *many* power centres. Yet others contrast pluralism with social atomism: too great a fragmentation would verge upon the 'mass society'. (Other forms of pluralism, as has been seen – and despite Eldridge's summation – are not primarily concerned with competition at all.) Clearly what is at issue is not some homogeneous doctrine, rather a set of overlapping but to some extent mutually incompatible theories and arguments. From the outset, moreover, pluralist analysis of social relations has combined description and prescription: reality and ideal have rarely been clearly differentiated. In the climate of the cold war, the problem of pluralism as ideology has inevitably been greatly accentuated.

In the field of industrial relations, Kerr's seminal paper is alone sufficient to reveal some of the difficulties raised by the notion of pluralism. Kerr explicitly defines himself as a *liberal* pluralist, in contrast to his American predecessors. The latter, he argues, 'were solicitous about the autonomy of the association vis-à-vis the state; the liberal pluralist must equally cherish the independence of the individual vis-à-vis the group'.[31] Absolutism could exist within the private association – and specifically, the trade union – as well as within the state, and was an equal danger and evil. In this respect Kerr is probably typical of the concerns of many American pluralists (which may reflect both the nature of the dominant social values, and the actual practice of trade unionism, in the contemporary United States). British pluralists, by contrast, have tended to insist that unions must be internally strong if they are to function effectively in their external relations as components of a pluralistic industrial relations system. In this issue, two distinctive conceptions of pluralistic industrial relations may be discerned: first, a focus on pluralism *within* industrial relations; secondly, an emphasis on the *autonomy* of industrial relations ('self-government in industry') as a major element in societal pluralism. The two conceptions are not necessarily compatible.

INDUSTRIAL RELATIONS ORTHODOXY: SOME BACKGROUND ASSUMPTIONS

If Kerr introduced the *concept* of pluralism to the analysis of the relations of unions with employers and with their own members, the approaches of many earlier writers contained assumptions – indeed often explicit assertions – which would normally be regarded as pluralist. These have subsequently been regarded by many commentators as integral components of industrial relations pluralism.[32]

Three such assumptions are of key importance. The first is that there are no undue concentrations of economic power, particularly in the labour market. Such power is either so extensively diffused that there exist no large accumulations; or else the power which, it is recognised, can be wielded by large corporations is more or less evenly balanced by that of organised labour. The second assumption is that, despite the plurality of sectional interest groups within contemporary society, it is meaningful to refer (usually without the slightest indication of the conceptual and theoretical difficulties entailed) to a 'public' or 'national' interest. Thirdly, the state is regarded as the more or less impartial guardian of this 'public interest', not subject to excessive influence from the economically powerful (precisely because no such homogeneous group exists), but on the contrary able to deploy its own power to buttress the weak and restrain any groups which may display signs of undue aggrandisement.

The proposition that there exists a public interest common to all groups and classes in the society, and that the state is its natural defender, is a principle of everyday commonsense which has from the very beginning informed the scholarly study of industrial relations. Thus the Webbs, in *Industrial Democracy*, note with approval the development of 'the view that, quite apart from the merits of the case, the stoppage of work by an industrial dispute is a public nuisance, an injury to the commonwealth, which ought to be prevented by the Government'. In like vein they predict that

> whenever an industrial dispute reaches a certain magnitude, a democratic state will, in the interests of the community as a whole, not scruple to intervene.... The State is a partner in every enterprise. In the interests of the community as a whole, no one of the interminable series of decisions can be allowed to run counter to the consensus of expert opinion representing the consumers on the one hand, the producers on the other, and the nation that is paramount over both.[33]

Some features of the Webbs' technocratic collectivism, and their faith in the rapid triumph of the Method of Legal Enactment, were evidently idiosyncratic and were to be transcended in the later development of British Fabianism. For a time their assumptions were to be more fundamentally contested among Fabian students of industrial relations, with the insistence of Cole and other Guild Socialists that the 'monstrous and irrefutable fact' of class antagonism within capitalism made notions of an overreaching public interest vacuous; and that the state was itself a repressive institution the action of which normally reflected the balance of forces in the economic sphere.[34] But such challenges to orthodoxy were soon muted; and the reconstructed Fabianism which formed the background to academic industrial relations in its 1950s renaissance showed few signs of unease at the notions of the 'community as a whole' and the state as its impartial representative.[35]

British students of industrial relations have often shown some reluctance to discuss the distribution of power in society: against the background of a strong empiricist tradition, such questions could readily be dismissed as metaphysical.[36] American writers (perhaps because many have shared with the labour economists a concern to develop theoretical analyses of 'bargaining power') have proved less reticent. The argument has been repeatedly rehearsed that a combination of full employment and (perhaps excessive) legislative support for collective organisation among workers permitted union power to equal, or even exceed, that of employers. This assertion is then commonly linked to the Webbian proposition that 'the public' or 'the nation' requires government intervention to protect its interests.[37] Three early post-war studies exemplify this approach admirably. Moore viewed the legislation of the 1930s (most notably the Wagner Act) as having achieved 'a roughly approximate equality in the power of the bargainers' and added that

> any further regulation of the course of industrial relations rests upon the thesis that in any conflict between special interest groups, the public willy-nilly becomes involved, and, indeed, that in the last analysis the public interest is preeminent. This amounts to saying that the government has the right (and some would say, the duty) to intervene and adjudicate disputes in the public interest.[38]

Slichter went further, describing American unions as 'the most powerful private organizations in the country'. He was thus moved to enquire:

What does the community propose to do to control the enormous power of unions. . .? When the public undertook to encourage unions, it thought that it was helping downtrodden and oppressed men to help themselves. It did not foresee the great power that it was placing in the hands of a few men. Now that this great power has been created, the community must decide what to do about it.[39]

Writing in the same year, Selekman insisted that 'the time has passed in which the dominating power of the employer had to be balanced by fusing the group strength of the rank and file workers. Instead, two great aggregates of industrial power now face one another'. His basic theme was that 'the public' would insist on government regulation of industrial relations unless union leaders themselves displayed 'maturity' and 'responsibility'.[40] It was not unusual, subsequently, for the Taft-Hartley Act to be explained (and commonly justified) in precisely such terms.[41]

Such an approach to the distribution of power between unions and employers has been reinforced by Galbraith's elaboration of the general principle that 'private economic power is held in check by the countervailing power of those who are subject to it', and his specific suggestion that 'the operation of countervailing power is to be seen with the greatest clarity in the labour market where it is also most fully developed'.[42] The view of economic power as more or less evenly divided between 'big labour' and 'big capital' naturally encourages the conception of the 'public interest' as the third party to collective bargaining, unrepresented unless through government intervention. The same view (or the variant which treats economic power as thinly spread among a multiplicity of groups and associations) also facilitates an unproblematic approach to government as an impartial agency easily able to 'set the rules of the game within which . . . conflict will occur, enforce these rules, and act as mediator'.[43] Notions of this kind constantly recur in the literature of American industrial relations pluralism, sometimes explicitly asserted, often as part of the unstated premises indicated by the general tenor of the analysis.[44]

THE DEVELOPMENT OF PLURALISM IN BRITISH INDUSTRIAL RELATIONS

The explicit elaboration of a pluralist approach to industrial relations is commonly identified with what has often been labelled the 'Oxford school'.[45] This label has usually been resisted by the putative members of the 'school', for understandable reasons. Despite some shared orientations among the most prominent students of industrial relations at Oxford in the 1950s and 60s – a readiness to contribute to the publications of the Fabian Society and/or *Socialist Commentary*, a concern to influence the formulation and application of 'public policy' (perhaps most notably through the work of the Donovan Commission) – there were evident divergences within the group. Most importantly, several writers based in Oxford during these decades were concerned essentially with practical and narrowly defined industrial relations 'problems' rather than with general issues of industrial relations (let alone broader social and political) theory. The theoretical background to their pragmatism was essentially *implicit*; if they are to be regarded as pluralists, it is by virtue of their apparent background assumptions rather than their explicit assertions.

Arguably there were only three Oxford academics in this period with an explicit concern for general questions of industrial relations theory and an unqualified commitment to an approach which in at least one of the senses outlined earlier is unambiguously pluralist: Hugh Clegg, Allan Flanders and Alan Fox. If these are to be regarded as the main British pluralists, it is interesting and perhaps surprising that the concept itself was not part of the regular vocabulary of the writings of the majority of the three. Clegg does not appear to have used the term in an academic publication before his defence of pluralism in 1975. The first use by Flanders would seem to be in his 'Internal Social Responsibilities of Industry' in 1966; the reference is to the business enterprise as 'a pluralistic society'[46] rather than to the more general role of trade unionism in economic life, and the implications of pluralism as a systematic social doctrine are not explicitly developed in Flanders' later writings. The one author to make pluralism by name a major focus of discussion is Fox; and in considering the nature of the pluralism of these three authors it is appropriate to commence with him.

Fox's distinction between the unitary and pluralistic conceptions of the industrial enterprise, made famous by his 1966 Research Paper *Industrial Sociology and Industrial Relations*,[47] was set out more briefly in an article three years earlier.[48] In both cases he refers to the view of the business organisation as a 'plural society' which Ross outlined in 1958.[49] As the most immediate source of British industrial relations pluralism, the analysis which Ross presents therefore merits explicit consideration.

Ross commences by criticising the 'unitary concept' of a firm as an integrated team; effective management, he argues, requires the 'recognition of and adaptation to group goals of many kinds'. What is needed, he continues,

> is a theoretical approach to management which treats the firm as a plural society rather than as the organic unity which most theorists appear hitherto to have represented it to be. The problem of government in a plural society is not to unify, integrate or liquidate sectional groups and their special interests in the name of some over-riding corporate existence, but to control and balance the activities of constituent groups so as to provide for the maximum degree of freedom of association and action for sectional and group purposes consistent with the general interest of the society as conceived, with the support of public opinion, by those responsible for its government.[50]

When Ross considers relations between workers *collectively* and their employers, he explicitly insists that power is evenly balanced: 'the development of the practice of collective bargaining, and the institutional arrangements associated with it ... has resulted in the establishment of parity of bargaining strength between employers and employed'.[51] Not only is this empirically the case, but necessarily so: one of the conditions of stable industrial relations is that 'the balance of power between the parties should not be markedly uneven'.[52] In general, however, the essence of pluralism as expounded by Ross is that employees should not be regarded as a single coherent group (let alone a *class*) but as fragmented among a multiplicity of sectional grouplets. The focus is not on the workforce as possessing common interests systematically antagonistic to those of the employer, but rather on internal conflicts and divisions which (by implication) are more significant than those between employees generally and those controlling the enterprise. On the familiar principle of this variety of pluralism, the existence of numerous cross-cutting sectional interests is a potential source of cohesion: Ross thus presents 'the concept of the firm as a system of dynamic equilibrium of a number of separate but interdependent group or sectional interests'.[53] Paradoxically, the specification of a plurality of interest divisions also permits Ross to refer without embarrassment to 'the general interest of the society' (even though, in the same sentence, he derides the notion of 'some over-riding corporate existence'). Hence management can be identified as the rational agent of an underlying collective purpose, rather than as the representative of interests opposed to those of subordinate employees: 'the task of management in this system of relationships is to reconcile individual and group objectives as closely as possible to the [firm's] central objective in order to enable the firm to work efficiently towards that end'.[54] Finally it may be noted that Ross provides a clear link between modern British industrial relations pluralism and the tradition discussed in the previous section: among the few references appended to his study is Kerr's paper 'Industrial Relations and the Liberal Pluralist'.

In his popularisation of the 'pluralistic frame of reference', Fox summarises several of the key points outlined above; he does not pursue (though neither does he disavow) the detailed ramifications of pluralism as presented by Ross. It may be noted that in his 1966 accounts of pluralism Fox shares with Ross a focus on industrial relations within the workplace rather than at the broader societal level. Like Ross he stresses the *multiplicity* of sectional interests within the enterprise; while conflicts between managements and other employees are treated as the outcome of functional differentiation rather than a structural antagonism of interests. The distribution of power and resources within the enterprise (and the way in which this is articulated with the wider social distribution of power) is not explicitly considered, and a balance of power is not therefore asserted; though such an assumption might appear to underlie such comments as: 'management has to face the fact that there are other sources of leadership, other focuses of loyalty, within the plural society it governs and that it *must share its decision making with them*'.[55] At the very least, it would appear that no conception of a radical disparity of power underlies the characterisation of the enterprise as 'a coalition of interests, a miniature democratic state composed of sectional groups with divergent interests over which the government tries to maintain some kind of dynamic equilibrium'.[56] It is interesting that in his more elaborate and systematic theoretical study *A Sociology of Work in Industry*, Fox employs the model of the firm as 'a coalition of stakeholders' in order to stress the diversity and multiplicity of intersecting interests. He goes on to enquire:

> What mechanisms exist through which the various stakeholders can hope to influence the ways in which management exercises its

discretion? Do these mechanisms favour some stakeholders as against others? By what values or ideologies are these mechanisms – or their absence – on the one hand justified, and on the other, challenged?

Such questions test pluralism where its vulnerability is greatest; and having raised them, Fox does no more than comment that 'these questions cannot be pursued here'.[57] Only with his critique of pluralism in 1973 and 1974 was a detailed reply attempted.

Flanders, as was noted above, did not engage in explicit discussion of the implications of pluralist theory; but his writings exhibit a number of the assumptions discussed in the previous section. The notion of a public interest of which the government is the guardian recurs, most particularly perhaps in his discussions of incomes policy. 'The case for a national wage policy', Flanders began an article in 1958, 'rests upon a single and simple premise, that there is an undefended public interest in the results of collective bargaining.'[58] Earlier he had written that

> the need for a national wages policy has arisen because there is a *public* interest in the outcome of negotiation and arbitration. It is no criticism of the trade unions to recognise that their majority view on wages policy ... may be at variance with the public interest, which only the Government can interpret in accordance with the mandate which it seeks and receives from the electorate.[59]

Subsequently one of the sections of his influential evidence to the Donovan Commission was headed 'Collective Bargaining and the Public Interest'. On occasion the uncritical use of the notion of a common national interest was linked to an explicit assertion of consensual national values. In *Industrial Relations: What is Wrong with the System?* he argued that the notion of a national industrial relations sytem was meaningful

> because the nation is an entity. The unity in this diversity is to be found in certain underlying principles, expressing value judgements, which are broadly accepted throughout the nation.... Fundamental to the argument of this essay ... is the thesis that the principles of any national system of industrial relations – and therefore their institutional consequences – are derived from the values by which the nation judges and legitimises the system's working and results.

The role of the state could itself be treated as one of the 'institutional consequences' of consensual values: 'the general legal framework of external job regulation is one manifestation of such principles, but so is the administrative role of government'.[60]

Like Ross and Fox, Flanders was willing to assume that despite the plurality of divergent interests within industrial organisations, it was nevertheless meaningful to speak in general terms of 'the ends of the enterprise'.[61] The conception of a single purpose underlying productive activity is closely related to an ambivalent use of such notions as 'rationality' and 'efficiency'. One important theme in Flanders' writings is that practices condemned by employers as 'restrictive' or 'inefficient' may represent rational strategies by workers pursuing their own divergent interests. This argument is vitally important: the concepts of efficiency and rationality apply properly to the evaluation of alternative *means* to given ends. Unless these ends are known, it is not logically possible to evaluate the rationality or efficiency of any act or practice as a means. Nor can it be assumed that the objectives of one party to a relationship necessarily coincide with those of others: what is rational and efficient for one may be irrational and inefficient for those with different aims and interests. Yet Flanders appears to contradict this insight with his identification of efficiency with the 'social function' of management.

Management's primary commitment is to efficiency; its job is to organize the use of human and material resources to produce the best results with an economy of effort. Working practices which are grossly inefficient are a challenge to management that it can ignore only at the price of professional incompetence.[62]

Also significant is Flanders' comment that 'the rationality implicit in planning appears to be an enemy of the sectional pressures unleashed by democracy'.[63] What such arguments neglect is the extent to which practices which for employers are 'grossly inefficient' may be *efficient* means to the distinctive goals of the 'human resources' (i.e. workers) who sustain them; or the possibility that increased control by shop-floor workers may alter the operation of production in ways which are highly *rational* in the light of their own interests, however much they obstruct the intentions of planners within companies or government agencies; or the fact that the priorities of capitalist industry (to which management is formally committed) are themselves only one (however dominant in practice) among a variety of 'sectional pressures'. One consequence of this ambivalent orientation to the concepts of rationality and efficiency is to bestow special endorsement on the 'logic' inherent in capitalist production; another is to confine within somewhat narrow limits the extent to which workers' interests may be recognised as diverging from those of the employer.[64]

In his references to the distribution of power in industry, Flanders indicated general agreement with the conclusions of earlier pluralist writers. 'The change in the state of labour markets, with employers competing for employees more strongly than the latter are competing for jobs, undermines the case that could once be argued that union organisation was needed to redress a position of bargaining inequality.' National economic planning reinforced the effect of full employment: 'the balance of power between employers and employees has been shifted very much more in the latter's favour. The trade unions have also gained a new place in society and its economic government which gives them a greater voice in the nation's affairs.' The reversal in power relations, Flanders often argued, was particularly apparent within the workplace: 'ill-prepared managements have found themselves faced with a much stronger, and often a new, bargaining power on the shop floor: not the bargaining power of trade unions as such, but of work groups who have their own sanctions ranging from the instant stoppage to bans on overtime or the withdrawal of co-operation'.[65]

Of the three 'Oxford' writers under consideration, Flanders was the most extensively versed in the literature of American industrial relations, making frequent reference to its theoretical contributions in his own analysis. At times he was critical of American theories – most notably in his discussion of Chamberlain in 'Collective Bargaining: a Theoretical Analysis'. (The same article also indicates both the extent to which he shared the viewpoint of the Webbs, and the extent of his divergence.) But his criticism did not extend to any fundamental challenge to the assumptions outlined in the previous section; indeed, as the quotations above indicate, he appeared to approach industrial relations with similar presuppositions. The distinctive contribution which Fox brought to industrial relations pluralism was a sociological orientation (at a time when sociology was regarded with some suspicion by leading British students of the subject). Most specifically, he drew from Durkheim a concern with the relationship between economic processes and institutions on the one hand, and the dynamics of normative cohesion or conflict on the other. Such issues were of course in the forefront of the Parsonian approach which dominated postwar academic sociology.[66]

The separate analytical backgrounds of Fox and Flanders were synthesised in their joint article 'The Reform of Collective Bargaining: from Donovan to Durkheim'.[67] The title precisely defines the direction of their argument: the conclusion of the Donovan Commission that the 'anarchy and disorder' of British industrial relations in the 1960s were directly attributable to the conflict between 'two systems'[68] is re-interpreted within the categories of Durkheim's major works. The central issue of their discussion is represented by the notion of 'normative order'. Fox and Flanders identify two 'ideal types' of society. In the first (which bears a close resemblance to Durkheim's pattern of 'mechanical solidarity') there is no scope for diversity of behaviour; 'the tasks of norm creation and enforcement are wholly centralised' and uniformity is imposed 'by the coercive powers of the state'.

At the opposite extreme we have the pluralistic society with the least possible statutory regulation of employment relations. Through the mechanisms of freedom of contract, freedom of association, an unrestricted traffic in ideas and ideologies, combined with a strong preference for voluntary action, there develops a wide varietyof relatively autonomous but inter-acting norm-creating groups and agencies. The result is a multiplicity of separate normative systems.[69]

The necessary consequence is some degree of disorder and conflict; the central problem for Fox and Flanders is how 'normative disorder' can be kept 'within socially tolerable bounds' (hence sustaining what Durkheim termed 'organic solidarity'). They interpret the pattern of industrial relations which formed the centrepiece of the Donovan analysis as 'a progressive fragmentation and breakdown of existing regulative systems';[70] this they attribute to a lack of articulation between the balance of shop-floor power, the substantive aspirations of employee groups, and the procedural norms and institutions designed to achieve some form of accommodation among the parties to collective bargaining. The Donovan proposals for the formalisation of bargaining at plant or company level are presented as a basis for 'building up agreement on procedural norms on how substantive relations are to be regulated'.[71] The ultimate objective is the 'reconstruction of normative order' in industrial relations through the creation of a new 'procedural consensus'.[72]

Pluralism, as Fox and Flanders present it here, is *not a theory of sovereignty but of social differentiation*; the key issue is the maintenance of social integration despite group autonomy and government non-intervention. This conception of pluralism contrasts radically with that of Clegg. The development of his analysis echoes the argument of Schumpeter; 'democracy is not only a matter of choosing who shall govern, it is a matter of making that choice more than formal by allowing opposition between parties, so that the elector may choose between men and between policies.'[73] A decade later Clegg added to electoral opposition an emphasis on pressure group politics as a constituent of democracy:

> Every important interest is organized and represented. As soon as its organization acquires some following it is recognized by the government and by one or more of the political parties (if not all). Its spokesmen are heard, its claims and grievances are studied, and those with authority in the administration and in the parties make strenuous efforts to come to terms with them. All the claims of all the pressure groups cannot be met. But so much of what they seek can be given to them, together with such good reasons for refusing to meet the rest, as to make them think that they are being treated fairly, and that their bargaining is giving them as much as they could reasonably expect. The consequence of this system is that most groups in society are integrated of their own free will into the political system.[74]

Clegg's distinctive contribution was to apply the competitive theory of democracy to industrial relations, with the argument that 'the trade union is industry's opposition'.[75] While accepting that 'there are important differences between politics and industry, and no analogy drawn from political democracy can be applied direct to industry without reference to them', his firm conclusion was that 'the main duty of a trade union is, and must remain, to oppose'.[76] Independent trade unionism – independent of both management and the state – had created, within capitalism, the only possible form of industrial democracy. Direct participation by trade unions in management would compromise their independence and hence subvert their effectiveness as an opposition;[77] while public ownership of industry was irrelevant to industrial democracy (indeed if applied comprehensively would concentrate within the state such economic power that democracy would be endangered).

Clegg's theories of democracy – industrial and political – he has described as 'both pessimistic and traditional': 'They are rooted in distrust – distrust of power. They argue that the political and industrial institutions of the stable democracies already approach the best that can be realized. They return to traditions of liberal thought which preceded the rise of socialism.'[78] 'Distrust of power' connects Clegg's pluralism far more closely than that of Fox or Flanders to the concerns of both British and American political pluralists. Accordingly, his main theoretical attention is to the *societal* role of trade unions as industry's opposition. But in consequence, his theory offers little illumination of the role of unionism within the workplace and in the detail of collective bargaining – a major analytical concern of the other authors. Clegg's treatment of issues arising at this level is essentially descriptive and pragmatic. This is evident in his argument that the trade union, while it must oppose, must not 'avoid responsibility at all costs' and thus embrace 'the easy but largely ineffective role of permanent opposition'; on the contrary he insists 'that it is necessary for a union both to oppose and to agree, and that industrial arrangements deserve to be called democratic only when these two functions are within the region of balance'.[79] He accepts as compatible with industrial democracy the view of the 'progressive employer' that 'the management of industry is fundamentally sound, and requires independent opposition only to guide it into the right course'; and concludes that 'as soon as we reject any simple and unique definition of industrial democracy we can see that a number of combinations of its elements – trade union opposition and willing participation of workers with management in a common enterprise – is possible'.[80] Clegg does not, however, offer a theoretical framework for the analysis of different modes of interaction of opposition and agreement, or criteria for identifying the 'region of balance'.[81]

BRITISH PLURALISM: CRITICS AND COUNTER-CRITICS

The distinctive background of Clegg's approach to industrial relations is of obvious relevance for any appraisal of his rejoinder to the criticism of pluralism which Fox develops in *Beyond Contract*. Clegg states that 'pluralism emerged as a criticism of the political doctrine of sovereignty'; and defines a plural society in terms of the legitimate existence and autonomous activity of pressure groups. The stability of such societies indicates that 'there must be some mechanism at work which binds the competing groups together and holds them back from rending their societies to pieces. For the pluralist this mechanism is the continuous process of concession and compromise.' This process in turn probably requires a society with sufficient material resources to permit concessions which keep the various groups reasonably satisfied.[82]

Clegg differentiates pluralism as 'mere description' from its role as a 'moral doctrine'. The latter 'gives moral force to a set of rules intended to facilitate and foster compromise in dealings between the many groups in society, including the government'. As in his previous writings, Clegg stresses the parallels between politics and industrial relations.

> Although most industrial and commercial managements are selected in a very different manner from democratic governments, they, like governments, claim a special authority and responsibility within their domain; and the doctrines of political sovereignty and managerial prerogative have much in common. Trade unions act as pressure groups both in politics and in industrial relations. There are many similarities between collective bargaining and the political processes of compromise and concession.... The rules of collective bargaining can be seen as the industrial equivalent of the political rules governing the operation of pressure groups.[83]

A key point in Clegg's presentation is his diagnosis of the 'paradox of pluralism as a moral doctrine'. While the various groups in society should recognise a moral obligation to seek compromise, for this to become an *overriding* commitment would negate the interests and aspirations underlying group organisation and hence the necessity for bargaining and compromise. Thus pluralist ethics 'cannot constitute a complete moral philosophy on their own. To make sense, they require that men also respect other moral imperatives.'[84]

Before turning to the main content of Fox's critique, Clegg notes the latter's argument that pluralism is a syndrome, any element of which may be embraced by some pluralists and rejected by others; and hence that 'a person subscribing to any one pluralist belief cannot be regarded as necessarily identifying with, or even being aware of, the others'.[85] Clegg insists that his own conception of pluralism agrees in matters of substance with that of Fox; the differences are only in 'matters of detail and emphasis'. The key area of contention involves the implications which, according to Fox, necessarily follow from the basic assumptions of pluralism. 'Since we agree on the essentials of the pluralist perspective', Clegg insists, 'his observations on the difficulty of describing an ideology cannot disarm my criticism. Either this agreed pluralist perspective implies what he says it does, or it does not. If he is right, I am wrong; and *vice versa*.'[86]

This argument is curiously disingenuous. As much of the preceding discussion has sought to demonstrate, pluralism is far from a homogeneous doctrine but is on the contrary pluralistic. Nor is there a clearly identifiable core of belief, theory or principle of which the various pluralisms are merely elaborations. Even within the restricted context of British industrial relations, pluralism is clearly differentiated. Clegg's own pluralism reflects different analytical roots from that of even his closest colleagues; it is convergent but not identical in the assumptions included and those excluded.[87] Hence only in the most superficial sense do Clegg and Fox 'agree on the essentials of the pluralist perspective'. What Fox criticises as 'pluralism' (including its 'fuller implications') appears accurately to reflect his own previous position; nor is it obvious that he misrepresents the approach of Flanders. The 'agreement' between Fox and Clegg on the definition of pluralism is asserted by the latter but unsupported by any evidence in his paper.[88]

It may also be noted that Clegg's specification of the content of pluralism as a 'moral doctrine' – the moral value of compromise and of rules facilitating compromise – is somewhat idiosyncratic. Most writers who seek to elaborate the normative implications of pluralism commence by emphasising the duty of governments (and other individuals and institutions occupying major positions of power in society) to tolerate sectional organisation and oppositional activity. The rules to be observed by interest groupings themselves are more commonly treated as a secondary issue, and one approached as often as not by implication rather than explicitly. It is precisely at this point that notions of balance of power, or of the neutral refereeship of the state, are introduced (or *appear* to be presupposed) as an explanation of both the actuality and the desirability of social stability despite inter-group competition. The empirical and normative connotations of pluralism's 'problem of order', and Clegg's treatment of them, are pursued further in the following section.

ORDER IN INDUSTRIAL RELATIONS: SOME PARADOXES OF PLURALISM

It is Fox's treatment of this issue – the source of stability despite competition and conflict – which attracts the main brunt of Clegg's attack. Fox refers briefly to the analysis and prescriptions of the Donovan Report, commenting that its optimistic assessment of the prospects for an agreed 'reform' of British industrial relations implies a somewhat narrow conception of the dynamics of industrial conflict. 'Clearly the assumption was being made of a widespread basic consensus which needed only the "right" institutional forms in which to emerge.' Fox continues by asking:

> What are the fuller implications of these attitudes? The first is that every industrial conflict situation can, in sufficiently skilled and patient hands, be made to yield some compromise or synthetic solution which all the interests involved will find acceptable and workable – that no group, for example, retains a continuing concern with maintaining what other groups define as disorder. This in turn requires that each party limits its claims and aspirations to a level which the other finds sufficiently tolerable to enable collaboration to continue. It would obviously be possible for one party to make claims which the other found totally unacceptable and on which compromise or synthesis proved impossible. The pluralist presumption would be that in such a case the consensual ethic governing joint regulation would be ruptured, and a forced collaboration would emerge when one party succeeded in coercing the other. The operation of a pluralistic system requires that such situations be the exception rather than the rule, and that in the main the claims of each party fall within the range found bearable by the other. On the basis that they both subscribe to this philosophy of mutual survival, the parties are able to operate procedures of negotiation and dispute settlement characterized by a consensual code of ethics and conduct.[89]

Clegg's response is that 'if pluralism implied this it would indeed be in trouble, for the evidence is that such a compromise cannot always be found, even in established plural societies. What acceptable and workable solution was available in the dispute between the miners and the mineowners in 1926, or between the miners and the Conservative government at the beginning of 1974?' He insists that 'pluralism implies that an acceptable compromise is not always and inevitably available. Without the risk that agreement will not be reached, collective bargaining is a sham, and the pluralist doctrine is meaningless and not worthy of discussion.' Thus Fox's notion of a 'basic procedural consensus' is fundamentally suspect, since it may imply that commitment to a compromise resolution of disputes overrides all other principles.[90]

To what extent do Clegg's objections demolish Fox's argument? It should be noted that Fox qualifies his suggestion that pluralism presupposes a 'basic consensus' by arguing that an agreed solution is not *always* attainable in disputes, merely that a 'coercive' outcome is treated as 'the exception rather than the rule'.[91] Thus qualified, the point Fox makes in this passage differs in no significant respect from assertions made elsewhere by Flanders;[92] or indeed from Clegg's own insistence that 'we expect a compromise to be reached; it usually is'.[93]

Nevertheless, the argument developed here merits more detailed scrutiny. At the outset it might be suggested that the notion of 'acceptable and workable' compromise is extremely ambiguous. The terms of the settlement of the 1926 lock-out were 'accepted' by the Miners' Federation, and formed the basis of subsequent working relationships. Likewise, the 1974 miners' strike ended in an agreed outcome. In neither case was the defeated party altogether destroyed, even though it may have been considerably bloodied. This points to the ambiguity of the very notion of 'agreement' in industrial relations. The terms of settlement of many disputes may diverge from what one or other (or both) of the parties initially regards as acceptable; but once the balance of forces becomes apparent they may appear preferable to a prolonged conflict. Agreement, in other words, does not occur in a political vacuum; to pose a dichotomy between 'voluntary' and 'coercive' outcomes in collective bargaining is to ignore the fact that the use of sanctions (or the possibility of their use) necessarily forms the background to the negotiating process. In one sense, the bitter and perhaps violent contestation of deeply opposed objectives, and the gentlemanly accommodation of marginal differences, are social processes altogether distinct in character. But in another sense they are merely opposite extremes of a continuum reflecting differences only of degree. Because the notion of agreement displays this ambiguity, differences of emphasis among analysts of union-employer relations may appear of greater substance than is actually the case.

To approach this issue from a slightly different perspective, it might be said that the negotiation of collective agreements is subject to both normative and pragmatic constraints. The latter have been emphasised by Chamberlain in his discussion of what he terms a 'conjunctive' bargaining relationship. Because an employer cannot normally dispense with the whole of his workers, nor they collectively with him, both parties are tied together and are under a practical necessity ultimately to resolve their mutual disputes.

> Collective bargaining in most instances today thus *requires* that some agreement be reached between the parties. . . . Conjunction, the coming together of union and management, in the sense used here arises not because of any sympathetic regard for the other, or because of a voluntary choice of the other as partner; it arises from the absolute requirement that some agreement – *any* agreement – be reached, so that the operations on which both are dependent and which give both their functional significance may proceed.[94]

To some extent Fox may be said to attribute the 'basic procedural consensus' in contemporary industrial relations to precisely such pragmatic considerations.[95] But in addition (as his reference to a 'consensual ethic' indicates) he argued that pluralism prescribes a normative basis to the pursuit of compromise. To this, Clegg responds that 'if a "basic consensus" at all times and in all circumstances takes precedence over any other commitment then, for the pluralist, acceptance of the rules of collective bargaining cannot be a "basic consensus" '.[96] This rejoinder appears to miss Fox's central point: the normative principle implicit (in his view) in pluralism is not that all other moral values must be sacrificed in the interest of compromise, but that the *substantive aspirations* articulated in the bargaining process must be such as to facilitate agreed solutions.

The containment of the substantive aspirations of trade unionists is one of the main themes developed by Fox in his subsequent analysis. He argues that they do not normally challenge

> the essential protections for wealth, privilege and power. . . . Their aspirations are for marginal improvements in their lot, not for eliminating private property, hierarchy, extreme division of labour, and the principles and conventions which support great inequalities of wealth, income, and opportunities for personal fulfilment.[97]

This might be regarded as a particularly significant paradox of pluralism in its own right. Given the conflicts of interest which pluralists diagnose within the sphere of employment and productive relationships, how is it that the normal operation of industrial relations institutions focuses on limited divergences (or even partial convergences) of interest, and serves to generate the commitment of trade union representatives and their members to rules which facilitate (or at least do not seriously obstruct) the pursuit of managerial priorities? How, indeed, can it be taken as self-evident that a natural outcome of new institutions of 'industrial democracy' will be the creation of 'a new legitimacy for the exercise of the management function'?[98]

Fox seeks to explain the constraints on trade unionists' aspirations partly in terms of the influence of an ideology which legitimises the existing economic order. In addition, he argues, 'they see the power arrayed against them as so overwhelming as to make that basic framework appear inevitable, or challengeable only at disproportionate cost to themselves and things they value'.[99] Pluralists themselves, he argues, accept as natural and inevitable that in collective bargaining trade unions should pursue restricted (and hence readily negotiable) objectives.

> Pluralists do not envisage as the outcome of joint regulation by management and labour any major change in the organization of industry, in the fundamental distribution of power and control, or in the broad objectives towards which the industrial effort is directed. Rather it is assumed that there is basic agreement on these issues and that pluralistic mechanisms must be valued, not only as ends in themselves, but also as means for articulating, institutionalizing, and resolving marginal discontents and disagreements which, though of considerable significance for the immediate parties, leave the essential structure of control basically intact.[100]

Fox adds that in his view pluralists assume that unions and employers bargain in the context of a balance of power – ignoring the fundamental imbalance which structures the whole agenda of collective bargaining in a manner conducive to employer interests – and hence insist that unions are morally bound to the terms negotiated (however far short of their members' interests these may in fact fall).

Clegg contests this argument with considerable vehemence. He denies that a balance of power is a necessary presupposition of pluralism, however many pluralists may actually have made such an assumption; and he insists that in any case the relative disposition of power in industrial relations is normally impossible to establish with confidence. In developing the latter point Clegg embraces a thoroughgoing empiricism which, in equating power with the overt use (or threat) of sanctions in the bargaining area, totally sidesteps the case which Fox seeks to construct.[101] The former argument involves the premise that pluralism is in its fundamentals a homogeneous doctrine; whereas one indication of its heterogeneity is the fact that the notion of balance which Clegg excludes is indeed *integral* to the pluralism of many (probably most) other pluralists. But in any event these questions are secondary to his central theme; for he insists that the moral obligation to adhere to collectively agreed terms is in no way dependent on equality of power in the bargaining relationship.

> The pluralist rules of pressure-group politics and collective bargaining guarantee that pressure groups and trade unions have scope to operate and to exercise such power as they have at their command. Rights imply obligations, and, in return for this guarantee, pressure groups and trade unions should deal honourably with governments and employers. In industrial relations this means that where an employer recognises the union, grants it reasonable facilities and bargains 'in good faith', the union is morally obliged to bargain in good faith with him – good faith including the honouring of agreements. The obligation on a union (or a pressure group) does not arise from negotiating with the employer (or the government) on equal terms, but because the employer (or the government) respects union rights (or pressure group rights). In some instances there may be a wide disparity of power between government and pressure group (let us say a group of village residents challenging a planning order) or between a manager and a union representative (say between a plant manager of a major company and the shop steward of a group of labourers) but the pluralistic ethic demands that the government should respect the villagers' right to put their case and to seek publicity and support, that the manager should respect the rights of the labourers and their steward to present their demands and deploy such strength as they possess, and that the villagers and labourers should in return honour their obligations.[102]

This argument raises as many problems as it answers. Is the assertion that 'rights imply obligations' an 'is' or an 'ought', a description or a prescription (two aspects of pluralism which Clegg seeks at the outset of his paper to segregate)? Or does such a statement in fact *combine* empirical and normative elements (in the same way that there is no clear-cut division between the thesis that pragmatically collective bargaining typically leads to agreement and the assertion that normatively a readiness to compromise is incumbent upon bargainers)? In any case, does the moral obligation which Clegg outlines rest primarily upon the macro-level desirability of stable collective bargaining institutions as a component of societal pluralism, or upon the micro-level reciprocity of rights and obligations among trade unions and employers? More specifically, what defines the calculus of rights and obligations: do unequal rights engender equal or unequal obligations? And do purely formal rights entail substantive obligations? In his *New Approach to Industrial Democracy*, it was seen earlier, Clegg explains the accommodation of pressure groups to the rules of the pluralist game by his belief that 'so much of what they seek can be given them, together with such good reasons for refusing to meet the rest, as to make them think that they are being treated fairly'. But now, seemingly, a pressure group (or body of trade unionists) might gain neither substantive concessions nor acceptable explanations; yet however strong the sense of injustice it is morally obliged to acquiesce, only provided that its right to present its case has been formally respected.

Here is a further paradox of pluralism – and in particular the pluralism of students of British industrial relations: the tendency to evaluate *procedural* rights far above *substantive* interests. This orientation might be seen in some respects as a simple reflection of the actual preferences and practice of the parties to industrial relations in Britain. 'The parties to collective bargaining in this country', wrote Flanders, 'have generally preferred to build their relations more on their procedural than on their substantive rules.' When the importance of procedural rules is emphasised, he added, 'a premium is being placed on industrial peace and less regard is being paid to the terms on which it may be obtained.'[103] Clegg made a similar point when he wrote that 'trade unionists may think that unions raise their wages; but they established unions as a means of giving themselves some part in the regulation of the conditions of their working lives, and even if it could be shown that unions have little effect on wages, they would continue to value them for the same reason as a method of regulating relationships between people in industry, and as the channel they wish wage changes to pass through, whatever these changes may be.'[104]

One suspects that the response of most trade unionists to such a suggestion would be unprintable. Whatever the limitations of sociological surveys of workers' attitudes (and they are considerable), there can be no serious grounds for questioning the evidence that the majority regard trade unionism primarily as a source of material advantage. They do not admire collective bargaining simply as an elegant ritual, a procedural *pas-de-deux* as significant for its aesthetic sophistication as for its substantive outcome. They value trade unionism, more prosaically, as an effective means of pursuing interests which differ significantly from those of the employer: at the very least, as a mechanism for 'maintaining or improving the conditions of their working lives'.[105]

  The procedural bias of both practitioners and theorists of industrial relations – the perspective within which 'the actual technique of bargaining, involving "give and take", making concessions, achieving a compromise solution, is accredited with a virtue'[106] – is intimately related to the conception of workers' *substantive* interests on which Fox focuses his critique. Although pluralists commence from the premise of a conflict of interests in industry, the logic of their whole analysis is to minimise the material basis of this conflict. (This is of course encouraged by an emphasis on the pluralistic diversity of sectional interests, as against a systematic antagonism of interests between employers and employees.) For most political pluralists, group competition is compatible with social stability and integration because there are limits to the free development of group organisation and action. 'There is a very sharp distinction in the public domain between legitimate interests and those which are absolutely beyond the pale,'[107] writes Wolff. This distinction is integral to Lipset's argument that 'a moderate state of conflict is in fact another way of defining a legitimate democracy'.[108] The effective articulation by disadvantaged social and economic groups of their distinctive interests through pressure for major alterations in the structure of society would necessarily provoke *immoderate* conflict and hence jeopardise political stability; hence such groups are necessarily 'extremist', 'undemocratic' and probably 'authoritarian', and cannot expect the indulgence extended to groups whose *substantive* aspirations for change are more modest (perhaps because their material interests are already well served). For as Schumpeter insisted, 'democracy cannot be expected to function satisfactorily unless the vast majority of the people in all classes are resolved to abide by the rules of the democratic game and . . . this in turn implies that they are fundamentally agreed on the fundamentals of their institutional structure'.[109] Dahl makes the implications of this premise admirably explicit: 'prior to politics, beneath it, enveloping it, restricting it, conditioning it, is the underlying consensus on policy that usually exists in the society among a predominant portion of the politically active members'. It is this prior consensus which gives point to Dahl's previously quoted argument that 'any active and legitimate group will make itself heard'. 'By "legitimate",' he writes, 'I mean those whose activity is accepted as right and proper by a preponderant portion of the active'.[110] The equation of pluralism with conservatism could scarcely be more clearly presented.

Industrial relations pluralism incorporates close parallels. Legitimate interests, it is normally assumed, are those commonly identified as such by 'responsible' participants in 'mature' collective bargaining: that is to say, they are interests which can in principle be accommodated in the give-and-take of bargaining between employers and union representatives. Hence Kahn-Freund, after insisting that 'the legitimate expectations of labour and of management belong to those which are inevitably in conflict,' defines the legitimate material interests of labour in remarkably narrow terms: 'steadily increased real wages', 'a reasonable measure of job security'. Workers who demand more, or who challenge the 'legitimate interest' of employers in exercising coercive control over the labour process in the pursuit of profit, are 'blinded by class hatred' and need not be taken seriously.[111] To regard trade union organisation and action as a means to radical social and economic transformation (as many trade union rulebooks envisage) and to *act* upon this basis (as contemporary British unions do not) would strain intolerably the institutions of pluralistic industrial relations. As Flanders argued,

> Joint regulation ... presupposes agreement on its aims. To achieve it neither management nor workers' representatives have to neglect or prejudice their own proper functions and the quite different responsibilities which they entail. They have only to take an enlightened view of how their functions may best be discharged, which means in particular abandoning the deeply-entrenched belief on both sides that if one wins the other must lose. They have to learn from experience that, given good will and fair dealing, they can better advance their diverging interests by appreciating that they are divergent and yet, by compromise, can be reconciled.[112]

Such reconciliation necessarily presupposes that the objectives of trade unionists do not diverge too far from the priorities of capitalist production; the expropriation of the expropriators would be the paradigm of a zero-sum game. Happily for the pluralist, trade unionists who employed collective action in the pursuit of the latter objective could properly be excluded from the normal bounds of pluralistic toleration, for the resulting conflict would be clearly 'due to irresponsibility or to agitation by eccentrics or by subversives'.[113]

CONCLUSION: PROCEDURAL BIAS AND JOINT REGULATION

The elevation of procedural principles above substantive outcomes, and the narrow specification of trade unionists' legitimate interests, accord particularly comfortably with the analytical approach to industrial relations in terms of 'joint regulation'. This approach derives from Dunlop's argument that 'every industrial relations system creates a complex of rules to govern the workplace and work community'.[114] In Britain the focus on rules and regulation has become a commonplace, with the extensive influence of the theories of Allan Flanders and his definition of industrial relations as the 'study of the institutions of job regulation'.[115]

To focus analytically on 'institutions of job regulation' is to assign primacy to the parties to collective bargaining and to the procedural arrangements in which they participate, and only secondary importance to the substantive outcome of their relationship. It is significant that Clegg uses the notion of regulation to revise the Webbs' classic definition of a trade union, replacing a substantive focus by a procedural bias. As was seen in the previous section, while the Webbs define the members' interest in their union as 'maintaining or improving the conditions of their working lives', Clegg's argument is that workers view unions as 'a means of giving themselves some part in the regulation of the conditions of their working lives'. The mere participation in job regulation may of course be wholly compatible with the stagnation or deterioration of material conditions; the analytical emphasis on regulation reinforces the pluralists' unconcern with workers' substantive interests. The very notion of rules itself suggests that the issues of industrial relations revolve around administrative detail rather than fundamental principle. The joint determination of rules fits the scenario of 'pluralistic industrialism' mapped out by Kerr and his associates: 'class war will be forgotten and in its place will be the bureaucratic contest of interest group against interest group.... The great battles over conflicting manifestos will be replaced by a myriad of minor contests over comparative details.'[116] To define industrial relations in terms of rules is to emphasise the relatively defined, stable and regular aspects of employer-worker and management-union relationships; by the same token it is to play down the significance of conflicts of control in the labour market and over the labour process as manifestations of a fundamental and continuous antagonism of interest.

There is indeed some ambiguity in the whole treatment of problems of control within pluralism. Flanders refers to 'regulation or control' as if the two terms were equivalents: as if control by rule (the dictionary definition of regulation) is the only form of control relevant to industrial relations.[117] *Workers'* control over production clearly transcends 'job regulation' in the conventional sense of the term; and whatever the differences apparent among industrial relations pluralists, they are at one in discounting the possibility or desirability of workers' control. Flanders distinguishes different methods of job regulation 'according to the parties participating in the authorship of its substantive rules';[118] but when he turns to the controls imposed autonomously by workers in the form of 'custom and practice' he describes them merely as 'social regulation by custom'.[119] The refusal to regard workers as in any sense the 'authors' of control by custom and practice is far-reaching in its implications: for if such 'social regulation' erodes the control of management over the labour process it can be characterised not as workers' control but as anarchy and disorder. No rational person can gain from a state of 'indecision and anarchy' (the main theme of the Donovan Report's analysis of workplace relations);[120] everyone can gain from a process of reform through which collective relations on the shop floor are 'effectively and jointly regulated'.[121] Just as 'a weakening of control by managements' can be readily interpreted as 'anarchy in workplace relations,' so there is no real paradox in the principle that managements 'can only regain control by sharing it'.[122]

A different perspective might however encourage different conclusions. Pluralist accounts of workplace relations in Britain, as Goldthorpe has argued, have been dominated by 'the blanket assumption that the removal of disorder in industrial relations must constitute a general good'.[123] But anarchy and disorder are not necessarily identical. As Eldridge suggests, 'what is described . . . as a loss of integration could from another perspective be analysed in terms of encroaching control – a response to inequalities no longer regarded and accepted as legitimate'.[124] The workplace bargaining in engineering and other British industries in the 1960s – however sectional, parochial, and divorced from any wider social purpose – did represent an area of autonomous control by ordinary workers and a means to more tolerable material conditions. The strategy for 'reform' articulated by the Donovan Report and by most academic commentators was designed to dilute and confine the autonomy of spontaneous collective action at the point of production. Goldthorpe identifies the kernel of the problem with the comment that 'when Flanders writes that managements "can only regain control by sharing it", the question which must arise is that of whether those with whom control is to be shared and those over whom control is to be reimposed are in fact the same people'.[125] The answer must be that the reformist objective was to reduce or eliminate a network of controls of which union officials (including shop stewards) were not the main initiators, through the involvement of a hierarchy of representatives (lay and/or full-time) in formalised and centralised bargaining at plant or company level. This strategy would clearly enhance the *procedural* status of trade unionism; the underlying aim was the erosion of direct workers' control over *substantive* conditions.

If the strategy has failed to achieve the objective, this is perhaps indicative of the inherent weaknesses in the pluralist approach(es) to industrial relations. The advantage to *all* parties of a more formalised and comprehensive 'joint regulation' must appear self-evident so long as form rather than content is emphasised, and substantive divergences of interest are narrowly conceived. The focus on 'job regulation', moreover, encourages a segregation of 'industrial relations' as an area of analysis from the underlying social relations of production, and hence facilitates an uncritical orientation towards managerial priorities of cost-effectiveness and technical rationality. It is the contention of this paper that understanding would be better assisted by a radically different approach: a sensitivity to the contradictory dynamics of capitalist production, the antagonistic structure of material interests within the labour market and the labour process, and the consequent and persistent generation of conflict and disorder within the very institutions and procedures designed to bring order and stability to employer–employee relationships.

Such a focus, it may be suggested in conclusion, would permit some of the emergent contradictions in pluralism as an intellectual doctrine to be located materially and historically. The development of pluralist ideas in industrial relations, as in the social sciences more generally, has tended to follow a distinct trajectory. Originally radical in orientation, or at least associated with reformist strategies designed to advance workers' material interests, pluralist ideas have increasingly tended to serve as a conservative legitimation of established institutions and ultimately as a cloak for essentially repressive programmes.

This paradox can be explained once the changing objective basis of pluralist thought is specified. The original plausibility of the notion that *all* can achieve concrete benefits from the pluralist operation of give-and-take was rooted in the conditions of an era of sustained capitalist expansion (backed by imperialist domination of world markets): there was a considerable margin available for concession by employers to trade unionists, or by governments to social interest groups.[126] (The same circumstances, it may be noted, lay behind the model of an 'industrial relations system' linked to other social institutions only by a limited and specific set of mediating processes.) Subsequent controversies among pluralists and ex-pluralists may be interpreted as reflections of the problem of adaptation to a far less favourable climate. Economic crisis and recession are in no way an opportune context for the peaceful and orderly accommodation of opposing interests: social and economic antagonisms are necessarily sharpened, the process of give-and-take becomes more manifestly zero (or even negative) sum. In such circumstances, however, 'participation' (though not *control*) may be offered to subordinate and disadvantaged groups without necessarily diminishing the dominance and advantages of those at the top. The procedural bias of British industrial relations pluralism – which has seemingly become accentuated in step with the malaise of the British economy – is thus an important ideological accommodation to material contradictions. But this accommodation of analysis to the growing difficulty of shoring up industrial stability carries with it a substantial intellectual price: for the increasing emphasis on form rather than content renders pluralism less and less adequate or relevant as an aid to understanding the real world of industrial relations.

Notes

1. S. H. Hodgson, letter to William James, 18 May 1909, quoted in R. B. Perry, *The Thought and Character of William James*, Vol. I, Little Brown, 1935, p. 651 (emphasis in original).
2. The interrelationship is discussed in R. Hyman and R. H. Fryer, 'Trade Unions: Sociology and Political Economy', in J. McKinlay, *Processing People*, Holt, Rinehart and Winston, 1975.

3. H. A. Clegg, 'Pluralism in Industrial Relations', *British Journal of Industrial Relations*, Vol. 13, 1975.
4. C. B. Macpherson, *The Political Theory of Possessive Individualism*, Oxford University Press, 1962, p. 4.
5. B. Crick, 'The Strange Death of the American Theory of Consensus', *Political Quarterly*, Vol. 43, 1972, p. 57.
6. Wiliam James, *A Pluralistic Universe*, Longmans, 1909.
7. D. Nicholls, *Three Varieties of Pluralism*, Macmillan, 1974.
8. K. Martin, *Harold Laski*, Cape, 1969, p. 65.
9. O. Gierke, *Political Theories of the Middle Age* (trans. F. W. Maitland), Cambridge University Press, 1900.
10. L. Duguit, *Law in the Modern State* (trans. J. and H. Laski), Allen and Unwin, 1921.
11. H. Laski, *The Foundations of Sovereignty*, Allen and Unwin, 1921, p. 169.
12. *Pluralistic Universe*, p. 321.
13. *Foundations of Sovereignty*, p. 169.
14. 'Note on L. Duguit', *Harvard Law Review*, Vol. 31, 1917, p. 191.
15. E. Durkheim, *The Division of Labour in Society* (preface to 1902 edn.), Macmillan, 1933, p. 28.
16. The most notable among the authors of the latter was of course G. D. H. Cole. As a Guild Socialist his theories were often imprecise, shifting and idiosyncratic; as Nicholls comments (p. 12), 'We find in his writings a significant departure from the pluralist position on the question of sovereignty.... Cole's position changed rapidly from year to year, and from book to book, and it is difficult to give a coherent account of his political theory at this period.' While Cole was later to exert a considerable influence on the academic study of industrial relations in Britain, he had by then discarded many of the radical elements in his original pluralism. For analysis of the pluralism of the Guild Socialist movement see S. T. Glass, *The Responsible Society*, Longman, 1966; L. P. Carpenter, *G. D. H. Cole*, Cambridge University Press, 1973.
17. 'Note on L. Duguit', p. 273.
18. *Three Varieties*, Ch. 3.
19. J. Schumpeter, *Capitalism, Socialism and Democracy*, Allen and Unwin, 1943.
20. *Ibid.*, p. 269. He subsequently specifies the criterion of democracy as 'free competition among would-be leaders for the vote of the electorate' (p. 285).
21. Schumpeter makes little attempt to document the 'classical' theory which he attacks; it has been argued that the theory as he presents it is largely a myth (C. Pateman, *Participation and Democratic Theory*, Cambridge University Press, 1970).
22. See in particular R. A. Dahl, *Preface to Democratic Theory*, University of Chicago Press, 1956.
23. *Three Varieties*, p. 25.
24. *Preface*, p. 137.
25. An interesting indication of the diversity of pluralist approaches is

that while cross-cutting and overlapping economic, political, religious and cultural groups are a vital element in the American political theory of pluralism, the anthropological model of the 'plural society' developed by J. S. Furnivall involves the coincidence of such group divisions and hence a rigid social segmentation. 'A plural society . . . is characteristic of the modern tropics. One finds there a society in which two or more groups live side by side but separately within the same political unit. . . . Each group holds by its own religion, its own culture and its own ideas and ways of life; the members of each group mix only in the market-place' ('Some Problems of Tropical Economy' in R. Hinden, *Fabian Colonial Essays*, Allen and Unwin, 1945, pp. 167–8).

26. R. Dahrendorf, *Class and Class Conflict in Industrial Society*, Routledge and Kegan Paul, 1959, p. 317. Since political theories of pluralism are not directly related to the main theme of this paper, no attempt at a critique is offered here. But see for example C. Wright Mills, *The Power Elite*, Oxford University Press, 1959, Ch. 11; G. W. Domhoff and H. B. Ballard, *C. Wright Mills and the Power Elite*, Beacon Press, 1968; W. E. Connolly, *The Bias of Pluralism*, Atherton Press, 1969; R. Miliband, *The State in Capitalist Society*, Weidenfeld and Nicholson, 1969; R. P. Wolff, 'Beyond Tolerance' in R. P. Wolff, B. Moore and H. Marcuse, *Critique of Pure Tolerance*, Cape, 1969; F. G. Castles, D. J. Murray and D. C. Potter, *Decisions, Organizations and Society*, Penguin, 1971; S. Lukes, *Power: a Radical View*, Macmillan, 1974.

27. C. Kerr, 'Industrial Relations and the Liberal Pluralist', *Proceedings of the Seventh Annual Meeting*, Industrial Relations Research Association, 1955.

28. *Ibid.*, pp. 5–6.

29. *Ibid.*, p. 7.

30. J. E. T. Eldridge, 'Industrial Conflict: Some Problems of Theory and Method', in J. Child, *Man and Organization*, Allen and Unwin, 1973, p. 159.

31. 'Industrial Relations and the Liberal Pluralist', p. 10.

32. Clegg has insisted ('Pluralism in Industrial Relations', p. 313) that while it may be possible to assemble 'an impressive number of statements by pluralists' asserting a given proposition, 'that, by itself, does not turn such statements into implications of the pluralist perspective'. This argument is considered later in the present paper.

33. S. and B. Webb, *Industrial Democracy*, Longmans, 1902 edn., pp. xxvii, 813–4, 823.

34. G. D. H. Cole, *The World of Labour*, Bell, 1913, Ch. 1.

35. An important link in this process was W. Milne-Bailey's influential study *Trade Unions and the State*, Allen and Unwin, 1934. Milne-Bailey, then head of the TUC Research and Economic Department, presents an elaborate exposition of the theories of Laski and other pluralists and on this basis asserts the necessity and propriety of a sphere of trade union autonomy vis-à-vis the power of the state. (The argument derived topicality both from the anti-union legislation of

1927 and from the fate of trade unionism under fascism and Stalinism.) But he proceeds to commend a scenario whereby trade unions provide expert assistance in the implementation of a consensually determined economic policy within a reformed and state-directed capitalism (an objective seemingly informing some of the participants in the Mond-Turner discussions, of which Milne-Bailey was joint secretary). His vision of trade unions as 'semi-autonomous functional groups within the State' (p. 378) neatly exemplifies the strain of Durkheimian functionalism underlying much of the early pluralist emphasis on the role of voluntary associations and groups within the broader society. At the same time it points forward to the wartime and post-war integration of British unions within the machinery of national economic planning. Milne-Bailey's analysis would seem to have exerted an important influence on the development of Flanders' conception of pluralism.

36. Thus Clegg ('Pluralism', p. 313) devotes some space to questioning the analytical utility of the notion of 'balance of power' in industrial relations. 'It is extremely difficult to measure bargaining power, as would have to be done to establish whether there was a balance of power or not. . . . In most instances the only means of establishing where the balance lies is to wait for a conflict in which both sides deploy all their resources, and to note which side wins, or whether the outcome is stalemate. We all know now that, under present conditions, the bargaining strength of the miners outweighs that of the Coal Board by a wide margin. . . . But in most industrial situations there is room for endless argument over where the balance of power lies.'

This argument illustrates neatly a number of important aspects of industrial relations pluralism. Most crucially, to take for granted that 'power' is the same as 'bargaining power' severely circumscribes the analytical focus: the power of the parties is to be assessed on the basis of the outcome of explicit demands and overt conflict. This approach was challenged by Alan Fox in *Beyond Contract* (Faber, 1974, pp. 276–80): 'it is in precisely those power relationships where the power disparity is greatest that its active exercise is least necessary'. The material and ideological dominance deriving from the ownership and control of capital, Fox argues, is such that unions normally challenge the existing structure of power, privilege and resources only at the margins. 'Labour often has to marshal all its resources to fight on these marginal adjustments; capital can, as it were, fight with one hand behind its back and still achieve in most situations a verdict that it finds tolerable. What many see as major conflicts in which labour seems often now to have the advantage are conflicts only on such issues as labour deems it realistic to contest, and these never touch the real roots of ownership, inequality, hierarchy, and privilege. Only if labour were to challenge an essential prop of the structure would capital need to bring into play anything approaching its full strength.'

A simple empiricist approach, in other words, cannot reveal the extent to which power relationships have already shaped the agenda of collective negotiations within which 'bargaining power' is exercised. Thus it is unclear by what means Clegg is able to determine that in 1974 the miners' opponents did in fact 'deploy all their resources' in a conflict in which colliers sought a wage level modest indeed by comparison with the salaries of the majority of professional and managerial employees engaged in far more congenial occupations. It is surprising, given that Clegg's paper is explicitly a critique of this section of *Beyond Contract*, that he wholly ignores this part of Fox's argument.

37. A rare example of unease at the taken-for-granted usage of 'the public' or 'the nation' can be found in N. W. Chamberlain, *Social Responsibility and Strikes*, Harper, 1953, p. 25. After asserting that 'public opinion is the force which supports sanctions enforcing social responsibility' he continues: 'but who is "the public"? A public consists of individuals having something in common which significantly associates them under given circumstances.' This is a somewhat insubstantial definition in view of the weight which the notion is commonly required to bear.

38. W. E. Moore, *Industrial Relations and the Social Order*, Macmillan, 1946, p. 445.

39. S. H. Slichter, *The Challenge of Industrial Relations*, Cornell U.P., 1947, pp. 25, 154.

40. B. M. Selekman, *Labor Relations and Human Relations*, McGraw-Hill, 1947, pp. 83, 173.

41. See for example, H. R. Northrup and G. G. Bloom, *Government and Labor*, Irwin, 1963, p. 490. 'To date, the function of government has been primarily to provide the basis for equality of bargaining power between management and labor. The Wagner Act sought to prevent large, strongly entrenched corporations from using their power to throttle unions in their infancy by resort to discriminatory practices. Then, as unions grew in membership and strength, the need for such one-sided intervention in the labor market lessened, and Congress enacted the Taft-Hartley Act in an effort to pare down some of the rights given unions and to equalize the bargaining power in the labor market.'

42. J. K. Galbraith, *American Capitalism*, Penguin, 1963, pp. 125, 128. (Galbraith's book was first published in 1952.)

43. C. Kerr, J. T. Dunlop, F. H. Harbison and C. A. Myers, *Industrialism and Industrial Man*, Heinemann, 1962, pp. 290–1. In an interesting footnote in 'Industrial Relations and the Liberal Pluralist' (p. 10), Kerr specifies that 'For a pluralistic system to work well, the state must be independent and impartial, and something more than impotent'.

44. For a variety of examples, see Fox, *Beyond Contract*, pp. 269–70.

45. See e.g. H. A. Turner, 'The Royal Commission's Research Papers', *British Journal of Industrial Relations*, Vol. 6, 1968; A. N. J. Blain and J. Gennard, 'Industrial Relations Theory: a Critical Review', *British Journal of Industrial Relations*, Vol. 8, 1970; J. H. Gold-

thorpe, 'Industrial Relations in Great Britain: a Critique of Reformism', *Politics and Society*, 1974.

46. A. Flanders, *Management and Unions*, Faber, 1970, p. 150.
47. HMSO, 1966. Fox elaborated part of his analysis in 'Managerial Ideology and Labour Relations', *British Journal of Industrial Relations*, Vol. 4, 1966.
48. 'What Does Morale in Industry Mean?', *Socialist Commentary*, March 1963.
49. N. S. Ross, 'Organised Labour and Management: the UK' in E. M. Hugh-Jones, *Human Relations and Management*, North-Holland, 1958.
50. *Ibid.*, pp. 101–2.
51. *Ibid.*, p. 104.
52. *Ibid.*, p. 131.
53. *Ibid.*, p. 113.
54. *Ibid.*, p. 114.
55. 'Managerial Ideology', pp. 371–2; emphasis added.
56. *Industrial Sociology*, p. 2. It may be noted that in the use of the notion of dynamic equilibrium, and in the conception of managerial power in functional rather conflictual terms, the pluralism of both Ross and Fox displayed close affinities with the harmonistic sociology of Talcott Parsons. There are evident Parsonian tendencies in Fox's later work, *A Sociology of Work in Industry* (Collier-Macmillan, 1971). For example, Fox writes (p. 139) that 'if unions are to stand any chance of forcing management to yield a share in decision-making ... their struggle and the methods used must be tolerated by society and the state. In the last resort, it is the values and norms, legal and otherwise, of the wider society which determine whether or not the collectivity is able to impose itself upon the organization's procedural system.' This suggests an essentially idealist perspective reminiscent of Parsons' emphasis on the central social role of a 'common value system'.
57. *A Sociology*, pp. 58, 61–2.
58. 'Can Britain Have a Wage Policy?', *Scottish Journal of Political Economy*, Vol. 5, 1958, p. 114.
59. *A Policy for Wages*, Fabian Society, 1950, p. 17 (emphasis in original). See also 'Collective Bargaining' in A. Flanders and H. A. Clegg, *The System of Industrial Relations in Great Britain*, Blackwell, 1954, pp. 318, 322.
60. *Management and Unions*, pp. 93, 100–1.
61. *Ibid.*, p. 89.
62. *The Fawley Productivity Agreements*, Faber, 1964, p. 235.
63. *Management and Unions*, p. 114.
64. From a narrow conception of workers' interests it is then easy to exaggerate the possibility of consensus on changes in work practices and organisation through 'productivity bargaining'. This point is considered further in a later section; see also Goldthorpe, 'Industrial Relations', especially p. 432.
65. *Management and Unions*, pp. 224, 134, 166–7.

66. See, for example, A. W. Gouldner, *The Coming Crisis of Western Sociology*, Heinemann, 1971.

67. *British Journal of Industrial Relations*, Vol.7, 1969; reprinted in *Management and Unions*.

68. Royal Commission on Trade Unions and Employers' Associations, *Report*, HMSO, 1968.

69. *Management and Unions*, pp. 249–50.

70. *Ibid.*, p. 253.

71. *Ibid.*, pp. 273–4.

72. It is important to locate the use of this term – regarded critically by Clegg in his subsequent paper – in its context. Fox and Flanders write (p. 251): 'out of manifest conflict may come agreement, but it is important to distinguish between normative agreement and normative consensus. Groups with different normative aspirations may negotiate an agreed compromise on what the prevailing norms are to be, but this does not necessarily imply a total consensus of values and principles. This is not to say that no element of consensus is present. Clearly the agreement to compromise expresses at the very least a consensus that the game should continue, and be played moreover according to certain rules. But within this procedural consensus, different groups may reach normative compromise on substantive issues while still retaining normative aspirations which markedly diverge.'

73. *Industrial Democracy and Nationalization*, Blackwell, 1951, p. 14.

74. *A New Approach to Industrial Democracy*, Blackwell, 1960, p. 20.

75. *Industrial Democracy*, p. 24.

76. *Ibid.*, pp. 23, 145.

77. While any alternative mechanism of worker representation in management decision-making, Clegg argues, would constitute a rival to trade unionism and hence weaken its oppositional effectiveness.

78. *New Approach*, p. 29.

79. *Industrial Democracy*, pp. 28, 30.

80. *Ibid.*, pp. 32, 36.

81. Arguably this would be even more difficult to demonstrate empirically than the existence of a balance of power in industrial relations!

82. 'Pluralism', p. 309.

83. *Ibid.*, p. 311.

84. *Ibid.*

85. *Beyond Contract*, p. 260.

86. 'Pluralism', p. 312.

87. It is of some interest that the main component of Clegg's definition of pluralism – competition among legitimate and autonomous pressure groups – was presented in his earlier writings as a definition of democracy. His use of the two terms as virtually interchangeable seems distinctive within the literature of industrial relations.

88. It is worth noting that at the time Clegg permitted the conception of pluralism developed by Fox and Flanders in 1969 to pass without public criticism – though their use of the notion of procedural consensus, and their more general Durkheimian framework, diverge

significantly from the account of pluralism which he now presents.

89. *Beyond Contract*, pp. 264–5.

90. 'Pluralism', p. 312.

91. It is interesting to compare this extract from *Beyond Contract* with the parallel section in 'Industrial Relations: a Social Critique of Pluralist Ideology' (in J. Child, *Man and Organization*, 1973). While Fox in much of this chapter follows closely the text of his earlier article, at this point he re-orders the argument so as to emphasise the qualifications to what might otherwise seem an assertion of the inevitability of consensual compromise.

92. For example in *Management and Unions*, pp. 113, 197.

93. 'Pluralism', p. 311.

94. N. W. Chamberlain, *Collective Bargaining*, McGraw-Hill, 1951, pp. 445–6; emphasis in original. For a similar analysis see E. Wight Bakke, *Mutual Survival*, Yale U.P., 1946.

95. *Beyond Contract*, pp. 263–4.

96. 'Pluralism', p. 312.

97. *Beyond Contract*, p. 278.

98. Committee of Inquiry on Industrial Democracy, *Report*, HMSO, 1977, p. 95.

99. *Beyond Contract*, p. 278.

100. *Ibid.*, pp. 281–2.

101. On this point see note 36 above.

102. 'Pluralism', pp. 314–5. One minor oddity in this argument may be noted: political pluralists who have made the assumption of balance have normally meant by this that no pressure group wields substantially greater power than any other; Clegg by contrast assumes that the argument about balance refers to the relative power of pressure groups and government.

103. *Management and Unions*, pp. 98–9.

104. 'The Purpose of Trade Unions', *The Listener*, Vol. 68, 1962, p. 500.

105. S. and B. Webb, *The History of Trade Unionism*, Longmans, 1920 edn., p. 1.

106. V. L. Allen, *Militant Trade Unionism*, Merlin, 1966, p. 30.

107. 'Beyond Tolerance', p. 52.

108. S. M. Lipset, *Political Man*, Heinemann, 1960, p. 83.

109. *Capitalism, Socialism and Democracy*, p. 301.

110. *Preface*, pp. 132, 137–8.

111. O. Kahn-Freund, *Labour and the Law*, Stevens, 1972, pp. 52–3.

112. *Management and Unions*, p. 197. Elsewhere, Flanders argued that a 'common purpose' in industry was possible and was indeed a precondition of stable industrial relations pluralism. Criticising Clegg's presentation of the 'pressure group' model of democracy, he asked: 'surely political democracy does not live by pressure groups or, to drop the euphemism, power groups alone? The mere division of power, which is all that the existence of opposition implies, does *not* suffice to create stable and enduring political systems. What happened to the Weimar Republic where power was certainly divided? Democracy . . . depends for its very survival on society having some

elements of common purpose. . . . In industry, too, even collective bargaining represents a mixture of "pressure group" and "common purpose" democracy' ('Meaning of Industrial Democracy', *Socialist Commentary*, April 1960, p. 14; emphasis in original). In some respects this argument anticipates the analysis developed with Fox in 'From Donovan to Durkheim'.

113. Royal Commission, *Report*, p. 137. For a more detailed examination of the limited conception of workers' legitimate interests as a feature of industrial relations pluralism see R. Hyman and I. Brough, *Social Values and Industrial Relations*, Blackwell, 1975.

114. J. T. Dunlop, *Industrial Relations Systems*, Holt, 1958, p. viii.

115. *Management and Unions*, p. 86.

116. *Industrialism and Industrial Man*, pp. 292–3.

117. *Management and Unions*, p. 41.

118. *Ibid.*, p. 94.

119. *Ibid.*, pp. 94, 223.

120. Page 33.

121. *Management and Unions*, p. 45.

122. *Ibid.*, pp. 196–7, 172.

123. 'Industrial Relations in Great Britain', p. 432.

124. 'Industrial Conflict', p. 165.

125. 'Industrial Relations in Great Britain', p. 440.

126. Both Kerr and Clegg, in their discussions of pluralism in industrial relations, note the importance of economic expansion for the original acceptability of traditional collective bargaining arrangements; but they do not pursue the implications for the analysis of a change in economic circumstances.

4 Pressure, Protest and Struggle: Some Problems in the Concept and Theory of Industrial Conflict*

This chapter examines a number of themes involved in the interpretation and analysis of 'industrial conflict', linked by critical concern with the questions of purpose and rationality in collective actions by workers. The first section challenges the value of the conventional category of 'industrial conflict' as applied by industrial sociologists and social psychologists to a diverse range of individual and collective behaviours. In so far as these approaches do not embrace an explicit managerial pragmatism, their focus implicitly assimilates actions of very different form and character merely on the basis that they constitute problems for the employer. The dominant orientation of such approaches is thus negativity. Moreover, the dimension of rationality that gives many forms of employee action their meaning and significance is largely or wholly ignored.

The second section examines conceptions of strikes common in 'industrial relations' analyses. Writers who adopt the perspectives of bargaining theory insist that conflict should be understood as rational action. Nevertheless, the nature and meaning of strike action are typically appraised within restricted parameters; goals and tactics not framed within the rules and presuppositions of 'mature' collective bargaining tend to be dismissed as pathological. While it may indeed be true that strikes in Northern Europe and North America are characteristically associated with the dynamics of union/employer negotiations, this is far from universally the case. Moreover, the growing political connotations of industrial relations imply that, even in the Anglo-Saxon context, the collective bargaining approach will yield diminishing returns.

Analyses that accept the latter argument are considered in the third

*First published as Chapter 20 in G. B. J. Bomers and R. B. Peterson (1982) *Conflict Management and Industrial Relations*, Kluwer-Nijhoff.

section. Recent literature has included a variety of attempts to develop 'political' interpretations of strike activity, in many cases seeking to establish the characteristics of national contexts in which workers' conflicts embrace 'industrial' or 'political' objectives. The growth of explicit state involvement in union/employer relations – discussed by some under the notion of 'corporatism' – has encouraged attention to certain forms of strikes (or their suppression) as a medium of 'political exchange'. The central weakness of such approaches is their tendency to assimilate the logic of worker collective action within the priorities of union leaders and representatives whose orientations and interests may be significantly different. The implications of this approach are thus unreceptive to the rationality of forms of worker struggle that challenge hierarchical control within the labour movement.

In the final section, an attempt is made to outline an interpretative framework premised on viewing collective struggle as working-class creativity. It is argued that such struggle is an essential basis for the autonomous definition of collective identity and interests and underlies the distinctiveness of labour organisation. The irony of such organisation is its tendency to routinise and attenuate oppositional action; thus, its effectiveness in articulating the antagonism between workers' interests and the dynamics of capital accumulation can atrophy. Tendentially, therefore, union organisation can represent the *object* as well as the *medium* of worker resistance. Any adequate theory of strikes must accommodate this inherent duality.

INDUSTRIAL CONFLICT: A CONCEPTUAL 'PUT-DOWN'

The notion of 'industrial conflict' is a somewhat elastic concept. Frequently used as a synonym for strikes, it is, however, generally employed by industrial sociologists with a far broader meaning. This ambiguity is neatly captured in the editors' introduction to the classic symposium *Industrial Conflict*. After an initial discussion of the 'problem' in terms of union/management disputes, they go on to comment:

> A true understanding of industrial strife and what should be done about it demands consideration of related, less spectacular manifestations as well. It may even be suggested that the general object of study is not the labor dispute, the strike, or the lockout, but the

total range of behavior and attitudes that express opposition and divergent orientations between industrial owners and managers on the one hand and working people and their organizations on the other hand. (Kornhauser, Dubin, and Ross, 1954, p. 13)

A broad conception of the term likewise underlies Kerr's (1964, p. 171) argument that, in addition to strike action, 'conflict with the employer may also take the form of peaceful bargaining and grievance handling, of boycotts, or political action, of restriction of output, of sabotage, of absenteeism, or of personnel turnover.'

What justifies the application of a single category to such diverse phenomena? To an important extent, this usage of the notion of 'industrial conflict' reflects the specifically managerial orientation of much industrial sociology and, in particular, social psychology. The most obvious common feature of the items in Kerr's list is that all constitute 'labour problems' since they interfere with managerial objectives in terms of control, production, and profitability. It is true that a catholic conception of industrial conflict has been given a seemingly more objective intellectual rationale with the theory of 'temporary withdrawal from work' (e.g. Hill and Trist, 1955). Put simply, the thesis is that all the specified forms of activity represent behavioural responses to stressful work situations. Moreover, it is often added, different types of 'organised' and 'unorganised' conflict appear to constitute functional alternatives. In other words, the tensions generated by a given work situation may cause workers either to go on strike, stay at home, hit the foreman, or smash (or be smashed by) the machine. And certainly there is some evidence to suggest that, other things being equal, a high level of collective militancy may be associated with a low level of 'unorganised conflict'.[1]

A crucial feature of such approaches, however, is their conception of industrial conflict as *negative*. The common element in the forms of activity so characterised is not what they are, but what they are not. From the simple perspective of the managerial pragmatist, the key aspect of all varieties of industrial conflict is their *divergence* from the 'normal' situation, in which employees attend their workplace assiduously, perform their tasks conscientiously, and obey instructions submissively. Conflict represents a failure to conform to the objectives and expectations of the employer. The more sophisticated academic formulations share this same characteristic of negativity: '*low* morale', '*withdrawal* from work', or – the most blatant example of this genre – '*suboptimal* system functioning'. Allied with this negativity of conceptualisation is a positivistic analytical bias; the various forms of industrial conflict, from strikes to absenteeism to accidents, are analysed behaviouristically as 'responses' to 'stimuli', the more-or-less mechanical outcomes of a given material situation, to be explained and interpreted along the same lines as a mechanical breakdown.

Such approaches divert attention from the fact that the various forms of conflictive activity in industry represent, to varying degrees, positive and purposeful labour action. Any adequate sociological analysis of such activity must locate its occurrence within the structure of opposing interests inherent in social relations of production in capitalist industry: between those who appropriate surplus value and those who sell their labour power, between those who are agents of the coercive priorities of capital and those who are subordinated to their control and surveillance. Within the context of antagonistic relations of production, industrial conflict cannot be fully understood except in terms of the opposing strategies of those whose interests, and hence whose underlying orientations and objectives, are themselves in opposition. A strike, overtime ban, or work to rule designed to achieve a wage increase, improved conditions, or greater control over the labour process is an example of rational and purposeful action. So is 'labour turnover', which entails finding a new work place at least marginally preferable to the old and, at the very minimum, represents a change. So is taking a day off to stay in bed or to go fishing. So is the strategic sabotage that may be the only easy respite from the tyranny of the line, or at least the simplest way of hitting back at the employer where it hurts. It is intellectual arrogance to dismiss the rationality of such forms of action – either explicitly, with such labels as 'aimless indiscipline' or 'mindless militancy', or implicitly, through a crude behaviourism that treats this merely as a deviation from managerially defined rationality and excludes workers' own purposes as analytically irrelevant.

Of course, some forms of conflictive action are *prima facie* more rational than others. There are likely to be variations in the degree of information and understanding on which the grievances or aspirations that inspire such actions are based. Some strategies are better calculated to achieve their objective than others; some, indeed, may actually be counterproductive. (It is one of the key tasks of a sophisticated trade union organisation to advise members when militancy is likely to bring success, when its efficacy is doubtful, and when it may even play into the hands of management.) A distinction may also be made in terms of levels of rationality: the extent to which grievances are consciously appraised in relation to their structural origins, and the extent to which strategies are oriented toward the alteration of underlying causes as well as immediate consequences.[2] (Thus, taking the odd day off brings only temporary respite from an oppressive work situation; joining with fellow workers to change conditions may bring a more basic relief. In general, it is obvious that collective strategies provide greater scope than individual ones for significant influence on the underlying sources of discontent.)[3] To insist on the rational status of industrial conflict, therefore, is not to assert the uniform or monistic character of its rationality. It is only through a problematic framed in terms of rational and purposeful strategies, and through a methodological refusal to accept 'industrial conflict' as an undifferentiated and coherent category, that the problem of variations in the rationality of different types and instances of action can be seriously confronted.

The previous paragraphs should not be interpreted as a simplistic identification of conflict with rationality. It is true that very powerful ideological influences operate in industrial relations to define militancy (itself commonly a pejorative expression) in terms highly inappropriate to workers' collective interests. 'Strikes . . . are conventionally described as industrially subversive, irresponsible, unfair, against the interests of the community, contrary to the workers' own best interests, wasteful of resources, crudely aggressive, inconsistent with democracy, and, in any event, unnecessary' (Allen, 1966, p. 27). Moreover, simple habituation to the existing mode of production is an important cause of industrial peace. 'The advance of capitalist production develops a working class, which by education, tradition, habit, looks upon the conditions of that mode of production as self-evident laws of Nature' (Marx, 1959, p. 737). Strikes and other types of oppositional activity that challenge workers' customary subordination to managerial control and their role within the labour process, though widespread and endemic, are not in this sense 'normal': they involve the deliberate rupturing of at least aspects of the normality in which capital dominates over living labour. Beyond the active impact of ideology and the passive effects of habituation there is, however, a more rational basis for industrial peace and order. The conflict of interests between labour and capital can be most clearly characterised at the level of analytical generality; it is not precisely and immediately refracted in the detail of social relations in industry. Within the individual work place, for example, employees are dependent on the continued survival and profitability of the enterprise; these would be jeopardised by demands and struggles to transcend certain limits. (Capitalism benefits from ideological pressures to define these limits with extreme narrowness and, more crucially, to ignore the fact that struggles that disrupt the antagonistic interdependence of wage labour and capital could engender other relations of production in which this antagonism is transcended.)[4] At a different level, this symbiosis of antagonistic interests is manifest in the dependence of both employers and trade union representatives on the maintenance of a 'bargaining relationship' that sets firm boundaries to permissible disorder. For workers' collective representatives, a necessary consideration in the formulation of objectives and strategies is the possible repercussion on organisational security of the articulation of demands or adoption of tactics that overstep the limits of tolerance on the part of the significant (and powerful) others with whom they interact.[5]

Such considerations cast further doubt on the adequacy of 'industrial conflict' as an analytical category. The strategies of workers (individually and collectively) and of their organisational representatives are framed within the context of contradictory social pressures and are partly shaped by complex processes of interaction within and without the work place. It is highly misleading to posit a simple dichotomy between industrial peace or order on the one hand, and conflict on the other. Rather, it is necessary to assume a continuum of modes of interaction within social relations of production and a similar continuum of strategies; moreover, one must appreciate that there may exist considerable divergence between the strategies pursued at different organisational levels or on different issues at a single level. (Thus, collaborative trade union/employer relations may coexist with guerrilla warfare between workers and supervisors, or wage militancy with acquiescence in managerial control over the labour process, or vice versa.) The complex ramifications of the possible patterns of strategy and interaction centring around the sale of labour power and the control of the labour process (conflict-in-order, order-in-conflict) require a dialectical analysis rather than a categorisation by crude dichotomy.

INDUSTRIAL RELATIONS PERSPECTIVES: THE LIMITS OF COLLECTIVE BARGAINING

Such arguments should be (relatively) uncontentious for most students of labour/management relations, who have long been accustomed to stress the purposeful nature of strikes and analogous collective actions as elements in bargaining strategy, and also the need to understand such phenomena not as discrete conflictive events but as episodes in a continuing bargaining relationship.

The rational and purposeful basis of 'industrial conflict' is a necessary premise of those who regard this as a fertile area for the application of game theory analysis. Schelling (1960) opens his classic discussion by contrasting his own approach with those that 'treat conflict as a pathological state and seek its causes and treatment'; he insists on the importance of an 'assumption of rational behavior' and goes on to argue that 'most conflict situations are essentially bargaining situations'. The same presuppositions clearly inform writers (e.g. Walton and McKersie, 1965) whose main purpose is to apply bargaining theory to industrial disputes. And implicitly at least, industrial relations writers more generally adopt a similar perspective. Indeed, this is evident from the very definitions commonly offered for the strike: 'a temporary stoppage of work by a group of employees in order to express a grievance or enforce a demand' (Griffin, 1939, p. 20); or 'a situation in which a number of workers collectively withdraw their labor in order to secure some immediate advantage' (Karsh, 1958, p. 1).

The view of industrial stoppages as 'functional' rather than pathological is a key feature of Coser's (1956) general analysis of social conflict. The same focus is developed by Dubin with his notion of 'institutionalisation' of conflict:

> Industrial disorder as a feature of industrial conflict is always temporary and limited. The strategic end of industrial conflict is to establish a new basis of order, a new set of rules governing management–men relationships. . . . But every industrial conflict is resolved, and with its resolution comes a new working code that guides the relationships during the period of the resulting agreement. One of the consequences of the institutionalization of industrial conflict through collective bargaining is that the limits of industrial disorder come to be institutionally determined. For any given conflict there is inevitably introduced a long-time perspective, a vista of continuing relations between company and union regardless of the outcome of the current controversy. (Dubin, 1954, p. 45)

Yet, paradoxically, such interpretations tend to define the parameters of 'rational' conflict so narrowly that their implications largely parallel the managerialism of the social psychologists. Indeed, the convergence is explicit in a recent article by Barbash, in which 'normal' conflict, which constitutes 'a means to induce agreement' and hence is functional in accommodating divergent socio-economic goals, is contrasted with 'pathological' forms:

> Normal conflict is the conflict essential to the maintenance of the system and without which the system is largely incapable of functioning. Pathological (or dysfunctional) conflict is not only not essential to the maintenance of the system, it may even be destructive of it. Although conflict is an element in the maintenance of equilibrium in the industrial relations system, there is a point beyond which conflict becomes 'aberrant', 'abnormal', 'dysfunctional', or 'pathological'. (Barbash, 1980, pp. 87–9)

Among instances of the latter, Barbash cites 'conflict which results in major social disorganization of a community or society', 'the persistence of a large hard core of absenteeism, tardiness, indiscipline', and 'persistent civil disobedience' – all of which result in 'major damage to the public interest in the process of asserting sectional claims'.

With exceptional candour, Barbash exposes the assumption underlying the conventional perspectives of most industrial relations pluralists – that is, the open articulation of conflict strategies in industry is tolerable and even desirable only because and in so far as the substantive aspirations of trade unionists and the means adopted for their pursuit do not radically challenge capitalist priorities.[6] Thus, strikes are legitimate only as a limited and routinised pressure tactic oriented toward relatively modest goals on the agenda of negotiation between trade unions and employers. For industrial relations orthodoxy there can be no canons of rationality, no vocabularies of motive, to justify more ambitious and more disruptive forms of struggle.

This conception accords closely with what has been long established as the dominant social reality of work stoppages in Anglo-Saxon countries. A strike is indeed normally a calculated act and an integral element in the processes of industrial relations – the pursuit of collective bargaining by other means. Yet, can workers' collective struggles be invariably understood merely in terms of strategies to achieve an 'immediate advantage' within the framework of collective bargaining? This is certainly disputed by Durand and Dubois, who challenge the perspective exemplified by Griffin and his successors:

This classic definition of the strike conflicts with spontaneist or political interpretations. The calculative strike with its precisely formulated objectives is different from the strike as a revolt expressing, quite apart from any specific demand, workers' accumulated discontent with their total situation. It is equally distinct from the strike as a social movement or general strike, which, through its extent, size, and gravity poses an explicit or implicit challenge to the policies or the very legitimacy of the political authorities. (Durand and Dubois, 1975, p. 9; this translation by the author)

What this argument indicates above all is the danger of a culture-bound conception of the nature and purposes of strike action. This is by no means a novel insight. Ross and Hartman (1960), in their analysis of strike statistics, emphasised the substantial international variations in the average length of stoppages and suggested that these indicated the occurrence of quite distinct social phenomena differing in their causes and consequences. Yet they, too, adopted the tacit assumption that the 'normal' strike was closely associated with bargaining between employers and trade unions and that in those countries where this was demonstrably not the case, this was *ipso facto* evidence of deviance or immaturity. What is clear from a genuinely international perspective is that the tradition of largely routinised strike activity, institutionally segregated from broader social and political conflicts – the basis of the conventional 'industrial relations' presuppositions – is itself atypical. Not only in many countries of the Third World, but also in a number in the developed West, formal trade union organisation covers only a limited proportion of the labour force, and workers' militancy is often loosely related, if at all, to collective bargaining institutions. In such contexts the primary function of trade unions themselves is often other than collective bargaining; negotiating relationships with employers are often limited in scope and stability, and unions may have a far more significant role as social welfare organisations or as representatives of the political aspirations of the working class. Where this is the case, it cannot normally be anticipated that strikes and their purposes will match the Anglo-Saxon stereotype. Nor – in light of the increasing politicisation of industrial relations even where 'mature' collective bargaining has long prevailed – can it be assumed that the traditional isolation of 'industrial' from 'political' conflict will survive here either.

POLITICAL EXCHANGE: A NEW MANAGERIALISM?

The limits of the 'industrial relations' approach to industrial conflict have been emphasised in a growing number of comparative studies of strike patterns, stimulated in part by the detailed interpretation by Shorter and Tilly (1974, p. 343) of strikes in France as 'an instrument of working-class political action'. Snyder (1975, p. 264), for example, has argued: 'There are major, often implicit, assumptions in the "bargaining approach" to strikes, which are reasonable only within certain institutional settings.' Only in the context of stable trade union representative status and established institutions of negotiation is it likely that work stoppages will be oriented primarily to employment conditions in individual enterprises; but in so far as these conditions exist only in a minority of countries, the 'rules for analysing and interpreting strikes' applied by industrial relations students are not generally relevant.

A more elaborate framework of contextual distinctions has been suggested by Hibbs (1978) in his attempt to relate international trends and variations in strike activity to the 'political economy of distribution'. Historical developments in conflict patterns can, in his view, be interpreted according to the extent and character of state involvement in the allocation of economic resources, allowing three basic paradigms:

> In nations where state intervention is comparatively low (passive) and the market is supported, the private sector is the primary arena of conflict over distributional outcomes, 'business unionism' is the dominant orientation of organised labour, and strike activity is relatively high and has shown no tendency to decline over the long run. Canada and the United States are examples of this pattern. Strike activity also stands at comparatively high levels and shows no signs of declining in countries where the state has intervened actively in the labour market in order to support the market: i.e., has actively participated in setting private-sector wages, hours, and conditions of work without socialising the consumption and distri-bution of a very large fraction of the national income. The distinctive feature of industrial relations in societies falling in this category is the politicisation of the strike. The state is an important actor in the system of industrial relations and, therefore, the strike is frequently used as a form of political action to exert pressure on the government, either to grant concessions to labour unilaterally

or to coerce a favourable settlement from recalcitrant employers. France and Italy are the exemplary cases. Only in societies where the state has actively (and successfully) pursued market-modifying policies has there been a massive displacement of conflict over distributional issues to the electoral arena and, as a result, the 'withering away' of the strike in the private marketplace. This historical configuration is of course best illustrated by the experience of the Scandinavian social democracies. (Hibbs, 1978, pp. 169–71)

Put simply, Hibbs views strikes as an important element of labour strategy in the first two contexts – in the one, to apply pressure against employers, and in the other, against hostile governments. Yet in the third context industrial struggle is a less rational strategy for workers:

> The political marketplace and the private marketplace can be viewed as alternative arenas for the maximisation of goals. Once the Social Democrats began to reshape fundamentally the political economy of distribution, the political process offered labour the greater marginal return on activity. Political pressure and bargaining was emphasised at the expense of industrial militancy, and strike activity in the market declined dramatically. (Hibbs, 1978, p. 172)

According to Shalev (1979), Hibbs has done little more than systematise arguments of such earlier writers as Ross and Hartman on the implications of political institutions for strike patterns, while his methodology for empirical validation is unconvincing. Moreover, Hibbs's entire formulation of the 'political economy of distribution' thesis rests on two unacceptable premises: that workers' struggles are oriented solely towards influencing the distribution of income, and that a choice between industrial and political strategies can be made unproblematically at the level of an entire labour movement. Yet there are significant parallels between the approach of Hibbs and the interpretation with which Shalev himself is associated – the latter based upon a (rather formalistically defined) notion of working-class organisational strength:

> With increasing relative strength of the working class, different courses of action can be expected to become open for the sellers of labour power. In particular, we anticipate that, with more extensive organisational power resources, the political arena will be-

come increasingly important for labour. To the extent that labour is successful in acquiring control over political institutions, it can exercise its power through these means and will not be limited to the industrial arena. On the other hand, the possibilities for employers to exercise political power will decrease. The availability of the political alternative for labour can therefore be expected to be of importance for the conflict strategies of both capital and labour. The exchange processes between them may now involve not only the industrial but also the political arena. (Korpi and Shalev, 1979, p. 170)

Referring specifically to Swedish experience, the same authors argue:

A labour movement which had developed sufficient organisational strength and political support to achieve durable control of the polity altered the balance of power in society in such a way that the contending classes were moved to fundamentally renegotiate their mutual interrelations. Of particular interest to the student of industrial conflict is the fact that Swedish labour in effect renounced the strike weapon in order to more effectively pursue its long-run class interests in the political arena.[7] (Korpi and Shalev, 1979, p. 177)

The notion of 'political exchange' employed by Korpi and Shalev is of obvious relevance to recent discussions of emergent forms of organised interchange between capital, trade unions and the state in many Western societies in recent years. For the purposes of this chapter, it is unnecessary to focus on the adequacy or coherence of the interpretation of such tendencies in terms of 'corporatism'.[8] What is at issue is the specific significance for strike activity of a growing influence of trade union concerns on the policies of the state as well as on discrete employers and growing governmental control of the macroeconomic effects of conflicts and agreements between employers and unions (particularly where unions are relatively strong but the economy is relatively weak).

There is an interesting ambivalence in the idea of political exchange; on the one hand, it can refer to a trade-off between unions and the state; on the other, to a switch in the locus of unions' own conflict strategy from the 'industrial' to the 'political' arena.[9] Clearly the 'internal' selection of trade union strategy and the 'external' patterns of collaboration between unions and state are interconnected; indeed, neither process can be adequately comprehended without reference to the other. Yet their dissociation is a common feature of recent analyses of 'corporatism'. Both separations tend, in turn, to encourage reifications of the organisational dynamics of trade unions and thus to suppress sensitivity to the role of workers' collective struggles.

As an example, it is possible to cite Streeck's often highly perceptive analysis of German trade union politics. He has argued:

> [The actions of German industrial unions, because of the size of their membership,] have direct and predictable macroeconomic consequences. They can calculate strategically that the cumulative effects of their bargaining can contradict their members' interests, so that their victories are counterproductive. Thus, for an industrial union the macroeconomic connections between the wage level on the one hand, and productivity, investment, employment, and price stability on the other, are relevant to a quite different degree than for workplace negotiators such as British shop stewards. In so far as the strategic perspectives of industrial unions include macroeconomic variables which are outside the concern and influence of more parochial agents, they are in agreement with at least the basic technical premises of a governmental incomes policy oriented towards growth and the fight against inflation. (Streeck, 1979, p. 208; translation here by the author)

Such an analysis – uncontentious and even banal at first sight – is, however, far from innocent. For writers on trade unionism who counterpose short-term against long-term strategies and micro against macro considerations typically divert attention from hierarchical differentiation of power and interests within the organisation. Moderation of goals and restraint in tactics are no more than the enlightened self-interest of trade union members. Thus, militancy of actions or objectives must reflect short-sightedness, sectional selfishness, or politically motivated irresponsibility that may, in the interests of 'the union as a whole', be suppressed.

Thus, ultimately the 'political exchange' perspective can easily lead to a restricted notion of the rationality and legitimacy of industrial militancy that differs little from industrial relations orthodoxy or the managerial positivism of social psychology. Where the logic of trade union power involves accommodation with the state, the persistence of industrial struggle must represent the illogical survival of outmoded orientations and practices.

COLLECTIVE STRUGGLE: MEANINGS AND PURPOSES

A more critical approach might regard far more sceptically the notion of uniform interests and criteria of relevance within a union as a whole. The advantages of acquiescence with the economic priorities of the state (or of particular employers) are not evenly distributed within a trade union. In so far as the rewards for moderation of union policy apply primarily to the security and status of 'the organisation' – possibly at the same time as members' own material interests are neglected – it is the representatives and officials directly involved in leadership functions who will be most strongly drawn towards accommodative practices. In short, a conflict of interests may occur *within* trade unions, in which event the internal distribution of power may be of crucial significance for the policy outcome. Yet this distribution may in turn owe much to external relations; more specifically, the 'political exchange' between union leaders and employers or the state may enhance their own power within their organisation, thus increasing their ability to maintain collaborative policies. [10]

Once again, it is clear that industrial struggle persists against imposing odds. Hence it is time to return to an appraisal of its nature, meaning, and significance. Two themes are of central importance: (1) Collective protest and resistance occur in the context of antagonistic social relations of production, and (2) they represent positive and purposeful initiative. Most strikes can be viewed as 'creative acts of an offensive kind' (Cronin, 1979, p. 9) or as 'the power of people directing their own action co-operatively towards common purposes' (Brecher, 1972, p. viii). Or, to quote Karsh:

The essence of the strike lies in the behavior of human beings acting together; it involves groups and their relationships between and among each other; it requires planning and organization, the strategy and tactics of collective action; it involves the forging of new forms of social structure and sometimes the emergence of new social institutions. It is not merely a cessation of work in pursuit of an economic goal; it represents an instance of social conflict in the form of a corporate refusal to participate in previously accepted social institutions. From its collective nature, the strike derives its power of coercion and the motives upon which its rests. (Karsh, 1958, p. 3)

This points to a factor of paramount significance – through struggle the distinctive character of workers' collective organisations is constituted. This process has recently received detailed attention from Offe and Wiesenthal (1979). Workers organise collectively, they argue, only after capital has *already* established a threefold dominance. First, each capital integrates a multiplicity of productive resources under unified command; a single capital is itself a collectivity. Second, workers relate to capital from a position of inequality within the labour market and explicit subordination within the labour process. And third, capital occupies a privileged position in relation to the state and society in general by virtue of the salience of its production and investment decisions for economic stability; since capital must be *induced* to perform functions necessary to the state, it rarely has to apply positive and active pressure to achieve policies conducive to its interests. Not only are workers, as bearers of distinctive interests, already subordinated to capital; they are also atomised by their mutual competition in the labour market. Each possesses to some degree a unique set of needs, aspirations and interests, and there exists no natural common denominator through which divergences between workers can be resolved; whereas differentiations within and between capitals 'can be reduced to the unequivocal standards of expected costs and returns – i.e., to the measuring rod of money' (Offe and Wiesenthal, 1979, p. 75).

Hence, the 'logic of collective action' relevant to workers' organisation is distinctive in two respects. Given workers' relative powerlessness, organisational strength derives not from the sum of their pre-existing resources but from the mobilisation of collectivity itself. As Offe and Wiesenthal (1979) put it, the members' 'willingness to pay' is less important than their 'willingness to act'. And this willingness may be seen as both cause and consequence of a social process through which workers' distinctive collective interests are defined and articulated. This process involves a practical and ideological struggle against the tendencies, on the one hand, to characterize workers' identities individually rather than collectively, and on the other to define their interests as identical to those of capital (or at least subject to appraisal by identical criteria). Thus, 'collective action is concerned with a redefinition of what we mean by "costs" and "benefits"'; and 'the logic of collective action of the relatively powerless . . . implies a paradox . . . that interests can only be met to the extent they are partly redefined' (Offe and Wiesenthal, 1979, pp. 96, 79).

This process of redefinition is sustained by moments of collective struggle and also is a precondition of effective militancy. To specify the purposes of workers engaged in conflict is a methodologically as well as an empirically complex task. For though it is a necessary starting point to recognise that 'workers strike because striking works and because they have grievances' (Cronin, 1979, p. 5), this insight is insufficient. How are grievances translated into strike action?

Individual unrest, frustration, or discontent represents a fluid condition which has the potentialities for differing lines of action. Indeed, the unrest is not social until it is organized; expressions of individual dissatisfaction need to be crystallized, defined, and focused. Most of all they need to be communicated and thus shared. . . . It is in these terms that leadership plays a crucial role. (Karsh, 1958, p. 6)

A very similar theme underlies the work of Shorter and Tilly (1974, p. 338). Individuals, they argue, 'are not magically mobilized for participation in some group enterprise, regardless how angry, sullen, hostile, or frustrated they may feel. Their aggression may be channeled to collective ends only through the co-ordinating, directing functions of an organization, be it formal or informal.'

Thus, the very notion of a 'spontaneous' strike is in many respects misleading; collective action by workers is impossible without some degree of leadership and organisation within the collectivity. A study of the 1973 South African strikes (Institute of Industrial Education, 1974) emphasised this point: 'Each worker does not just coincidentally decide that he or she is not going to go into the factory on that particular day.' The authors point to the indirect influence of various organisations and movements developing 'black consciousness' and stimulating an awareness both of economic and political grievances as well as of potential collective strength in acting for redress. Against this background 'activists' among the workforce could generalise a belief in the desirability and feasibility of strike action, making use of 'pre-existing, informal communication networks such as friendship groups, "home-boy" groups, groups of people who habitually commute together, and so on.' While the notion of politically motivated and tightly knit 'agitators' is wide of the mark, the romantic conception of absolute spontaneity is likewise inadequate.

If organisation of some form necessarily underlies the initiation of a strike, it also shapes the definition of the meanings and purposes of collective struggle. It follows from the antagonistic social relations of production within capitalism that workers typically experience a multiplicity of grievances directly related to the terms of their employment and the conditions of their labour as well as to their more general social situation. This means that in any employment relationship there exists the *potential* for organised conflict, but it also follows that workers may engage in a common struggle for a variety of motives, more or less articulate and explicit, which may contain important divergences between individuals and groups. Moreover, a stoppage precipitated by a specific episode or grievance (perhaps of a relatively trivial nature) may occur only because of the prior accumulation of a multiplicity of other discontents.

Thus, the identification of the causes of a specific strike is often a methodologically as well as empirically complex endeavour. Paradoxically, the predominant purposes of collective action may become explicit only after a stoppage is already in progress, by the articulation of a rationale that selects one or more salient complaints or demands from among the strikers' pre-existing grievances and aspirations. Such a process of selective articulation is inevitably influenced to an important degree by opinion leaders among the participants, by influential outsiders, and by the more general industrial and social environment in which the dispute occurs. For example, union organisers may seek to develop a stoppage by unorganised workers into a struggle for membership and recognition – a process familiar to the historian of British labour, and notable particularly in the rise of general unionism around the turn of the century. Political activists may seek to develop disputes into mass support for demands reflecting the perspectives of their own organisations (their success will reflect the extent to which these do encapsulate aspects of the strikers' own priorities).

When strikes occur within an established institutional framework of industrial relations – rather than being initiated by unofficial activists or discontented non-unionists – their social organisation is throughout commonly overt and formalised. This may involve, for example, public discussion and mass meetings; recommendations by shop stewards, convenors, or full-time officials; or at times the elaborate ritual of strike ballots. At the same time, as Batstone, Boraston, and Frenkel (1978) have shown, the formal procedures of collective decision-making are interlinked with less overt processes of social organisation. Workplace activists and leaders will mobilise networks of communication and influence to shape collective attitudes and orientations; will deploy organisational, informational, and

other resources to unify or isolate sectional groups; and will attempt
to structure the lines of discussion and decision in work group,
factory, or joint shop stewards' meetings. Hence, those in positions
of workplace influence and leadership can, within limits, determine
whether a stoppage occurs as well as which workers and what issues
will be involved and along what lines it will be settled. Where
shop-floor union organisation is less strongly developed, external
officials may exercise a less pervasive but at times decisive influence.

At this point a further paradox arises. While collective militancy
presupposes organisation, organisation can also impose quantitative
and qualitative restraints on the articulation of militancy. One cannot
overgeneralise the basic argument of Shorter and Tilly (1974, p. 192)
that 'in France unionization increased the propensity to strike'. The
thesis of 'institutionalisation of conflict', like all half-truths, *is* half
true. In the context of established procedures of negotiation between
unions and employers (or governments), union representatives
typically embrace a commitment to an 'orderly' bargaining relationship. Thus, their role is more often to inhibit or resolve disputes than
to initiate and mobilise. No less significant is their tendency to
encourage the formulation of grievances relatively susceptible to
peaceful settlement within the routines and conventions of negotiation. Hence, various studies have indicated the transformation of
strikes reflecting a diversity of grievances into negotiations for
straightforward wage increases – these offering the easiest basis for
an uncomplicated compromise settlement. And even Shorter and
Tilly, despite their belief in a generally positive link between
militancy and unionism, note that interwar strikes in France were
more likely to focus around limited bread-and-butter issues when
trade unions were officially involved:

> Strikes waged over job control issues tended to fail more often than
> strikes in general, and a lost strike could devastate a struggling
> union. Bureaucratization meant for union leaders a greater con-
> cern for preserving the integrity of the organization above all other
> objectives, and leaders who thought this way would avoid the
> explosive authority issues that could shatter their unions into
> fragments. (Shorter and Tilly, 1974, p. 167)

Without resorting to Michelsian 'iron laws', it is thus possible to
identify a contradiction. Workers' organisations are defined and
constituted through collective struggle; yet they tend also to contain
and inhibit such struggle.

Offe and Wiesenthal (1979, p. 102) characterise this tendency as the 'uncoupling of *representation* of interests and *activation* of interests', the 'dissociation of representation and struggle'. The inevitable consequence is that the distinctive logic of working-class collectivism atrophies, and union organisation, losing its power base in (potential) membership mobilisation, becomes increasingly dependent on the support and goodwill of those external agencies it was created to combat.

There are interesting affinities with Gramsci's (1977) discussion of Italian union organisation six decades ago. Workers' struggles and organisational strength, he argued, force capital to yield significant concessions: 'It obliges the employer to acknowledge a certain legality in his dealings with the workers.'

The emergence of an industrial legality is a great victory for the working class, but it is not the ultimate and definitive victory. Industrial legality has improved the working class's standard of living, but it is no more than a compromise – a compromise which had to be made and must be supported until the balance of forces favours the working class. (Gramsci, 1977, p. 265)

Yet union officialdom typically regarded 'industrial legality as a permanent state of affairs'. They even joined with employers when the balance of forces altered, defending the sanctity of agreements against challenge by the membership. Organisational forms established through earlier struggles may thus become an obstacle to further advance, either because workers' collective solidarity or aspirations expand or because activism and representation become detached. Glaberman expresses this point succinctly:

The victories of the working class and their organizations all become transformed. There is a dialectical process at work. So long as the struggle ends short of the socialist revolution, every codification of victory, every kind of organization, becomes absorbed and institutionalized into capitalist society. In a sense the class struggle consists of overturning past victories. (Glaberman, 1973, p. 83)

This argument is clearly relevant to an appraisal of the upsurge in industrial militancy (in terms both of the number and extent of stoppages and the content of demands expressed) that occurred in many Western economies in the late 1960s and early 1970s. To an important extent many of the struggles may be interpreted as a 'revolt against institutionalisation'. Pressure from below, at times directed as much against the union as the employer, either bypassed existing processes of representation or else compelled them to articulate interests previously sublimated (for a detailed discussion, see Crouch and Pizzorno, 1978). Yet the subsequent downturn in struggle may be viewed in part as a reflection of the 'reinstitutionalisation' of those groups and strata that led the upsurge a decade ago. In Britain the largely autonomous shop steward organisation of the 1960s has become far more closely integrated within the official structures of trade unionism and collective bargaining (a necessary precondition to the effectiveness of the pay curbs of 1975). In Italy rank-and-file activism has been formalised within a recognised framework of factory councils, and workplace militants have been brought into line with the 'historic compromise'.

Reinstitutionalisation of militancy is facilitated where its initial impetus involves the more aggressive pursuit of existing collective bargaining objectives rather than radically new strategies and definitions of collective interest. Thus, Herding has commented on the limits of the 'rank-and-file revolts' in American unions in the 1960s:

> Wherever feasible, they did not leave the ground of the formal rules of collective bargaining, union constitutions, and the legal environment (which, on the contrary, they use effectively against its intentions). Due to this formal adaptability, as well as to their instrumentalism, successful revolts have in some cases been susceptible to the very same routine and ritualism of collective bargaining they had fought – even though on a higher level. (Herding, 1972, p. 302)

Seeking to generalise from a wider range of historical reference, Montgomery has concluded:

> Union structures, leaders, and demands have been successfully incorporated into American capitalism time and again. So have workers' parties (reformist and revolutionary alike), cooperatives, and works councils here and in Europe. Whenever a revolutionary tide is checked and workers' organizations are forced to continue functioning within the capitalist framework, they become to some extent part of that framework. No one form of organization is any more immune to this process than any other. Shop committees and works councils, for example, were handily incorporated into the employers' American Plan in the 1920s. Even when shop councils

arose amid a general crisis of plant closings, heavy layoffs, and employers' sabotage of production – conditions which propelled them into the most immediate exercise of workers' control – such councils quickly succumbed to what the Germans of 1919 called 'factory patriotism'. (Montgomery, 1973, pp. 74–75)

Accommodation to external power – the explanation of so many aspects of the internal dynamics of trade unionism (see Hyman, 1975, pp. 87–92) – is thus a key to the analysis of the 'natural history' of strikes. Capital impinges, both directly and through manifold institutional mediations, on the social process through which workers' collective identities and interests are defined and pursued in struggle.

CONCLUSIONS

A recent survey (Edwards, 1979) has argued for the integration of structure and process in the analysis of strikes. In this paper, that task has been attempted through a focus on the social processes within which antagonistic social relations of production generate specific definitions of interest and strategies of protest and pressure.

The central emphasis has involved the *contradictory* constitution of 'industrial conflict'. Its nature and significance can be adequately comprehended only if its creative and purposeful character receives proper emphasis. As Cronin (1979, p. 195) argues: 'Social and industrial conflict are the means used by ordinary working men and women to assert their changing needs and aspirations in the face of trends and problems that even their rulers and employers cannot control.' More profoundly, such actions also generate the distinctive logic which informs authentic working-class organisation. Yet the consolidation of hierarchical representational structures is itself associated with the attenuation of this subversive logic; external pressures contain and domesticate the oppositional thrust of collective demands and struggles – hence the cyclical trajectory that workers' militancy commonly displays. As traditional weapons become blunted, new forms of resistance must be created in what is often a painful and subterranean process.

A persuasive theory must be grounded in this central contradiction of industrial struggle and must sensitively map the complex dialectic of institutionalisation, reinstitutionalisation, and counterinstitutionalisation.

Notes

1. See for example Scott *et al.* (1963). This argument has been challenged; thus Bean (1975, p. 101) suggests that it 'appears that organized and unorganized expressions of conflict are linked by means of a direct and additive, rather than an inverse, connection.' But it may well be true that a particular work place, industry, or period of time may generate a high level of *all* forms of conflict, and also that, in a given and stable context, changes in one form of conflict may be inversely related to changes in others.

2. For one attempt to pursue these questions see Hyman (1977) and compare the notion of 'strike sophistication' discussed by Stearns (1974).

3. This is, of course, part of the basic rationale of trade unionism, a point pursued further in the discussion of meanings and purposes in collective struggle.

4. 'To say that the interests of capital and those of the worker are one and the same is only to say that capital and wage labour are two sides of one and the same relation. . . . As long as the wage worker is a wage worker, his lot depends upon capital. That is the much-vaunted community of interests between worker and capitalist' (Marx, 1959, p. 93).

5. This has, of course, been a persistent theme in the post-war sociology of industrial relations. Initially developed in Mills's (1948, pp. 8–9) interpretation of the role of the national union leader as a 'manager of discontent', a similar perspective has been elaborated in a number of recent British studies of workplace organisation. What is not always emphasised is that the resulting 'institutionalisation of conflict' reflects not simply the emergent properties of (trade union) organisation but also a process of accommodation to external power within the environment in which trade unions operate and hence the interpenetration of internal and external hierarchical control.

6. This aspect of 'industrial relations pluralism' is analysed in detail in Hyman (1978).

7. Korpi and Shalev also discuss the economic context of trade union political strategy and the implications of organisational strength for internal discipline; their model is thus significantly more complex and sophisticated than that of Hibbs. Nevertheless, the affinities between their approaches remain noteworthy.

8. For a useful critique of the main usages of this term, see Panitch (1980).

9. Pizzorno (1978) coined the term as part of his argument that trade unions increasingly trade 'consensus or moderation' against 'political power' – sustaining the political credibility and/or economic effectiveness of government policies in return for influence on their formulation. While Korpi and Shalev note that the notion is taken from Pizzorno, they do not make clear that their own usage (concerned with a change in the locus of struggle) is significantly different.

10.   Whereas Korpi and Shalev appear to treat disciplinary control within a union as a product of its 'autonomous' organisational strength, it seems more illuminating to view hierarchical control within unions as associated with the distribution of power outside.

References

Allen, V. L. (1966) *Militant Trade Unionism*, London, Merlin.

Barbash, J. (1980) 'Collective Bargaining and the Theory of Conflict', *British Journal of Industrial Relations*, Vol. 18, pp. 82–90.

Batstone, E., Boraston, I. and Frenkel, S. (1978) *The Social Organization of Strikes*, Oxford, Blackwell.

Bean, R. (1975) 'The Relationship between Strikes and "Unorganised" Conflict in Manufacturing Industries', *British Journal of Industrial Relations*, Vol. 13, pp. 98–101.

Brecher, J. (1972) *Strike!*, Boston, South End Press.

Coser, L. A. (1956) *The Functions of Social Conflict*, London, Routledge and Kegan Paul.

Cronin, J. E. (1979) *Industrial Conflict in Modern Britain*, London, Croom Helm.

Crouch, C., and Pizzorno, A. (eds) (1978) *The Resurgence of Class Conflict in Western Europe since 1968*, London, Macmillan.

Dubin, R. (1954) 'Constructive Aspects of Industrial Conflict', in A. Kornhauser, R. Dubin and A. M. Ross (eds) *Industrial Conflict*, New York, McGraw-Hill.

Durand, C., and Dubois, P. (1975) *La grève*, Paris, Armand Colin.

Edwards, P. K. (1979) 'The "Social" Determination of Strike Activity'. *Journal of Industrial Relations*, Vol. 21, pp. 198–216.

Glaberman, M. (1973) 'The American Working Class in Historical Perspective'. *Radical America,* Vol. 7, pp. 81–90.

Gramsci, A. (1977) *Selections from Political Writings 1910–20*, London, Lawrence and Wishart.

Griffin, J. I. (1939) *Strikes*, New York, Columbia University Press.

Herding, R. G. (1972) *Job Control and Union Structure*, Rotterdam, Rotterdam University Press.

Hibbs, D. (1978) 'The Political Economy of Long-Run Trends in Strike Activity'. *British Journal of Political Science*, Vol. 8, pp. 153–77.

Hill, J. M. M. and Trist, E. L. (1955) 'Changes in Accidents and Other Absence', *Human Relations,* Vol. 8, pp. 121–52.

Hyman, R. (1975) *Industrial Relations: A Marxist Introduction*, London, Macmillan.

Hyman, R. (1977) *Strikes*, London, Fontana.

Hyman, R. (1978) 'Pluralism, Procedural Consensus, and Collective Bargaining', *British Journal of Industrial Relations*, Vol. 16, pp. 16–40.

Institute of Industrial Education (1974) *The Durban Strikes 1973*, Durban, Ravan Press.

Karsh, B. (1958) *Diary of a Strike*, Urbana, Illinois University Press.

Kerr, C. (1964) *Labor and Management in Industrial Society*, New York, Doubleday.

Kornhauser, A., Dubin, R. and Ross, A. M. (eds) (1954) *Industrial Conflict*, New York, McGraw-Hill.

Korpi, W. and Shalev, M. (1979) 'Strikes, Industrial Relations and Class Conflict in Capitalist Societies', *British Journal of Sociology*, Vol. 30, pp. 164–87.

Marx, K. (1958) 'Wage Labour and Capital', in K. Marx and F. Engels, *Selected Works*, vol. 1, Moscow, Foreign Languages Publishing House.

Marx, K. (1959) *Capital*, Vol. 1, London, Lawrence and Wishart.

Mills, C. W. (1948) *The New Men of Power*, New York, Harcourt Brace.

Montgomery, D. (1973) 'Spontaneity and Organization', *Radical America*, No. 7, pp. 70–80.

Offe, C. and Wiesenthal, H. (1979) 'Two Logics of Collective Action', *Political Power and Social Theory*, Vol. 1, pp. 67–115.

Panitch, L. (1980) 'Recent Theorizations of Corporatism: Reflections on a Growth Industry', *British Journal of Sociology*, No. 31, pp. 159–87.

Pizzorno, A. (1978) 'Political Exchange and Collective Identity', in C. Crouch and A. Pizzorno (eds) *The Resurgence of Class Conflict in Western Europe since 1968*, London, Macmillan.

Ross, A. M. and Hartman, P. T. (1960) *Changing Patterns of Industrial Conflict*, New York, Wiley.

Schelling, T. C. (1960) *The Strategy of Conflict*, Cambridge, Mass., Harvard University Press.

Scott, W. H., Mumford, E., McGivering, I. C. and Kirkby, J. M. (1963) *Coal and Conflict*, Liverpool, Liverpool University Press.

Shalev, M. (1979) 'Strikes and the State: a Comment', *British Journal of Political Science*, Vol. 8, pp. 479–92.

Shorter, E. and Tilly, C. (1974) *Strikes in France, 1830–1968*, London, Cambridge University Press.

Snyder, D. (1975) 'Institutional Setting and Industrial Conflict', *American Sociological Review*, Vol. 40, pp. 259–78.

Stearns, P. N. (1974) 'Measuring the Evolution of Strike Movements', *International Review of Social History*, Vol. 19, pp. 1–27.

Streeck, W. (1979) 'Gewerkschaftsorganisation und industrielle Beziehungen', in J. Matthes (ed.) *Sozialer Wandel in Westeuropa*, Frankfurt, Campus.

Walton, R. E. and McKersie, R. B. (1965) *A Behavioral Theory of Labor Negotiations*, New York, McGraw-Hill.

5 Theory in Industrial Relations: Towards a Materialist Analysis*

Analysis of the organised interrelationships between employers and the collective representatives of labour was once conducted overwhelmingly in pragmatic and empiricist terms; the subsequent elaboration of 'industrial relations theory' was firmly rooted in the harmonistic presuppositions of functionalist sociology. But in recent years this field of study has attracted a variety of more radical interpretations, and in particular has become an arena for a growing range of Marxist and neo-Marxist arguments. This chapter explores the significance of such developments, raising in the process questions concerning both the nature of Marxism and the adequacy of the conventional category of industrial relations.

TRADITIONAL APPROACHES TO INDUSTRIAL RELATIONS

The very term 'industrial relations' is indicative of the character of the subject which it denotes. It forms an area of study with no coherent theoretical or disciplinary rationale, but deriving from a directly *practical* concern with a range of 'problems' confronting employers, governments and their academic advisers in the pursuit of labour stability.[1] On this pragmatic basis, research and teaching in industrial relations became established (often with the employer and/ or governmental sponsorship) in institutions of higher learning in the US and Britain. Doubtless the location reflected material factors: the existence of a 'labour problem' stemming from relatively strong and stable trade unionism, and a *laissez-faire* tradition inhibiting direct strategies of containment by the state. The acceptability of this new field, within the framework of respectable academic endeavour, equally may be related to factors specific to these countries: most notably, the theoretical sterility of much academic work in other

*First published as Chapter 2 in P. Boreham and G. Dow, *Work and Inequality*, Macmillan Australia.

disciplines ensured that a new and unashamedly atheoretical subject would not appear out of place.[2]

At first sight, the past two decades have witnessed a marked shift in orientation. Dunlop's pointed critique of his fellow-students – 'facts have outrun ideas. Integrating theory has lagged far behind expanding experience'[3] – attracted a ready response; so too did his proposal that the concept of an 'industrial relations system' might offer the theoretical centrepiece of a coherent and distinctive discipline.

Why Dunlop's shoddily constructed essay should have assumed such seminal status is perhaps puzzling: undoubtedly he must have articulated an extensive malaise within the industrial relations establishment. Possibly, with the decline of the post-war strike wave, American academics were less necessary to employers and governments in an immediate trouble-shooting role, and thus required a longer-term rationale for their existence; perhaps also, the influx of students with a range of social science backgrounds encouraged a search for a theoretical framework which would justify industrial relations academics to their colleagues in other disciplines.[4] In any event, the 'theory' which was to become so widely and so rapidly embraced neatly combined the advantages of ready availability, academic acceptability, and complete compatibility with the existing focus of teaching and research.

Dunlop derived his model of the 'industrial relations system' explicitly from Parsons's delineation of the 'social system'.[5] Arguably, he failed seriously to comprehend the Parsonian project[6]; but it is clear that he drew from it a number of orientations – idealism, formalism, conservatism – very convenient for the task of rationalising and legitimising a field of inquiry which had developed primarily to assist capital in ensuring the productive, predictable and profitable exploitation of labour. As has been argued:

> systems analysis offers an ideologically acceptable alternative to those who embrace the perspectives of the pragmatist but eschew his unsophisticated language and concepts. The selfsame problems of efficiency, practicality, constructive adaptation to change and the 'orderly' reform of industrial relations can be tackled in either framework. The principal concerns of Parsons' sociology parallel closely the chief worries of those in authority in industry.[7]

In their search for intellectual legitimacy, industrial relations academics borrowed in other ways (though equally uncritically) from current social science orthodoxy. The notion of 'institutionalisation of conflict' – elaborately theorised by Coser in his commentary on Simmel's *Conflict*[8] – has been fundamental to a whole series of post-war exercises in the sociology of industrial relations: Dubin's much-quoted contribution to the symposium *Industrial Conflict*[9]; the diagnosis of Kerr and his associates of an irresistible development of 'pluralistic industrialism' whereby workers' resistance 'gets organized, channelled, controlled'[10]; or Dahrendorf's thesis of 'the institutional isolation of industry and industrial conflict', highly influential in Britain in the 1960s.[11] The basic theme of all these analyses – that conflict of interest between workers and employers, once openly articulated by representative institutions whose legitimacy is conceded, can be relatively easily contained and accommodated – also underlies the most famous of all predictions in industrial relations: Ross and Hartman's 'withering away of the strike'.[12]

In Britain, resistance to explicit theory in industrial relations proved more tenacious than in the US; only in the late 1960s (at a time when research and teaching in the subject were expanding rapidly) did the 'need for theory' become a regular cry in the journals of the trade. While some writers have embraced the elaborate cybernetic models of recent 'systems thinking', the dominant framework has become a notion of 'industrial relations pluralism' often imprecise in its assumptions, heterogeneous in its lines of argument and varied in its derivations. The intellectual origins of British industrial relations pluralism include Dunlop, Chamberlain and other writers on American labour relations; political scientists such as Schumpeter and Dahl; Durkheimian sociology as construed by the Parsonian school; and the diffuse doctrines of Fabianism.[13]

The Anglo-American tradition, it is evident, is both complex and internally differentiated. Nevertheless, it is possible to discern an underlying paradigm which comprises three key assumptions. The first involves a naturalistic conception of interests: the fundamental actors in the 'industrial relations system' are a multiplicity of individuals and groups; larger collectivities are recognised only in the form of organisations and alliances established by these primary actors.[14] The second core characteristic is an empiricist conception of power: those determinations of social action are alone meaningful and significant which involve the actual or potential mobilisation of sanctions to influence identifiable decisions. A third premise (more overt in some writers than others) reflects an ethnocentric view of the nature and purpose of trade unionism: from a restricted conception of workers' legitimate interests stems a virtual apotheosis of collective bargaining and a definition of unions as almost by nature economistic, accommodative and hierarchical. These three suppositions lead without difficulty to a view of industrial relations as a set of stable institutions through which the 'inputs' of divergent goals and interests are routinely transformed into a 'web of rules' underwriting the smooth progress of capitalist production. [15]

The dominance of these assumptions within academic approaches to industrial relations is easy to understand once they are located historically. First, the ideological climate of the cold war created intense pressures for academics to develop an explicitly anti-Marxist explanatory framework (pressures assisted by the vulgarisation and stultification of most that passed for Marxist thinking during the Stalinist era). This climate affected social analysis in general, but may well have been reinforced for those students of industrial relations who required respectability not only within their own academic institutions but also in the eyes of the companies and governments whom they served. Second, and perhaps more importantly, the *material* context in which academic industrial relations spread its roots was that of expanding post-war capitalism and the hegemony of US imperialism: an exceptionally favourable basis thus existed for the 'positive-sum' resolution of conflicts between capital and organised labour. The model of 'pluralistic industrialism' was a product of the same conjuncture which gave birth to such constructs as 'the affluent society', 'the end of ideology' and the 'common value system'. Theory assumed the timelessness of conditions which were historically specific.

The material context has indeed altered dramatically since the first two post-war decades. Recession and the profits squeeze have reduced the margin for concession in wage bargaining at the same time as price inflation has heightened workers' expectations; employers' rationalisation strategies have brought job control issues – typically less susceptible to compromise – firmly onto the agenda; state initiatives and controls have challenged traditional assumptions of the autonomy of industrial relations institutions; new forms of social and political instability have seemingly been replicated in an enhanced radicalism of goals and methods in labour struggles. The complacent theories and formulae of post-war industrial relations academics have accordingly been thrown into some disarray. [16] Concurrently, *détente* in great power politics has been reflected in a certain loosening of cold-war constraints in intellectual life. Thus in industrial relations analysis, as in the social sciences generally, there has been a growing tendency to seek theoretical insights in more radical – and more specifically, Marxist – approaches.

MARXISM AND 'INDUSTRIAL RELATIONS': THE TRADITIONAL DETACHMENT

' "Industrial relations", the consecrated euphemism for the permanent conflict, now acute, now subdued, between capital and labour':[17] Miliband's dismissive comment typifies Marxist reactions to an area of study which appeared both manipulative and narrow-minded. For the post-war American left, most work in industrial relations followed the example of managerial 'cow-sociology' in assisting the repressive strategies of the industrially dominant. Wright Mills's denunciation still rings eloquent:

> The new practicality leads to new images of social science – and of social scientists. New institutions have arisen in which this illiberal practicality is installed: industrial relations centers, research bureaus of universities, new research branches of corporation, air force and government.[18]

To the charge of managerialism, Marxist writers have subsequently added a critique of the subject's intellectual foundations. Understanding is obstructed, not advanced, by positing a (relatively) autonomous sphere of social relations involving bargaining and 'rule-making' between unions and employers; the processes of 'job regulation' can be adequately comprehended only as part of an analysis, on the one hand of the dynamics of production and accumulation, on the other of the broader pattern of social and political relations.[19] For Marxists, the activities of employers and unions are to be construed in terms of such concepts as relations of production and class struggle; the term 'industrial relations' is at worst vacuous and at best incoherent.

Yet even if the typical mode of academic industrial relations analysis (let alone pretensions of its disciplinary status) is dismissed, the empirical realities which the label mystifies remain of considerable practical and theoretical importance to Marxists. Whatever the difficulties of defining Marxism (and some are considered later), there are clearly two basic assumptions which necessitate a reformulation of the industrial relations problematic. The first is that capitalist social relations of production reflect and reproduce a structured antagonism of interests between capital and labour. The second is that capitalism simultaneously organises workers collectively (since the capitalist labour process is essentially collective in character), and hence generates the material basis for effective resistance to capital and the priorities of the capitalist mode of production. What is conventionally studied as industrial relations may thus be conceived as a fetishised presentation of the class struggle and the various forms in which it is (at least temporarily) contained, fragmented and routinised. Thus one might expect Marxists to have made substantial attempts, not merely to criticise, but also to re-analyse, re-interpret and re-apply what is produced under the name of industrial relations. There is, in other words, an obvious need for Marxist theory in 'industrial relations'.[20]

It is surprising how limited were the attempts, in much of the post-war period, to develop a systematic alternative framework at the level of the concrete reality with which academic industrial relations is concerned.[21] This may in part reflect the lack of detailed support for such a theorisation within the classic Marxian literature. Marx and Engels were not working and writing in a context of routinised trade unionism and institutionalised collective bargaining; their comments on these themes represent in the main responses to immediate issues rather than intensive analysis.[22] The insights to be gained *directly* from the 'blue books' are therefore limited. An inclination to develop *original* Marxist theory in this area was almost certainly inhibited by the tendency – in an era of post-war class collaboration and compromise – to 'write off' the organised working class as a potential agency of revolution. This context encouraged a variety of developments within Western Marxism which despite radical differences were at one in assigning at best minor significance to working-class organisation and action. Examples are the popularity of forms of academicised structuralism in which human agency is virtually excluded; voluntarist and substitutionist emphases on the party or the combat group; and attempts to locate the motor of world revolution in 'marginal' social groups or the 'Third World'. Implicitly or explicitly, all such approaches accepted much of the argument of conventional industrial relations analysts: that industrial struggle in the developed West had become securely contained and institutionalised.

RECENT DEVELOPMENTS: TOWARDS CONVERGENCE?

The challenges to stable institutionalisation which in the past decade have forced reappraisals within academic industrial relations have, predictably, brought a shift of focus in the work of many Marxists. Recently there have been significant moves towards a materialist analysis which assigns appropriate weight to workers' collective organisation and struggles and to the processes of institutional mediation of labour conflicts: exploring their character, sources and internal contradictions. Yet paradoxically, recent changes – both in the material relationships studied as 'industrial relations' and in their analysis and theorisation – have in many respects accentuated the difficulties of characterising theory in general, and Marxist theory in particular, within the field of industrial relations.

In part this reflects the notorious ambiguities of that much reified construct, 'Marxism'. Commenting on the incompleteness of Marx's achievement, Rosa Luxemburg argued that

> the most valuable of all his teachings, the materialist-dialectical interpretation of history, presents itself to us as nothing more than a method of investigation, as a few inspired leading thoughts, which offer us glimpses into an entirely new world, which open to us endless perspectives of independent activity, which wing our spirits for bold flights into unexplored regions.[23]

The differentiation process noted by Korsch – 'there exist, both nationally and internationally, very different theoretical systems and practical movements which go by the name of Marxism'[24] – has escalated considerably in the subsequent half-century. Recent decades have seen the rise of a variety of 'new lefts'; the tolerance of theoretical heterodoxy within official Communist parties; and the growing acceptability of at least elements of Marxist analysis within academic social science. There is a substantial and fundamental divergence between, say, efforts to construct on the one hand a phenomenological Marxism from the epistemology and ontology of the 'young Marx', and on the other a structuralist Marxism which abstracts the categories of *Capital* from human practice and historical process. Less momentous points of division acquire heightened significance when embodied in the conflicts between self-declared Marxist parties and *groupuscules*.[25] Concurrently, the belated sanctification of Marx as one of the 'founding fathers of sociology' – a guide to the understanding of new problems of crisis, conflict and change which post-war orthodoxy was not designed to explicate – raises acutely the questions whether, and how, Marxism constitutes a self-contained and distinctive body of theory, concepts and analysis. Is it possible – or helpful – to assert a rigid demarcation between Marxist and 'bourgeois' theoretical practice, or is there a continuum of approaches each to a greater or lesser extent 'marxisant'?[26]

In the context of a specific field of study such as 'industrial relations', these problems are compounded by yet another: that of differentiation of levels of analysis in terms of generality and concreteness. If Marxism attains its essential distinctiveness as a *general* theory of capitalist production and class relations, can it *directly* and *exclusively* generate an adequate theorisation at the specific level of contemporary management–employee relations? Or is it possible for Marxist (neo-Marxist?) analysis to utilise certain of the concepts and theories of 'bourgeois' social science without succumbing to shallow eclecticism?[27]

It could be argued that the integrity of Marxist analysis is indeed inversely related to the specificity of the concrete issues which concern the student of 'industrial relations'. It is precisely those researchers who descend from the higher levels of generality and abstraction – who accept the challenge of *relating* the general to the specific, the concrete to the abstract – who face problems of analytical innovation which seem to require various forms of 'revisionism'. What is it that identifies Huw Beynon's *Working for Ford*[28] as a Marxist work? (If indeed it is: for one reviewer 'it objectively functions as part of the left reformist wing of institutional sociology by its partial failure to become Marxist sociology'.) Does Kern and Schumann's much cited study[29] represent a development of, or a withdrawal from, Marxism? Can the members (some? most? all?) of the *Groupe de Sociologie du Travail* be regarded as Marxist scholars? It is difficult to believe that such questions can be answered helpfully, if at all.

Perhaps the problem could be restated. It seems impossible to specify a clearly differentiated and homogeneous set of Marxist theories or explanations which systematically elucidate relations between unions and employers, workers and managers. Nor do Marxist researchers bring to the study of such relations a distinctive methodology: if many British Marxists regard the elaborate quantitative analysis of, say, strike statistics as unduly positivistic, and many Germans reject conventional survey techniques as authoritarian, their French or Italian counterparts reveal few such scruples.

Ultimately, it could be argued, the major contribution of Marxists has been as much in the questions asked as in the answers given or the methods of their attainment. It is the framework of what is taken for granted and what is regarded as problematic that most clearly differentiates Marxists from conventional 'industrial relations' analysts. In principle, 'bourgeois' researchers might raise similar questions: but a background in Marxian political economy creates a natural sensitivity to structures, problems and processes traditionally neglected within orthodox analysis – at least until a changed material context forces them importunately into view.

THREE SUBSTANTIVE ISSUES: THE SIGNIFICANCE OF MARXIST ANALYSIS

It is possible here to explore three such areas of enquiry: the dynamics of capital accumulation; the nature of the working class; and the changing forms of state involvement in relations between labour and capital. Recent work in these areas clearly demonstrates the major theoretical contribution of Marxist analysis; but indicates at the same time the heterogeneity of interpretations (and hence the acuteness of controversy *among* Marxists) and also points of convergence with non- (or semi-) Marxist approaches.

It is a notable paradox that while the dynamics of capital accumulation are a necessary starting-point of any distinctively Marxist discussion of class structure and class struggle within capitalism, there has traditionally been very little attention to the specific agencies and strategies of capital in its relations with labour. In contrast, bourgeois writers have long emphasised the historic significance of the so-called 'managerial revolution', have erected a grandiose pseudo-discipline of 'management science', and more recently (at least in Britain) have sought to develop a theory of industrial relations in which managerial policies and initiative constitute the key determinant.[30] The fundamental weakness of such approaches is that typically they assume or imply an exaggerated *autonomy* of managerial strategy from the structural dynamics of commodity production and capital accumulation. An important contribution of recent Marxist writing has thus been to confront the theses of managerialism with an analysis which explicitly emphasises the linkages involved.[31]

Criticism of managerialism has converged with more general

developments in the field of political economy. The breakdown of the relative stability of post-war capitalism has stimulated vigorous reassessment of some of the basic principles of Marxian economics, with much attention (often highly abstract) to the categories of value and price and to the famous 'transformation problem', and with considerable debate over the character and conditions of Marx's law of the tendency of the rate of profit to fall.[32] Of great importance is the growing willingness to link such theoretical discussion to the analysis of the current dynamics of the class struggle. On the one hand, workers' collective resistance to capital has itself been theorised as a source of crises of profitability; on the other (though most fruitfully *in conjunction* with the latter perspective), specific managerial strategies towards labour are related to the uneven development of patterns and problems of accumulation.[33]

One aspect of this emergent reconstruction and revitalisation of Marxist economics is a growing attention to the labour process. It is ironical that conventional writers on industrial relations have developed often sophisticated discussions of 'job regulation' and 'systems of rules' without any apparent recognition that the elaborate procedural and institutional superstructure on which they focus has its foundation in the sphere of *production*. Marx's discussion of the labour process – somewhat neglected in much post-war Marxist economic literature[34] – has received renewed attention following the appearance of Braverman's influential study.[35] It has accordingly become clear that sensitivity to the specific character of the capitalist labour process – to its function as the motor of valorisation and accumulation, to its dependence on a necessarily coercive system of control and surveillance – provides a basis for elucidating theoretical problems which bourgeois approaches can scarcely begin to formulate. Thus such a focus illuminates the concreteness and inherently antagonistic nature of what orthodox industrial relations writers term 'managerial relations'; and, more generally, exposes the class character of the managerial function.[36] It recognises that the inherent dynamism of the capitalist mode of production is reflected in a constant revolutionising of the labour process, which in turn threatens the stability of institutionalised forms of conflict resolution.[37] Of crucial importance, it helps deflate the ideology of 'technology' as a neutral, autonomous and irresistible force, revealing the technical organisation of production as an element in the struggle for control over production and thus demonstrating the need to locate materially and historically the contemporary experience of 'rationalisation'.[38] In addition, attention to the labour process underlines the need to analyse occupational changes within the working class in relation to the material basis of production rather than by reference to such epiphenomena as 'white collars'.[39]

This latter consideration connects closely with the central theme of a second major area of recent Marxist analysis: the patterns of divergence and differentiation within the working class. The basic postulate of the unity of the working class (*in* even if not *for* itself) – a unity constituted from a common relationship of antagonistic class interests as against capital and the bourgeoisie – implies a level of analysis distinct from that involved in specifying the immediately conceived structure of interests of particular groups of workers. Marx himself devoted only limited attention to hierarchical divisions within the working class, which in his view rested 'in part on pure illusion or, to say the least, on distinctions that have long since ceased to be real'; and whose material basis would be further eroded by the spread of the detail division of labour and the real subsumption of labour to capital. Yet it is clear that while some traditional differentiations have disappeared,[40] others have retained their significance and yet others have arisen. To analyse the nature and significance of such internal divisions and variations is at the same time to explore a number of general questions of great theoretical importance: what is the working class? how are its boundaries identified? what meaning (if any) can be attributed to the notion of 'middle class' within Marxist theory?

Much discussion of these issues in post-war sociology has been cast within a 'vulgar Weberian' framework. Typical features have been a subjectivist focus (studies of 'self-assigned class'); an emphasis on life-styles or consumption patterns to the neglect of the sphere of production; or analysis in terms of abstracted notions of 'authority' and purely market-related aspects of occupational differentiation.[41] While the more sensitive of such studies illuminate important areas of social relations traditionally neglected by Marxists, the fundamental weakness of neo-Weberian approaches is their failure to accommodate the *production of surplus value* as an integral component of the processes under examination.[42]

In recent years there have been important attempts to interpret the changing composition and structure of the working class, and the implications for collective labour organisation and action, against the background of Marx's analysis of the production of absolute and relative surplus value.[43] One major theme has been the evaluation of the significance of occupational strata and sectors to which sociological orthodoxy has attributed key importance: most notably, 'white-collar' and 'service' labour. While certain Marxists have sought legitimacy for identifying such groups as a 'new middle class',[44] the predominant concern has been to reject as obfuscatory such designations, and to emphasise the heterogeneity of the occupational changes which have occurred,[45] while at the same time locating these developments within the more general dynamics of capitalist production.[46] Of particular relevance for students of 'industrial relations' is the analysis of *contradictory* aspects in the position of certain occupational groups whose significance is currently increasing: what Carchedi terms 'those agents who, while not owning the means of production, perform the global function of capital and the function of the collective worker'.[47] Such a focus offers considerable potential for the theoretical understanding of the extent and boundaries of collective organisation among 'new' occupational groups, and the type of goals and strategies which are collectively pursued; and this in turn can assist in comprehending collective action within the 'traditional' working class.[48]

In this latter context, recent years have seen an engagement between Marxist economists and conventional accounts of labour market segmentation within the manual working class. In the 1950s, American labour economists and industrial relations writers[49] pointed to the development within major firms of job hierarchies in which recruitment to higher positions was made internally, and outward mobility was inhibited by the company-specific nature of workers' experience and expertise. The early accounts of 'neo-feudalism' in employment structures were essentially descriptivist, involving little significant theoretical advance on nineteenth-century notions of non-competing groups. Subsequent attempts – that of Doeringer and Piore[50] being the best known – to characterise the American economy as a whole in terms of 'labour market dualism' were also weak in developing theoretical explanations of the patterns identified.

Recent work by Marxist (and other 'radical') theorists has had two main objectives: to elucidate forms of segmentation in national labour (power) markets which diverge from those in the US; and to inform the specific analysis of market differentiation with a historical understanding of the dynamics of capitalist production. The basic premise is that the structure of labour (power) markets must be comprehended as the outcome of a complex dialectic between the unevenness of capitalist development (reflected in divergent tendencies among industries, regions and indeed nations); consequential variations in employer strategies towards labour; and patterns of worker organisation and resistance (which may themselves predominantly involve the pursuit and defence of *sectional* advantages).[51]

The general issue of labour (power) market structure assumes especial significance in relation to the position and struggles of two pre-eminently 'secondary labour market' groups: women and black or migrant workers. In both cases, the heterogeneity of approaches within radical and Marxist analysis – indeed the intensity and often acrimony of current debates – requires little emphasis. Some issues of contention may be noted: how far the *specificity* of the oppression and of strategies for liberation of women and blacks can be theorised in terms of *general* processes of marginality and disadvantage; the relative importance of deliberately discriminatory practices, patterns of institutionalised racism or sexism, and more fundamental socio-economic processes and structures; the extent to which the main dynamics of 'secondary' status are to be located within the operation of labour (power) markets themselves or externally (for example, historical and contemporary imperialist relationships; 'patriarchy' and the role of women within social reproduction and domestic labour); the direct utility to capital of the specific forms of subordination imposed on women, blacks and migrants (and hence the extent to which their current struggles are *necessarily* anti-capitalist).[52]

As far as the theme of this chapter is concerned, the significance of the expanding literature on these issues is twofold. On the one hand it has explored lacunae in Marxian political economy, effectively combating a traditional 'vulgar' tendency to reduce all social and economic oppression to a simple polarity of classes. In particular, Marxist feminists have exposed the economistic neglect of all forms of social production within capitalism except capitalist production itself: they have taken seriously Marx's dictum that 'the maintenance and reproduction of the working class remains a necessary condition for the reproduction of capital', elaborating some of the implications which Marx himself failed to pursue.[53] On the other hand, these theoretical debates (perhaps rather the *practical* struggles of women and black workers) have obliged students of industrial relations to attend seriously to aspects of work, wages and collectivism which have traditionally been largely ignored.[54] More crucially, this has in turn revealed the inadequacy of the 'industrial relations' perspective itself: for the 'industrial relations' of black workers reflect international structures of the exploitation of labour power by capital, and are not located merely within the framework of employer–employee institutions in a single national 'industrial relations system'; while women's 'industrial relations' cannot be meaningfully analysed except in terms of the highly complex interaction between institutions of wage-labour and more general processes of social production and reproduction.

The notion of a (relatively) autonomous 'industrial relations system' is thrown further into question by the pervasive role increasingly performed by state institutions in the conduct of union–employer relations. Such developments create obvious scope for Marxist interpretations, for Marxist critics of industrial relations orthodoxy have long insisted that there is an elaborate dialectic between capitalist production, class struggle and state power which cannot be grasped by a mechanical dichotomy between the 'economic' and the 'political'. From this perspective, an absence of direct and systematic state intervention in the organised relationships between labour and capital (the traditional pattern in Britain and North America) should be viewed as *itself a form of involvement*: for the 'abstention' of law and government permits the working out within 'industrial relations' of a particular balance of class forces in civil society. As a corollary, a more actively interventionist role is to be interpreted as a change in the form rather than the reality of state implication in the capital–labour relation.

The detailed contribution of recent Marxist analysis to what might be termed a 'political economy of industrial relations' is difficult to characterise. The relationship between state power and capitalist production is one of the most contentious issues in contemporary Marxist controversy: partly because, as Miliband has noted, 'the available classical writings are simply silent or extremely perfunctory over major issues of politics and political theory';[55] partly because of the overwhelming and immediate political significance of even relatively abstract theoretical debates;[56] partly because it is here that Marxist structuralists have engaged most violently with what are denounced as 'historicist' or 'positivist-empiricist' interpretations.[57] Without attempting here to enter into this controversy, it may be noted that the quasi-functionalist tendency within structuralist theories of the state (involving, for example, the unproblematic specification of trade unions among the 'ideological state apparatuses') make it extremely difficult to theorise the *changing* forms of interaction of employers, unions, governments and legislation. (Indeed, even to raise such questions may be denounced as evidence of a faulty problematic.)

By contrast, other Marxists have taken such developments as their main focus of analysis. One major issue has been the interpretation of the rapid growth of the state sector within many Western economies (thus in the role of government as an employer, as a direct actor within 'industrial relations'). As against conventional accounts of the 'welfare state' as the outcome of essentially 'political' decision-making processes, Marxists have explored the intimate connections between state employment and relations of production within contemporary capitalism. Thus it can be shown that much state expenditure contributes indirectly to the expansion of surplus value through providing the necessary infrastructure for advanced monopoly capitalism and through facilitating the reproduction of labour power; while the remainder predominantly helps underwrite the reproduction of the capitalist mode of production itself through what has been termed the 'warfare-welfare state'.[58] While such analyses are at their weakest when confronted with the substantial international *variations* in both the extent and the rate of growth in state expenditure,[59] they contribute powerfully to an understanding both of the relative social and economic stability of the first two post-war decades, and of the subsequent cycle of crises.

Against the background of a *combined* theory of the internal contradictions of state employment and expenditure as a source of 'fiscal crisis', and of the origins of the crisis of profitability within the development of monopoly capital itself, the dynamics of 'interventionism in industrial relations' are readily apparent. What is less directly explicable is the specific selection of strategies for state intervention: the imposition of wage controls, the enactment of legislative restraints on worker militancy and union action, the promotion of 'safe' channels of employee representation (e.g. works councils), the co-optation of unions within governmental policy-making, or the various possible combinations of these methods. A genuinely materialist analysis recognises that such strategies are not adequately explicable merely in terms of the internal workings of 'the political'; that the emergent institutional linkages and tensions between employers, unions and the various agencies of state power must be located concretely within the dynamics and contradictions of capitalist production in its current conjuncture. But the precise characterisation of this conjuncture, and the detailed elucidation of the multi-faceted relationship between state and 'industrial relations', receive only the most limited guidance from a generalised commitment to Marxist theory.[60]

MARXISM, TRADE UNIONISM – AND SOME POINTS IN CONCLUSION

It has already been suggested that many of the problems which affect the development of theory in industrial relations are, in part at least, problems of integrating different levels of generality. The state of 'industrial relations' or of class struggle cannot be simply 'read off' from a generalised characterisation of the economic and political conjuncture, but equally cannot be understood except against this background. What is at issue is the specificity of *institutions and processes of mediation* which are in some respects distinctive in each nation, industry, company and individual workplace; and which can alter in their effects over time. The contrasts in patterns of development in the various West European countries in the past decade (to make a relatively restricted geographical and temporal comparison) must be grasped as in large measure the outcome of differences at the level of mediation.

Trade unions themselves are obviously among the most crucial of such mediating institutions. The distinctive traditions of their historical development in each country – often reflecting the long superseded material context of their origins and early growth – help determine the degree to which union organisation encompasses the working class, the internal structural delineations within the movement, the nature of the linkages between unions, the types of attachment to political ideologies and parties, the orientation towards collective bargaining as a dominant mode of activity, the extent of internal democracy and the forms of articulation between membership and leadership. Such factors in turn have a profound bearing on each of the areas of analysis discussed previously: the extent to which unions intensify or help damp down crises of profitability and struggles over the labour process; their contribution to the unity or the internal hierarchisation and division of the working class; their accommodation or resistance to different strategies of state intervention. Unless the mediating role of unions can be adequately analysed and theorised, there will be severe limits to the value of the most impressive advances of theory in the areas discussed above.

It is therefore noteworthy how modest is a distinctive Marxist contribution to the understanding of trade unionism. The 'classic' Marxist writers in their discussions of union organisation and action were largely concerned to generate recipes for intervention and leadership in immediate working-class struggles, rather than to develop sensitive, systematic and generalisable theory. (Hence ironically there is considerable evidence of a mirror-image of the pragmatism of more orthodox commentators.) Accordingly, the terms in which Marxists have typically analysed unionism have been largely derivative. Lenin's notion of 'economism' – one of the most commonly repeated concepts in Marxist trade union literature – derived primarily from his reading of the Webbs' *Industrial Democracy*. The reactive and accommodative character of stable, 'pure-and-simple' unionism was stressed as strongly by such authors as Commons, Perlman and Hoxie (though their *evaluations* were of course very different) as by Marxists – whose detailed familiarity with actual trade union practice was often far less. Marxist commentaries on the relationships between leaders and led owe much to Michels and the 'elitist' school of political analysis. In particular, the familiar dichotomy between 'rank and file' (a conventional military metaphor) and 'trade union bureaucracy' (an almost ritual incantation popularised by the Red International of Labour Unions) normally reflects mere sloganising rather than serious theoretical intent.[61] Finally, the notion of corporatism – much in vogue as a characterisation of the growing intimacy of employer–union–state relations – lacks either analytical clarity or obvious Marxist credentials.[62]

The readiness of Marxists to embrace such categories and characterisations reflects the fact that all denote – though in a partial and mechanical manner – genuine tendencies within trade union development. The key question must therefore be: does Marxist theory offer the possibility of a distinctive and more scientific understanding of these tendencies than can be achieved through borrowed concepts and propositions? One obvious path to analytical insight is through an appreciation of the *historically contingent* character of what conventional commentators often treat as 'iron laws' of trade union development. A major component of the interface between antagonistic class forces, trade unions embody a contradictory potential which consigns on their organisation and action a persistent dualism: a dualism moreover which derives not merely from the *internal* dynamics of unionism but from the material interests and relations of production which they mediate.[63] The dominance of a particular tendency (militancy or acquiescence, democracy or oligarchy...) should thus be interpreted as the determinate, but to some degree always *provisional*, outcome of a particular combination of circumstances. Sensitivity to such dualism is uncommon. Most Marxist writing on trade unionism displays one of two opposing forms of one-sidedness. Either overwhelming weight is placed on the determinant effect of the logic of capitalist development, depicting as inevitable and uncontradictory the subordination of the working class to bourgeois hegemony and the integration of working-class organisations within the priorities of the capitalist state. Or else the contradictions within capitalism are treated as a source of almost unqualified openness for working-class collective action, spontaneous worker resistance to capital being viewed as a virtually undetermined agency of economic and political instability and transformation. The one approach effectively denies the potential or significance of conscious human (and specifically working-class) *practice* in the face of the structural determinations of capital; while in the other, the scope for working-class creativity is treated as unlimited regardless of the material context.

Both tendencies find partial legitimation within the corpus of classic Marxism; each on its own is clearly inadequate. Marx's theoretical stature derives essentially from the creative tension between his *dual* emphasis on the structural determinacy of capitalist production and the historical agency of the working class in struggle. The interpenetration of these contradictory facets of the social reality of capitalism demands sensitivity, insight and qualitative richness from the analyst of trade unionism. It is no exaggeration to suggest that the advances made on the existing tentative and exploratory essays in the theoretical understanding of unionism – in its manifold variations over time and place – will provide a critical test of the vitality and fertility of contemporary Marxism.

Yet it also remains true (as was suggested previously) that such advances are likely to display considerable parallelism with other interpretations – provided only that these are sufficiently attuned to the complex and contradictory nature of current mediations between labour and capital – even though derived from very different theoretical traditions. But in admitting the possibility of a certain convergence between Marxism and academic orthodoxy in the analysis of institutions and processes of mediation, is it necessary to concede the *autonomy* of 'industrial relations' as an area of material reality and intellectual endeavour? It is indeed correct to insist that this is a level of social relations which *partially* follow their own (contradictory) laws of development, and which accordingly require serious analysis in their own right. But today, more than ever before, it is fallacious to *exaggerate* the autonomy of the processes of institutional mediation of the capital-labour antagonism. On the contrary, in an epoch of crisis the interconnections between the various levels and elements of the social formation (national and international capitals and their various fractions; state and civil society; material and ideological relations), whose *superficial* independence once encouraged attempts to develop a self-contained theory of the 'industrial relations system', are now increasingly transparent.[64]

Notes and References

1. The term appears to have acquired widespread currency with the appointment by the US Congress in 1912 of a Commission on Industrial Relations. Its final report, in eleven volumes, was published in 1915. It took some time for the phrase to attain popularity in Britain (thus the source of the famous Whitley Reports of 1917–18 was the Committee on Relations between Employers and Employed); the first significant official usage was in the *Survey of Industrial Relations* published by the Board of Trade in 1926.
2. It is noteworthy that specialist industrial relations departments are uncommon in European universities, with their far stronger commitment to theory; and indeed, literal equivalents of the term 'industrial relations' have an alien ring in most European languages.
3. J. T. Dunlop, *Industrial Relations Systems*, New York, Holt, 1958, p. vi.
4. Some of the dilemmas which American industrial relations academics faced at this time are indicated – albeit in a somewhat mystificatory manner – by Clark Kerr, 'Industrial Relations Research: a Personal Retrospective', *Industrial Relations*, Vol. 17, No. 2 (May 1978).
5. His definition of a system is taken from *Economy and Society* (Parsons and Smelser), published two years earlier; and he spends four pages outlining the AGIL paradigm.
6. See, for example, S. J. Wood *et al.*, 'The "Industrial Relations System" Concept as a Basis for Theory in Industrial Relations', *British Journal of Industrial Relations*, Vol. 13, No. 3, November 1975.
7. Richard Hyman and Bob Fryer, 'Trade Unions: Sociology and Political Economy', in McKinlay, *Processing People*, London, Holt-Blond, 1975, p. 165.

8. L. A. Coser, *The Functions of Social Conflict*, London, Routledge & Kegan Paul, 1956.
9. R. Dubin, 'Constructive Aspects of Industrial Conflict', in Kornhauser *et al.*, *Industrial Conflict*, New York, McGraw-Hill, 1954.
10. C. Kerr *et al.*, *Industrialism and Industrial Man*, London, Heinemann, 1962, p. 233.
11. R. Dahrendorf, *Class and Class Conflict in Industrial Society*, London, Routledge & Kegan Paul, 1959. A best-seller in British academic circles, Dahrendorf's book made little impact in Germany where the original version appeared two years earlier: an indication, perhaps, of the theoretical vacuum then existing in British industrial sociology.
12. A. M. Ross and P. T. Hartman, *Changing Patterns of Industrial Conflict*, New York, Wiley, 1960. It is only fair to note that in this work Ross and Hartman presented the 'withering away of the strike' thesis in a far more guarded and qualified form than many subsequent writers.
13. The Fabian background to industrial relations analysis in Britain helps explain the – at first sight paradoxical – trend from sympathetic interest in the labour movement to a managerialist focus. The pioneering studies of the Webbs displayed *both* a commitment to what they identified as the goals of unionism, *and* an insistence on the virtues of industrial stability, the rationality of bureaucratic routine, and the selfishness of proletarian class strategies. More recent writers with a similar political and intellectual background to the Webbs, in a period of shop-floor worker resistance to the *common* bureaucratic control of management and union hierarchies, have identified naturally with the goals of 'order' as against 'anarchy'. This trend is explored in more detail in Richard Hyman, 'Pluralism, Procedural Consensus and Collective Bargaining', *British Journal of Industrial Relations*, Vol. 16, No. 1, March 1978. A certain parallel in the development of industrial relations studies in the United States is discussed by George Strauss and Peter Feuille, 'Industrial Relations Research: a Critical Analysis', *Industrial Relations*, Vol. 17, No. 3, October 1978. Early students – the 'Wisconsin school' – 'sought to describe, explain and legitimate the then struggling trade union movement'. By the 1940s, stability in labour relations had become a major concern: 'combined with sympathy for unions was a desire to understand and reduce the causes of industrial unrest'. Increasingly, Strauss and Feuille argue, 'industrial relations scholars ... became technicians and defenders of the status quo'.
14. The identification of industrial relations in terms of essentially *micro-sociological* processes is well represented by a work extremely influential among those seeking enhanced sophistication within the framework of traditional orthodoxy: R. E. Walton and R. B. McKersie, *A Behavioral Theory of Labor Negotiations*, New York, McGraw-Hill, 1965.
15. An explicit development of the 'input-output' model is provided by Alton W. J. Craig, 'A Framework for the Analysis of Industrial Relations Systems', 3rd World Congress of the International Relations

Association (September 1973). There are parallels in the writings of Allan Flanders.

16. A small but significant example may be noted: in the three successive editions of H. A. Clegg's standard textbook (*The System of Industrial Relations in Great Britain*, Oxford, Blackwell, 1970, 1972 and 1976) the concluding chapter appears in turn as 'The Reform of Collective Bargaining', 'The Reform of Industrial Relations', and 'The Crisis in British Industrial Relations'.

17. Ralph Miliband, *The State in Capitalist Society*, London, Weidenfeld & Nicholson, 1969, p. 80.

18. C. Wright Mills, *The Sociological Imagination*, New York, Oxford University Press, 1959, p. 95.

19. See, for example, Richard Hyman, *Industrial Relations: A Marxist Introduction*, London, Macmillan, 1975, Ch. 1.

20. This is *not* to suggest the desirability or possibility of a Marxist theory of industrial relations. To argue thus would be to accept the theoretical coherence of 'industrial relations' as an area of analysis: to endorse the material and theoretical *autonomy* of institutionalised management–union relations. For the same reason, any search for a radical *redefinition* of 'industrial relations' must be self-defeating. The formula 'processes of control over work relations' (*ibid.*, p. 12) fails not only through over-simplification (an expanded version might read 'processes of institutional mediation of collective labour conflicts deriving from antagonistic social relations of production'), but because the principles of inclusion and exclusion which determine the normal usage of the term 'industrial relations' are themselves theoretically inadequate.

21. The one British example of note in the first two post-war decades is V. L. Allen, 'The Need for a Sociology of Labour', *British Journal of Sociology*, Vol. 10, No. 3, September 1959. This brief essay reappeared in 1971 (in *The Sociology of Industrial Relations*, London, Longman) when the most significant change was in the title; Allen's subsequent *Social Analysis* is not largely concerned with industrial relations issues.

22. For a comprehensive collection of their writings on trade union questions see Karl Marx and Friedrich Engels, *Le syndicalisme* (2 vols) Paris, Maspero, 1972; and for a brief discussion see Richard Hyman, *Marxism and the Sociology of Trade Unionism*, London, Pluto Press, 1971.

23. 'Stagnation and Progress of Marxism' (1903) in *Rosa Luxemburg Speaks*, New York, Pathfinder, 1970, p. 107.

24. Karl Korsch, 'Why I am a Marxist' (1935) in *Three Essays on Marxism*, London, Pluto Press, 1971, p. 60.

25. Two factors have contributed to the distinctive form of such differentiations in Britain. Firstly, the traditional weakness of Marxism within the labour movement, and in particular the relative insignificance of Communist organisation, has allowed a greater detachment between theoretical controversy and organised political division than in continental Europe. Secondly, the problem of language has led to a

curious periodisation of theoretical development: for example, major writings of Lukács and Gramsci, of the Frankfurt School, and of the French structuralists have been published in English only in the past decade; while among the works of Marx himself, the *Grundrisse* and the *Resultate* have been available only in the 1970s. Theories and concepts emerge as the arcane possessions of a polyglot minority, assume on translation a rapid vogue, but are usually soon displaced by a different cult.

26. 'Moi, je ne suis pas marxiste': Marx's famous rejoinder is still a powerful caution against attempts to systematise his writings into a body of dogma. It is perhaps significant that most attempts to define Marxism are more convincing in characterising what it is *not* rather than what it *is*. What is at issue is not the acceptance of Marx's *specific* analyses and predictions (which after a century cannot but require extensive revision); Lukács exaggerated, but no more than this, in arguing that one could 'dismiss all of Marx's theses *in toto*, without renouncing Marxism.' But neither is Marxism (as Lukács went on to propose) primarily a question of *method*: efforts to formulate Marxism as methodology are typically either trite or circular, or else fail adequately to differentiate Marxism from other approaches. To posit Marxism as *tradition* (as Edward Thompson has suggested) is also unsatisfactory: a tradition is identifiable only retrospectively, and offers no adequate orientation towards *new* problems and situations. Yet it is even more unacceptable to regard Marxism as a *resource*: to assume, in Thompson's words, that 'all human culture is a supermarket in which we may shop around as we choose'. To believe that particular Marxian ideas can be wrenched out of context to assist explanation of a specific current problem, or can be combined promiscuously with other arguments from Comte, Durkheim or Weber, is to abandon any notion of Marxism as a coherent totality. The difficulty stems partly from the fact that while Marx's work possesses a genuine unity it is nevertheless incomplete and internally differentiated (indeed at times contradictory). The lack of a clear basis for a strategy which avoids dogmatism on the one hand, eclecticism on the other, is in part also a reflection of the paradox of 'armchair Marxism'. Marxist theory cannot be adequately defined and constituted through academic contemplation: 'all mysteries which mislead theory to mysticism find their rational solution in human practice'.

27. In a different context, Peter Worsley has commented that while Marxism represents 'the best world-view available in terms of its capacity to define the most relevant "problematic" for analysis and practical solution, it is markedly more problematic – in a different sense – in its capacity to cope with the more forbidding problem of operationalizing that general theoretical critique' ('The Reification of Marxism', *Sociology*, 9, 3 (September 1975), p. 499). Referring to British Marxist analyses of class and industry, John H. Goldthorpe has described as 'a rather curious situation' their tendency 'to denounce institutionalised social science, more or less indiscriminately, as "bourgeois ideology" serving only to legitimate the capitalist order.

Yet they are at the same time led to draw very heavily upon it in seeking to make the case that British society remains fundamentally differentiated and divided on class lines' ('Class, Status and Party in Modern Britain: Some Recent Interpretations, Marxist and Marxisant', *Arch. europ. sociol.*, 13, 2 [1972], p. 343).

28. Harmondsworth, Penguin, 1973.
29. H. Kern and M. Schumann, *Industriearbeit und Arbeiterbewusstsein*, Frankfurt, Europäische Verlagsanstalt, 1970.
30. See, for example, Ian Boraston *et al.*, *Workplace and Union*, London, Heinemann, 1975; and Hugh Armstrong Clegg, *Trade Unionism Under Collective Bargaining*, Oxford, Blackwell, 1976.
31. For example, Theo Nichols, *Ownership, Control and Ideology*, London, Allen & Unwin, 1969; and Robin Blackburn, 'The New Capitalism', in Anderson and Blackburn, *Towards Socialism*, London, Fontana, 1965.
32. For an extensive – though necessarily partisan – survey of the British literature see Ben Fine and Laurence Harris, 'Controversial Issues in Marxist Economic Theory', in Miliband and Saville, *Socialist Register 1976*, London Merlin, 1976. Continuing debates can be followed in the pages *New Left Review* and of the Conference of Socialist Economists *Bulletin* (published since 1977 as *Capital and Class*).
33. Andrew Glyn and Bob Sutcliffe, *British Capitalism, Workers and the Profits Squeeze*, Harmondsworth, Penguin, 1972, unleashed an intense controversy; debate continues among British Marxists as to the sense in which – if at all – workers can be considered partially 'responsible' for economic crises. Discussions of managerial strategy towards labour include Tony Cliff, *The Employers' Offensive*, London, Pluto Press, 1970; and Andrew L. Friedman, *Industry and Labour: Class Struggle at Work and Monopoly Capitalism*, London, Macmillan, 1977.
34. At least, in Britain and the US; the labour process has long been more central to Marxist discussion in Italy and other European countries. It is plausible to assume that emphasis on the labour process varies according to the importance of rationalisation of production as an element in capitalist strategy and class struggle.
35. Harry Braverman, *Labor and Monopoly Capital*, New York, Monthly Review Press, 1974. In Britain there has been a tendency – in line with a certain one-sidedness in Braverman's analysis – for writers who have 'rediscovered' the labour process to fetishise the concept: seeking in effect to *reduce* capital accumulation to the labour process, and thus neglecting the interdependent operation of the valorisation process. This criticism is developed by Tony Cutler, 'The Romance of "Labour"', *Economy and Society*, Vol. 7, No. 1, February 1978; Tony Elger, 'Valorisation and "Deskilling"', *Capital and Class*, No. 7, Spring 1979.
36. An important though excessively formalistic analysis is provided by G. Carchedi, 'On the Economic Identification of the New Middle Class' and 'Reproduction of Social Classes at the Level of Production Relations', *Economy and Society*, Vol. 4, Nos 1 & 4, February and November 1975.

37. This forms one of the central themes of Friedman's study.
38. See, for example, Braverman, Part II; Ernest Mandel, *Late Capitalism*, NLB, 1975, Ch. 16; CSE Pamphlet No. 1, *The Labour Process and Class Strategies*, 1976. Particularly important are the German compilations which have appeared roughly annually since 1972: Otto Jacobi *et al.*, *Gewerkschaften und Klassenkampf*, Fischer, Frankfurt, 1972 to 1975 and *Gewerkschaftspolitik in der Krise*, Berlin, Rotbuch, 1978; and Rainer Duhm and Ulrich Mückenberger, *Krise und Gegenwehr* and *Arbeitskampf im Krisenalltag*, Berlin, Rotbuch, 1975 and 1977.
39. Carchedi's analysis has been particularly influential among British Marxists; and see also Terry Johnson, 'What is to be Known? The Structural Determination of Social Class', *Economy and Society*, Vol. 6, No. 1, March 1977.
40. In Britain, notable examples are the virtual disappearance of the sub-contractor in mining and manufacturing, the erosion of the rigid Victorian dichotomy between craftsman and labourer, and the decline of domestic service. In many countries, the fall in agricultural employment has similarly reduced differentiation within the working class.
41. An early but sophisticated example of the neo-Weberian approach is David Lockwood, *The Blackcoated Worker*, London, Allen & Unwin, 1958. While Lockwood considers the 'work situation' of clerical labour, the notions of authority and bureaucracy dominate his analysis.
42. For an important comparative discussion of the Marxian and Weberian approaches to the analysis of class, and of recent developments in both traditions, see Anthony Giddens, *The Class Structure of the Advanced Societies*, London, Hutchinson, 1973.
43. In particular, Parts III–V of Volume 1 of *Capital*.
44. See Martin Nicolaus, 'Proletariat and Middle Class in Marx', *Studies on the Left*, Vol. 7, No. 1, January–February 1967, and Paul Walton, 'From Surplus Value to Surplus Theories', *Social Research*, Vol. 37, No. 4, Winter 1970; also the exchange between the two in Walton and Hall, *Situating Marx*, Human Context Books, London, n.d. [1972]. Both draw primarily on the *Theories of Surplus Value* which Marx himself, of course, never completed for publication.
45. Braverman (pp. 325–6) insists that 'the traditional distinctions between "manual" and "white-collar" labor, which are so thoughtlessly and widely used in the literature on this subject, represent echoes of a past situation which has virtually ceased to have meaning in the modern world of work'. Mandel (pp. 383–4n) emphasises 'the great variations in the economic structure of the so-called services sector. The function of middle-men, which expands in the course of the growing social division of labour and which can be ascribed in capitalism to enterprises dealing with trade, transport, storage, credit, banks and insurance, only constitutes a part of this sector, which sociologists and bourgeois political economists make into a pot-pourri of the most various activities, stretching from pure commodity pro-

ducers (gas, water and power production) to pure parasites and crooks.'

46. Many attempts have been made to analyse these developments in terms of Marx's somewhat ambiguous distinction between productive and unproductive labour. Despite the undoubted theoretical importance of this controversy, the degree of abstraction involved limits its relevance for the understanding of the organisation, strategies and struggles of particular collectivities within the working class.

47. 'The New Middle Class', p. 1. Carchedi identifies the function of capital in terms of control and surveillance, that of the collective worker in terms of coordination and unity. He insists – without evidence – that while a specific position may involve both functions, they cannot be performed simultaneously. If this assumption is rejected, it is possible to recognise as even more radical than Carchedi suggests the contradictions inherent in many of the rapidly expanding technical-managerial roles. For this reason, Carchedi's characterisation of those in such occupations as a 'new middle class' is an oversimplification – as, in the other direction, is Serge Mallet's famous thesis of the 'new working class' (*La nouvelle class ouvrière*, Paris, Seuil, 1963). Some of the ambiguities in such positions are explored by André Gorz, 'Technology, Technicians and Class Struggle' in Gorz, *The Division of Labour*, Brighton, Harvester, 1976.

48. For a survey of recent debates on the significance of occupational change for collective organisation and action see Richard Hyman, 'Occupational Structure, Collective Organisation and Industrial Militancy', in Crouch and Pizzorno, *The Resurgence of Class Conflict in Western Europe since 1968*, Vol. 2, London, Macmillan, 1978.

49. The extensive involvement of labour economists in the development of academic industrial relations in the US contrasts with their far more limited role in Britain.

50. Peter B. Doeringer and Michael J. Piore, *Internal Labor Markets and Manpower Analysis*, Lexington, DC Heath, 1971.

51. A good example of American attempts to radicalise 'dual labour market' analysis is Richard C. Edwards *et al.*, *Labor Market Segmentation*, Lexington, Heath, 1975. The varying endeavours of European Marxists to incorporate trade union action within the theory of labour (power) market structure are exemplified by Massimo Paci, *Mercato del laboro e classi sociali in Italia*, Bologna, il Mulino, 1973; Richard Herding, *Job Control and Union Structure*, Rotterdam, Rotterdam UP, 1972; Friedman, *op. cit.*; Jill Rubery, 'Structured Labour Markets, Worker Organisation and Low Pay', *Cambridge Journal of Economics*, Vol. 2, No. 1, March 1978.

52. Any selection of references would be partial and idiosyncratic. In the US, the *Review of Radical Political Economics* is a forum for many of these controversies. In Britain – in addition to the sources mentioned in note 32 – it is possible to cite the journal *Race and Class* and, for a range of Marxist and *marxisant* approaches, Diana Leonard Barker and Sheila Allen, *Dependence and Exploitation in Work and Marriage*, London, Longman, 1976.

53. One consequence of such work is to demonstrate important difficulties involving Marx's treatment of the value of labour power and hence the labour theory of value itself: see Veronica Beechey, 'Some Notes on Female Wage Labour in Capitalist Production', *Capital and Class*, No. 3, Autumn 1977.

54. The 'invisibility' of women in most industrial sociology – as in most labour history – has often been noted; see, for example, Richard Brown, 'Women as Employees', in Barker and Allen, *op. cit.*

55. Ralph Miliband, *Marxism and Politics*, Oxford, Oxford UP, 1977, p. 2.

56. Criticism or justification of the emergent political strategy of the Communist Parties – eventually graced with the label 'Eurocommunism' – provides the practical point of reference for many of the theoretical controversies; others revolve around the detailed political perspectives of particular leftist groups.

57. The most notable example being Nicos Poulantzas, *Political Power and Social Classes*, London, NLB, 1973.

58. James O'Connor, *The Fiscal Crisis of the State*, New York, St Martin's, 1973. There are interesting affinities in the analysis developed by Claus Offe, *Strukturprobleme des kapitalistischen Staates*, Frankfurt, Suhrkamp, 1972.

59. It could reasonably be argued that such variations might be explicated by *combining* Marxist interpretations with more conventional political theories of state expenditure.

60. To take one of the most substantial of recent studies which explore this relationship: Joachim Bergmann *et al.*, *Gewerkschaften in der Bundesrepublik*, Europäische Verlagsanstalt, Frankfurt, 1975. The authors' starting point is clearly a commitment to Marxist political economy, but it is hard to specify on what grounds their detailed documentation and analysis are to be regarded as distinctively 'Marxist'.

61. See Richard Hyman, 'The Politics of Workplace Trade Unionism', *Capital and Class*, No. 8, Summer 1979.

62. *All* stable trade unionism inevitably involves some form of accommodation with the superior power wielded by agents of capital and the state, and some degree of disciplinary control over the rebellious tendencies of the membership. In this sense, unions cannot escape 'incorporation' to a greater or lesser extent. The crucial analytical issues thus involve questions of modes, levels and outcomes of the incorporation process: issues which few discussions of corporatism attempt seriously to elucidate. One of the more sophisticated of recent treatments – Colin Crouch, *Class Conflict and the Industrial Relations Crisis*, London, Heinemann, 1977 – does pursue a range of conceptual differentiations; but though a few Marxist notions are grafted onto an essentially Weberian framework, this work (despite its title) gives little attention to class conflict or to production relations more generally. Alessandro Pizzorno, 'Entre l'action de classe et le corporatisme', *Sociologie du travail*, No. 2/78, avril-juin 1978, provides an interesting measure of convergence with Crouch (though his primary focus is at company rather than national level); his comparative analysis is very

firmly rooted in the categories of orthodox political science and industrial relations.

63. One recent attempt to explore this dualism is Rainer Zoll, *Der Doppelcharakter der Gewerkschaften*, Frankfurt, Suhrkamp, 1976: for a pointed critique see Walther Müller-Jentsch, 'Die Neue Linke und die Gewerkschaften', *Das Argument*, No. 107, Januar–Februar 1978. Failing to locate the contradictions of trade unionism which Marx recognised, and those apparent in its contemporary role as *Ordnungsfaktor*, in their altogether different material contexts, Zoll neglects the *specificity* of trade union dualism in different social and political environments. In this way, argues Müller-Jentsch, 'historical process is dissolved into analogy'.

64. Because of the declining margin of autonomy within any given element or level of this complex totality, the scope for a theory *of* 'industrial relations' will necessarily diminish – whatever advances may be made in theory *in* industrial relations. The owl of Minerva?

Part II

Problems of Contemporary Trade Unionism

6 The Politics of Workplace Trade Unionism: Recent Tendencies and Some Problems for Theory*

The aim of this chapter[1] is above all to stimulate discussion: firstly about the nature and significance of the changes which have occurred in British trade unionism (particularly at shop-floor level) since the 1960s; secondly about the implications of these changes for the analyses of union democracy and union leadership which are popular on the left.[2] Much of the argument is tentative or exploratory; constructive criticism will be very welcome.

It has long been common to discuss internal political relations within unions in terms of a dichotomy between 'bureaucracy' and 'rank and file'. Often closely associated has been a strategy which emphasises workplace struggle and shop steward militancy as an objective (even if unintended) agency of advance towards socialism.[3] Not infrequently, such a perspective has involved a somewhat idealised and romanticised conception of shop-floor organisation and action; and the controversy surrounding this position has not always been marked by a high degree of theoretical coherence. On the one hand, the notion of 'trade union bureaucracy' has normally represented a descriptive category or derogatory slogan rather than an analytical concept adequately embedded in a serious theory of trade unionism.[4] In effect, the term can be employed to present trade union officialdom as scapegoats for contradictions inherent in trade unionism as such. But conversely, critics of this position have at times treated the limitations inherent in trade unionism under capitalism as an alibi for the actions and inactions of trade union leadership (or at least a favoured group within this leadership).[5]

For the traditional critique of 'bureaucracy' does reflect a genuine and important problem within trade unionism. To put a complex argument extremely briefly:[6] those continuously engaged in a representative capacity perform a crucial mediating role in sustaining tendencies towards an accommodative and subaltern relationship

*First published in *Capital and Class*, No. 8, Summer 1979.

with external agencies (employers and state) in opposition to which trade unions were originally formed. No doubt *some* form of accommodation with external forces is inevitable (at least outside a revolutionary situation). But those within unions who primarily conduct external relations do not merely react to irresistible pressures; they help shape and channel the nature and extent to which trade union goals and methods adapt to external agencies which seek to minimise the disruptive impact of workers' collective resistance to capital.

Three important influences on this process may be noted. Those in official positions in trade unions possess a direct responsibility for their organisations' security and survival, a role encouraging a cautious approach to policy. In particular, this is likely to induce resistance to objectives or forms of actions which unduly antagonise employers or the state and thus risk violent confrontation. Because of their *ongoing* relationship with external parties, officials normally become committed to preserving a stable bargaining relationship and to the 'rules of the game' which this presupposes. And finally, the rationale of the officials' positions is typically a competence to perform specialist functions. To sustain a belief in the significance of their own role, there is a natural tendency to define trade union purposes in a manner which emphasises officials' own expertise and activities: stressing 'professional' competence in collective bargaining rather than militant mass action.[7] These three powerful (though not necessarily irresistible) tendencies help explain why union officials, though often politically and socially more advanced or progressive than many of their members, frequently perform a conservative role in periods of membership activism and struggle.

If the notion of 'union bureaucracy' is an unsatisfactory specification of what is nevertheless a real set of problems within trade unionism, the term 'rank and file' also lacks obvious theoretical foundation: indeed, it represents no more than a military metaphor.[8] The main implication is the lack of differentiation of interests and of hierarchical control within the main body of union membership. Just as, in military usage, privates and corporals might be classed together, so the notion of trade union rank and file has normally included 'lay' officers and representatives.[9] Discussion in the 1960s often treated shop stewards, in particular, as an essential component of the rank and file, sharing the same employer as the ordinary membership, participating in the same experiences and aspirations and subject to their control.

From this fairly unsophisticated perspective, discussion on the left has often stressed three aspects of shop steward organisation and action. First, that unionism within the workplace – as at national level – was predominantly economistic in orientation; yet because of its direct engagement at the point of production, it was necessarily involved in struggles against managerial control of the labour process. This concern with issues of job control could be viewed as a basis for more ambitious movements towards workers' control of production. Second, the very intimacy of the links between shop stewards and the small groups of workers they represented could accentuate the problem of trade union sectionalism; isolated militancy over parochial issues made workplace union power highly vulnerable to a concerted counter-attack by the employers. This problem of fragmentation was, however, mitigated by the development of joint shop stewards' committees[10] and – usually against the opposition of national officials – combine and other multi-plant bodies. Third, the proximity of shop steward organisation to the shop floor inhibited bureaucratic tendencies and corporatist developments. Indeed, the existence of autonomous workplace unionism represented a key defence against the incorporation of the national organisations; for if the official leadership were to compromise too far (by collaborating, for example, in government wage controls) they would be faced by a rank-and-file revolt spearheaded by the stewards' movement.

It is interesting that a somewhat parallel conclusion was drawn by conventional writers on 'industrial relations', particularly in their role as government advisers. Thus the central proposition of the Donovan Report of 1968 was the existence of 'two systems' of British industrial relations. Whereas conditions of employment were ostensibly determined at industry-wide level in negotiations between national officials of unions and employers' associations, it was bargaining within the workplace (at least in key sectors of manufacturing industry) which was in practice more significant. Such bargaining was typically piecemeal and sectional, remote from the control of full-time union officials or senior management, and commonly resulted in unwritten understandings and 'custom and practice' rules. To this divorce between official institutions and actual practice were attributed several consequences. Small-scale, unofficial negotiation was matched by a similar pattern of strikes. Upward pressure on earnings (particularly where payment by results applied) could not readily be contained by managerial resistance or governmental policies. And employer control over the labour process was substantially eroded. For many commentators, the combination of these features was considered a major barrier to the profitability and competitiveness of British capital.

Some sections of the ruling class proposed a solution primarily in terms of direct legal repression. Others advocated greater reliance on gradualist institutional transformation. Thus the major recommendation of the Donovan Commission was the formalisation and centralisation of collective bargaining at plant or company level. In this process employers should assume the main initiative, reconstructing payment systems and bargaining machinery and elaborating their internal procedures of management information and control. Unions for their part should appoint far more full-time officials in order to intervene actively in workplace negotiations and supervise the work of their shop stewards. The priority, Donovan insisted, was for employers and trade unions together 'to recognise, define and control the part played by shop stewards in our collective bargaining system' (1968, p. 120).

In the subsequent decade, the relations between unions, employers and the state have of course exhibited several major upheavals. Today it is possible to argue that the Donovan strategy has proved far more effective than is generally appreciated. At the same time, developments have not precisely matched the scenarios drawn by both advocates and opponents of 'reform' during the 1960s. Moreover, the 'offensive' of employers and the state, though clearly significant, has not alone been the decisive influence. No less important have been the emergent tendencies within workplace unionism itself, which have interacted with the strategies of employers, governments, and full-time officials.

A central feature of the past ten years has been the consolidation of a hierarchy within shop steward organisation. The tightening of internal management controls and the introduction of new payment systems, job evaluation structures, 'productivity' agreements and formalised negotiating and disciplinary procedures have often reduced significantly the scope for bargaining by individual stewards at section level. Workplace negotiation has become a far more centralised process, often involving the application to individual issues of an explicit set of 'rationalised' principles. But in the main this has *not* – as Donovan anticipated – become the responsibility of full-time officials from outside the company; in a period of rising union membership, the rate of new appointments has been limited. Rather, the introduction and operation of centralised bargaining arrangements has been the responsibility of a new layer of full-time convenors and shop stewards. The number of such representatives, it would appear, has quadrupled during the past decade, and considerably exceeds the number of ordinary union officials. And no longer can it be suggested, as Donovan argued (p. 107), that 'it is the exception, rather than the rule, for a chief shop steward to have a room put at his disposal as an office'; facilities provided by employers for senior stewards have expanded as substantially as their numbers.[11]

This trend has been paralleled by a centralisation of control within stewards' organisations. In the past, joint shop stewards' committees have tended to fulfil the functions of co-ordination rather than control, to depend upon the voluntary agreement of the various sections and their representatives rather than upon the exercise of sanctions. Today it is far more common for such committees to exercise a disciplinary role, forcing dissident sections of the membership into line. But at the same time, the small cadre of full-time or almost full-time stewards within a committee often possess the authority and the informational and organisational resources to ensure that their own recommendations will be accepted as policy by the stewards' body.[12]

These developments have in turn coincided with a significant degree of integration between steward hierarchies and official trade union structures. In the past there existed a considerable detachment (though exaggerated by some commentators) between workplace organisation and the branch-based decision-making machinery of most unions. Union rulebooks were slow to recognise the negotiating functions of shop stewards, and few even mentioned the position of convenors. Often those elected as lay representatives at different levels in trade union government were branch administrators rather than shop-floor bargainers. But in the past decade there have been extensive changes, often carried through under the slogan of greater union democracy. In some cases, workplace leaders have been given an official role within union constitutions; they have become represented on many national negotiating bodies; some unions have created industrial committees and conferences composed of workplace activists. Rulebooks have begun to define the rights and obligations of convenors and joint shop stewards' committees. Education and training schemes for shop stewards (typically emphasising the importance of negotiating expertise and orderly procedures rather than membership mobilisation) have burgeoned.

Against this background it is not fanciful to speak of the bureaucratisation of the rank and file. The developments of the last ten years, in those unions and industries where workplace organisation has long been strongest and most autonomous, have made possible a considerable degree of articulation beween union policy and national and shop-floor level. A key mediating role is now performed by a stratum of shop steward leaders who have become integrated into the external union hierarchies and have at the same time acquired the power, status and influence to contain and control disaffected sections and sectional stewards. This fact is crucial in explaining the effect of the TUC/government wage curbs since 1975. The very limited opposition and resistance on the shop floor during the first two (or even three) years of pay controls cannot be explained simply in terms of the level of unemployment, or political commitment to a Labour government, but owe much to the new ability of national union leaders to win the backing of major convenors, and of these in turn to deliver the acquiescence of their own workplace organisations. The internal politics of trade unionism today involves a complex system of linkages between the relatively inactive membership on the shop or office floor and the top leadership in the TUC Economic Committee. The ability of national leaders to contain, control and manipulate the ordinary membership depends to an important extent on their success in establishing loyalties, understandings or trade-offs with groups at different levels in this elaborate hierarchy who are able to deploy a variety of forms of influence and sanctions.

These developments have more general implications for a theoretical understanding of trade unionism in contemporary British capitalism. In the past, the existence of 'two systems' of industrial relations contained important limitations to the influence of national leadership and the corporatist tendencies of trade union organisation, in those areas of industry where relatively autonomous workplace struggle provided a power base largely independent of both management and full-time officialdom. As the duality always inherent in shop steward organisation[13] has become accentuated, so its potentiality as an agency of control over the membership has emerged more clearly. There is every reason to assume that this process will continue. The very rapid concentration and centralisation of British capital since the early 1950s entails persistent pressures for greater centralisation within British union organisation. Recent labour legislation, and union/employer moves to broaden the scope for collective bargaining, have generated a powerful impetus for the 'professional-isation' of workplace representation. Any serious moves towards 'participation' machinery (whether by legislation or through incorporationist strategies by major companies) are likely to extend such developments still further.

At this point, two qualifications are called for. The first is that the force of any generalisation concerning British trade unionism is limited by the immense variety of traditions, institutions and contexts. The trends so far discussed have been widespread and important, but far from universal. In particular, it must be noted that shop steward organisation deriving substantial autonomy from an active and extensive process of workplace bargaining has traditionally been confined to a relatively small proportion of British trade unionists. Its strongest roots were in sections of engineering, and a few other manufacturing industries, characterised by fragmented piecework systems and a general lack of sophisticated managerial controls (often because of 'soft' product market conditions in the 1940s and 1950s).[14] Multi-unionism was often an additional factor inhibiting effective control by outside union officials.[15]

A considerable contrast existed in much of the public sector, within most 'white-collar' occupations, and even among a wide range of private-sector manual workers. For most trade unionists it is reasonable to argue that national agreements determined fairly closely the actual earnings and conditions of employment, that shop steward organisation was relatively weak or even non-existent, and that full-time officials played an important role in whatever plant negotiations occurred.[16] In many such contexts, the main trend of the past ten years has involved a certain *de*centralisation of collective bargaining and union organisation. Paradoxically, sophisticated employers have recognised a *need* for the existence of workplace union representation. Recent years have seen major strategies of capitalist rationalisation and intensification of the labour process (encouraged by a variety of state agencies), typically involving the introduction of new production and manning standards and the tightening of the nexus between pay and performance.

The successful introduction of such schemes, with the minimum of worker resistance, was seen as dependent on their *negotiation* with representatives familiar with workplace conditions and able to exert authority over the labour force. If shop stewards did not exist, they had to be invented. In some cases, employers themselves took the initiative in providing recognition, facilities and 'training' for workplace representatives. In others, shop steward organisation was 'sponsored' by national union leaderships: at times anxious to collaborate with such managerial strategies, at times motivated by a genuine interest in greater membership involvement in union affairs, at times alarmed by the militant revolts against national negotiators which were a feature of the late 1960s and early 1970s. Introduced largely from above, steward machinery in such circumstances is normally far more closely integrated into the official structures of trade unionism and collective bargaining than where its origins lie in independent initiative from below. Nevertheless, the implications are potentially contradictory: such organisation, once established, may develop an unanticipated degree of autonomy, perhaps providing an effective basis for resistance to the policies of management or union leadership.[17]

This leads to the second qualification which must be specified. Arguably, the previous discussion of centralisation in shop steward organisation was unduly negative in tone. The traditional fragmentation of workplace struggles has always been a major source of weakness, and has become increasingly debilitating as capital itself has directed a co-ordinated attack on workers' conditions. The detachment of powerful shop stewards' organisations from national trade union politics was a reflection of the dominance of economism in the 1950s and early 1960s. Even in terms of workplace action, this could create a fatal vulnerability;[18] in a period of rapidly developing direct state intervention in industrial relations, with the close involvement of national union leaderships, continued detachment is impossible. Moreover, it would be unrealistic to deny the need for both leadership and discipline *within* shop-floor union organisations. Effective strategies to advance workers' collective interests at every level cannot be expected to emerge spontaneously; arbitrary acts of opposition by isolated individuals or groups may dissipate the strength of factory unionism or prove dangerously divisive.[19] Such considerations have been influential in encouraging the emergent tendencies towards centralised control within shop steward bodies themselves.

Who says organisation says, firstly discipline, secondly routinisation. This virtual truism is less dramatic than Michels's dictum yet at the same time perhaps more fateful. Analogous tendencies are apparent within trade union organisation at national and workplace levels. The resources of discipline and control which are a precondition of effective collective struggle contain the potential to be turned back against trade union members in the interests of capital: channelling and containing workers' resistance to the exploitation of their labour power, facilitating and reinforcing managerial control over the labour process. If the notion of corporatism – currently much in vogue – possesses a coherent meaning (and its usage is often somewhat vacuous), it is to indicate the *dominance* of this repressive potential over the explicit purposes of unions as agencies through which workers collectively pursue their own distinctive interests by mobilisation and struggle. No trade union movement can become wholly an agency of repressive discipline, for this would destroy its pretentions to independence and thus its claims to workers' loyalty to the instructions and recommendations which it issues. Conversely, no trade union movement can be wholly autonomous, for this would render its activities and indeed its very existence intolerable to capital. There is a radical dualism within trade union practice; and the balance between autonomy and incorporation (and hence in unions' role as an agency of power *for* workers or power *over* them) can vary within wide margins.

This fact gives vital significance to the trends discussed in the preceding pages. Traditionally, shop-floor organisation has been viewed primarily in terms of opposition and resistance to capital; and in so far as this view, even if oversimplified, reflected the dominant tendency within shop steward activity, the incorporation of trade unions as national organisations faced imposing obstacles. But if the balance between autonomy and containment within workplace organisations themselves has shifted – if their disciplinary powers are increasingly applied according to the logic of accommodation with the power of capital rather than workers' independent class interests – then it has become far easier for British trade unionism as a whole to move substantially towards the corporatist pole.

If this is a genuine danger (and the trends in trade unionism within most of Western capitalism offer few grounds for complacency), then a precondition of effective resistance is a correct identification of its nature. A central theme of this paper has been that the dichotomous conception of power in trade unions misrepresents the problem and thus obstructs analysis and ultimately confuses strategy. Between 'trade union bureaucracy' and 'rank and file' there exist many forms and processes of mediation. One may, for example, identify a stratum of 'rank-and-file leadership': the shop steward hierarchy, the respected and influential activists at branch and district level.

Participating far more regularly and extensively than most members in the unions' representative machinery, such activists organise and articulate the experiences and aspirations of the membership; but the influence which this gives them can on critical occasions be used to contain, control and manipulate members' reactions. Or the term 'semi-bureaucracy' might seem appropriate to designate the stratum of 'lay' officialdom on whom full-time union functionaries are considerably dependent but who in turn may be dependent on the official leadership. (For the full-time officials they perform a range of administrative tasks, act as channels of information, and may mobilise electoral support; they in turn may seek the backing of full-timers in sustaining their reputation with the membership and sponsoring their advancement within the union structure.) These two categories are themselves involved in relationships of interdependence; indeed they may largely overlap and in some unions virtually merge. The interconnections between national union leadership and the twelve million members in the workplace are thus manifold, complex and often contradictory.

A second inadequacy of the dichotomous conception of trade union politics is that the problem is not simply (although certainly it is partially) one of hierarchical control. The trends discussed in this paper cannot be properly comprehended (as some of the left appear to suppose) merely in terms of a layer of workplace leadership 'going over to the bureaucracy'. For there is an important sense in which the problem of 'bureaucracy' denotes not so much a distinct *stratum of personnel* as a *relationship* which permeates the whole practice of trade unionism.[20] 'Bureaucracy' is in large measure a question of the differential distribution of expertise and activism: of the *dependence* of the mass of union membership on the initiative and strategic experience of a relatively small cadre of leadership – both 'official' and 'unofficial'.[21] Such dependence *may* be deliberately fostered by an officialdom which strives to maintain a monopoly of information, experience, and negotiating opportunities, and to minimise and control the collective contacts among the membership. But what the authors of *The Miners' Next Step* termed the 'bad side of leadership'[22] still constitutes a problem even in the case of cadres of militant lay activists sensitive to the need to encourage the autonomy and initiative of the membership. Hence the predicament of the stewards whose relationships are explored by Beynon: 'torn between the forces of representation and bureaucratization'.[23]

The implication is not that union democracy is a utopian ideal, but that its attainment will always be partial and always against the odds. Given the necessity of some form of leadership within the unions, the style and character of that leadership can exert a critical influence on its responsiveness to general membership aspirations; or more crucially, its willingness and ability to *stimulate* the collective awareness, activism and control of the mass of workers, to *combat* their dependence on its own superior commitment and expertise. And given that the centralisation of workplace organisation is both inevitable and desirable – an argument which this paper has not intended to dispute – the issue of democratic centralism (to misapply the term) has become a vital question for shop-floor union leadership.

Posed at this level of organisation, it is clear that the democratisation of trade union practice – or the defence of existing democratic processes and traditions – is a question of the relationship not merely between full-time officialdom and 'lay' activists, but between *both* these categories and the general membership. The types of strategy long associated with 'unofficial' struggles must now be re-interpreted and re-applied within shop steward organisation. And here the irony is of course that influential local activists traditionally most committed to the struggle for democracy within the national union organisation may well recognise a vested interest in *resisting* pressures for greater democracy within the lower-level organisations which they dominate.

Ultimately, though, the problem of vested interests is probably the least substantial – if only because the most obviously visible – obstacle to strategies for 'democratic centralism' in contemporary unionism. A more insidious problem is what is conventionally termed the 'apathy' of the majority of union members. If the mass of trade unionists – except perhaps on occasion of a major dispute or wage negotiation – have little or no interest in participating in the mechanisms of discussion and decision-making, they can scarcely be in a position to control the policies and activities of those who exercise leadership. At best, the latter can be *indirectly* accountable to the membership through lower-level activists who may themselves be unrepresentative, or whose ability to oppose the leadership may be reduced by their members' passivity. It is of course a commonplace that most trade unionists take a far more active interest in workplace unionism than in the branch, district or national levels. It is also important to resist the tendency to treat membership 'apathy' as a scapegoat for mechanisms of union debate and decision-making almost calculated to deter any but the most dedicated, and for more basic structural sources of detachment between ordinary workers and the institutional mediations and articulations of their collective interests. But even if the term 'apathy' does not explain so much as mystify, the problem it denotes is a real one which even at the level of shop steward organisation is important in its implications.

The issues of apathy as against commitment, of union democracy as against the repressive imposition of centralised discipline, cannot be dissociated from conceptions of the nature and purposes of trade unionism as such. If the whole rationale of unionism is conceived as nothing more than negotiating with employers over wages and conditions – the pursuit of relatively marginal adjustments to the form of the capital/wage-labour relation – then the implications for unions' internal political life can be readily specified. Collective bargaining will assume a focal status within trade union practice; those who actually undertake negotiations will acquire an important basis for power within the organisation; a decisive influence on policy will be the maintenance of amicable bargaining relationships, which in turn entails the maintenance of 'orderly industrial relations' and the containment of 'undisciplined' resistance by workers to capitalist priorities. Conversely, a trade unionism defined in these terms offers no persuasive motive for active membership involvement in its internal government; most workers will quite legitimately feel that they have better things to do than to devote time and energy to meetings, controversies and decisions which will have only a minor effect on their own circumstances.

The goal of union democracy acquires significance only within a more radical conception of the objectives (at least potential) of unionism: as a basis for collective struggle *against* as well as *within* capitalism, as an agency which ultimately can be effective only as a means of collective *mobilisation* of the working class. It is scarcely necessary to add that, among British trade unionists, such a conception is at best an extremely subsidiary element within a tradition and an ideology powerfully dominated by the centrality of collective bargaining. Even militant and oppositional movements within unions are typically directed towards more ambitious aims and more aggressive methods within collective bargaining, rather than seeking to transcend the limits of collective bargaining itself. Accordingly, their strategies have rarely involved serious concern with developing sustained mass involvement.[24]

Trade union consciousness interrelates intimately with powerful external influences – both material and ideological – on the character of union action. The politics of trade unionism constitute a complex totality highly resistant to major strategies of radicalisation and democratisation – which, to be effective, must go hand in hand. But it is important not to end this paper (and to initiate any discussion which may ensue) on a fatalistic note. 'The trade union,' wrote Gramsci (1977, p. 265), 'is not a predetermined phenomenon. It *becomes* a determinate institution, i.e. it takes on a definite historical form to the extent that the strength and will of the workers who are its members impress a policy and propose an aim that define it'. The determinations to which British unions today *are* subject imply the closure of many of the options to which some romantic conceptions of the possibilities of trade unionism aspire. Nevertheless, the politics of trade unions today contain sufficient internal contradictions to make their scientific analysis and theorisation – involving the reformulation of many of the categories and assumptions traditional on the British left – an urgent and important task of theory and practice.

Notes

1. The chapter originates from a contribution to a BSA Industrial Sociology conference in Birmingham in the spring of 1978; a brief synopsis was produced under the title 'Double Agents? Some Problems of Workplace Trade Unionism'. This developed into a paper 'British Trade Unionism in the 1970s: the Bureaucratisation of the Rank and File?', discussed at the Bradford CSE Conference in July 1978.

2. Possibly this needs locating autobiographically. In the period before leaving the International Socialists (which was then in the process of its identity change) I was becoming increasingly aware of inadequacies – accentuated by the developments discussed in this paper – in the analysis of trade unionism current within the organisation. Since then I have felt less restricted in thinking through my heterodoxy. Although I have sharpened my criticisms, it should be clear from what follows that I do not share the simple rejection of 'rank-and-filism' articulated within the Communist Party.

3. As an example one may cite Cliff and Barker (1966). While noting the weaknesses of shop steward organisation in terms of fragmentation and economism, they concluded (p. 106): 'To defend and extend the shop stewards' organisations of today is to build the socialist movement of tomorrow; to fight for the socialist movement of tomorrow is to strengthen the shop stewards of today.'

4. The Red International of Labour Unions, which in the 1920s turned the three words 'trade union bureaucracy' into an incantatory epithet, was presumably not guided by sociological theories of bureaucracy. Certainly it would be difficult to construe the influence of union leaders over the membership primarily in terms of Weber's conception of 'legal-rational authority'. It is ironical to read in Beatrice Webb's *Diaries* of the period repeated complaints that British union leaders were extremely *inadequate* bureaucrats.

5. For an example see Roberts (1976). After correctly criticising those who attempt to subsume the problem of trade unionism within that of bureaucracy, he goes on to perpetuate precisely the reverse error. Thus Roberts argues (p. 378): 'What defines trade union leaders as a group is *not* . . . that they have special interests of their own distinct from those of the working class, but their *function* which is in turn structurally determined. . . . What is problematical for revolutionaries is not the role of trade union leaders but the nature of trade unionism itself.' What Roberts ignores is the fact that *both* can constitute important and interconnected problems. By virtue of their distinctive functions, union officials *do* possess special interests (though whether, to what extent, and in what circumstances these are *opposed* to those of ordinary members is a separate issue). One may also note that Roberts' view of the 'determination' of the nature of trade unionism and its limits would seem to be somewhat mechanical.

6. I have tried to treat some of the issues in more detail in my *Industrial Relations: A Marxist Introduction* (Hyman, 1975, Ch. 3).

7. These three points may be said to underlie Mills's famous characterisation of the union leader as a 'manager of discontent' (1948, pp. 8–9). For a more recent discussion of the contradictory pressures on the union official see Lane (1974).

8. Ranks and files were the horizontal and vertical lines of infantry drawn up for battle; as early as the sixteenth century the portmanteau term 'rank and file' was used to denote the common soldiery. The *OED* notes its application outside the military context in Mill's *Considerations on Representative Government* (1865). The term was used with reference to trade union members at least by the 1890s.

9. The Webbs commented in the second edition of their *History* (1920, p. 577) that the 'annually elected branch officials and shop stewards may be regarded as the non-commissioned officers of the Movement'.

10. Lane comments (1974, p. 204) that 'joint shop stewards' committees emerged as a means of regulating the otherwise "free market" of sectional groupings'. However, as Beynon (1973) insists, unification normally occurred in any meaningful sense only within the confines of the workplace; what resulted, he argues, was a form of 'factory consciousness'.

11. In general, a notable feature of the literature on shop stewards in Britain is the *absence* of serious discussion of the development of shop steward hierarchies and the ensuing problems of control. For some useful details of recent developments see Brown and Terry (1978).

12. For a painstaking documentation and analysis of such processes – though interpreted within a highly idealist problematic – see Batstone *et al.* (1977).
13. A much quoted comment is the conclusion of the Donovan Commission's own research, that 'for the most part the steward is viewed by others, and views himself, as an accepted, reasonable and even moderating influence; more of a lubricant than an irritant' (McCarthy and Parker, 1968, p. 56). A major study of the car industry suggested that the stewards' organisation 'has assumed, in relation to managements on the one hand and the rank-and-file of operatives on the other, many of the characteristics that the official unions once displayed under the earlier developments of national or industry-wide collective bargaining' (Turner *et al.*, 1967, p. 222).
14. Friedman's differentiation (1977) between centre and periphery is of obvious relevance here.
15. In this context, the series of major trade union amalgamations in the 1960s and 1970s may be seen as a further tendency encouraging the integration of workplace within national union organisation.
16. An indication of this variety of practices and relationships can be obtained from Boraston *et al.* (1975).
17. Such a tendency may perhaps be discerned in the development of the 'union stewards' established by the National Union of Public Employees in response to the introduction of bonus schemes in local government and the health service. In a very different context, Nichols and Beynon (1977, Part III) discuss ICI's strategy of sponsoring shop steward organisation in a 'greenfield' site, and indicate some of the latent contradictions resulting from the creation of a (partially) independent collective structure.
18. For example, when Ford management, with the collaboration of national union leaderships, smashed the powerful Dagenham shop stewards' organisation in the early 1960s. As Beynon (1973) indicates, this was a lesson which the stewards at Halewood subsequently took to heart.
19. The realities of such considerations, and the contradictory pressures which result, are sensitively discussed in Beynon (1973); see, for example, p. 140. The debates among Italian revolutionaries in 1919–20 remain surprisingly relevant; see Gramsci (1977).
20. This formulation of the problem was indicated by Bob Fryer in the discussion at the Bradford CSE Conference.
21. The notion of rank-and-file leaders as part of a 'cadre' which includes the full-time officialdom has been explored by Mick Carpenter in an unpublished paper.
22. See Unofficial Reform Committee 1912, pp. 13–15. The antileadership theories current in the unofficial movements in many British unions in this decade are often cited as a reason for their ultimately limited success. Perhaps more crucially, the tendency to consider 'leadership' in highly abstracted terms inhibited sensitive analysis of the requirements of militant union organisation in respect of centralised co-ordination, planning and decision, and the possible

strategies for their attainment while avoiding hierarchical domination and manipulation.

23. Beynon's argument (1973, p. 206) deserves quoting at greater length: 'The tension between the need for trade union organization and mass participation in that organization is a vital and irresolvable one. A gap exists between the shop stewards and the rest. A gap created by the very fact of sustained activism and enforced by its organization. Ultimately there is no way out of this. The complexity of modern society coupled with the physical and mental strains of factory work make some form of "full-time" activism essential. Even at the shop floor level. In coping with this the shop steward finds himself torn between the forces of representation and bureaucratization. Between the need to represent the immediate wishes of the members and to provide a long-term strategy that will protect the interests of those members.' There is a certain fatalism about this passage which belies Beynon's previous insistence (p. 202) that 'apathy, like commitment, doesn't fall from the skies'. While the gap between activists and others will never be fully or definitively bridged, there can at least be strategies to *reduce* it – strategies which, to an important extent, will need to transcend the boundaries of the individual workplace.

24. An important absence from this paper is a discussion of the role of Communist Party activists, who have long held positions of leadership within many workplace organisations. While I lack systematic and widely based information, it is clear that CP-dominated shop steward hierarchies rarely differ substantially from their non-CP counterparts in respect of the tendencies I discuss. Some CP trade union activists seek to justify this with a fatalistic assertion of the inherent limits of trade union action: treating 'Communist politics' as a sphere of practice totally dissociated from the narrow routine of 'trade union work'. Thus CP convenors are economistic or manipulative because, this side of the revolution, they can do no other: a thesis for which Lenin is sometimes cited in support!

References

Batstone, E. V., Boraston, I. G. and Frenkel, S. (1977) *Shop Stewards in Action*, Oxford, Blackwell.

Beynon, H. (1973) *Working for Ford*, Harmondsworth, Penguin.

Boraston, I. G., Clegg, H. A. and Rimmer, M. (1975) *Workplace and Union*, Oxford, Blackwell.

Brown, W. and Terry, M. (1978) 'The Future of Collective Bargaining', *New Society*, 23 March 1978.

Cliff, T. & Barker, C. (1966) *Incomes Policy, Legislation and Shop Stewards*, London Industrial Shop Stewards Defence Committee.

Donovan (Lord) (1968) Royal Commission on Trade Unions and Employers' Associations, *Report*, Cmnd 3263, HMSO.

Friedman, A. (1977) *Industry and Labour*, London, Macmillan.

Gramsci, A. (1977) *Selections from Political Writings 1910–1920*, London, Lawrence & Wishart.

Hyman, R. (1975) *Industrial Relations: A Marxist Introduction*, London, Macmillan.

Lane, T. (1974) *The Union Makes Us Strong*, London, Arrow.

McCarthy, W. E. J. and Parker, S. R. (1968) *Shop Stewards and Workplace Relations*, HMSO.

Mills, C. W. (1948) *The New Men of Power*, New York, Harcourt Brace.

Nichols, T. & Beynon, H. (1977) *Living with Capitalism*, London, Routledge & Kegan Paul.

Roberts, G. (1976) 'The Strategy of Rank and Filism', *Marxism Today*, December 1976.

Turner, H. A., Clack, G. and Roberts, G. (1967) *Labour Relations in the Motor Industry*, London, Allen & Unwin.

Unofficial Reform Committee (1912) *The Miners' Next Step*, Tonypandy, Davies.

Webb, S. & Webb, B. (1920) *History of Trade Unionism*, London, Longmans.

7 The Sickness of British Trade Unionism: Is There a Cure?*

This brief assessment of the present crisis of the British labour movement is analytical rather than descriptive in purpose; detailed evidence of the nature of British trade unionism and industrial relations processes cannot be presented within the space available.[1] It is important, though, to stress at the outset the complexity and diversity of the union movement in Britain, and the unevenness of the effects of the current crisis. The reluctance of native writers on industrial relations to engage in high-level theorisation reflects not only the powerful tradition of British empiricism but also the difficulty of establishing *any* generalisation to which some exception cannot be found. It follows that the general arguments set out below are tentative and schematic: a fuller account would need to develop many qualifications. The argument is moreover at the level of the underlying and general, rather than the immediate and concrete (and hence constantly altering) problems which beset the movement.

This chapter begins with a brief sketch of the distinctive traditions of unionism in Britain, suggesting their historical roots and the implications of a changed material environment. The industrial, political and ideological dimensions of unions' current weakness are then analysed. Particularly significant features of their present demoralisation, it is argued, are the alienation of much of the membership from the official organisations, and the divisive effects of fragmented demands and struggles. Underlying these problems, it is suggested in conclusion, are the related weaknesses of bureaucracy, fetishism of the state, and a more general vacuum of policy.

ORIGINS OF THE PRESENT CRISIS

British trade unionism is founded on a profound contradiction of

*Originally published in German as 'Die Krankheit der britischen Gewerkschaften: Gibt es ein Heilmittel?', *Prokla*, 54, März 1984; and in Italian as 'La malattia del sindacalismo britannico: c'é una cura?', *Prospettiva sindacale*, 52, giugno 1984.

practice and theory. Class consciousness in Britain has long involved a strong sense of workers' distinctive identity and interests, but unrelated to a conception of the working class as the agent of social transformation. Most of the main unions are indeed affiliated to the Labour party, and their leaders express socialist rhetoric on conference platforms; but the actual practice of trade unionism is circumscribed by the day-to-day relationship with capital. As bargainers with capital, union representatives at every level express a form of business unionism. Not, however, in the American sense: for as well as pursuing often militant wage policies, unions (and in particular their members acting 'unofficially') assert considerable control over the labour process, contesting management's right to make uninhibited use of workers' labour power. The enforcement of a rich variety of 'custom and practice' (often denounced as 'restrictive practices') is seen by some commentators as a source of British capital's poor record in terms of productivity and international competitiveness.[2] Certainly it is true that British unions have been far less circumscribed than many of their European counterparts by social democratic ideologies of macroeconomic rationality and social harmony. In this sense, union assertiveness over wages and job controls probably *has* affected the profitability of British capital – an anti-capitalist outcome of policies *not* informed by anti-capitalist principles.

'Free collective bargaining' has been the fundamental slogan of modern British unionism. The slogan encapsulates an argument that the state and the law should as far as possible be excluded from involvement in union–employer relations; that the spheres of 'politics' and industrial relations could and should be segregated. Certainly the unions for at least a century have seen some need to engage in parliamentary politics; and their finance is essential for the existence of the Labour Party, in whose policies they often exert decisive influence. But the decision of the Trades Union Congress (TUC) in 1899 to delegate political activity to a separate organisation reflected the dominant view that too much direct involvement in 'politics' would distract trade unions from their primary concerns. The attempt to establish a clear division of labour between Party and unions – Party leaders should not initiate policy on 'industrial relations' questions, but union leaders should not seek to dictate Party policy on broader 'political' issues – is a constant theme. This division is reflected, too, in the relation between Party and union opposition tendencies. Traditionally, rank-and-file union militancy has involved different issues, and different individuals and groups, from left-wing activity in the Labour Party. And even in the case of individuals who *are* active in both contexts – some leftist shop-stewards, for example – the two forms of struggle are rarely integrated. This segmentation of opposition naturally enhances the control of the leadership in both Party and unions.

This dominant tradition had its roots in the nineteenth-century development of capitalism and trade unionism. British unions emerged early, the product of the early rise of industrial capitalism. Because of British capital's dominance in world markets, there was an adequate surplus for employers and unions to reach agreement on questions of wages and conditions. Because of its 'spontaneous' development, British capital was typically characterised by relatively small employers with no elaborate managerial structure; responsibility for the organisation of production was in large measure sub-contracted to the various work groups, themselves often composed of skilled craftsmen. Thus workers' commitment to 'custom and practice' was reciprocally conditioned by a style of 'unscientific management' on the part of British employers. Fragmentation and decentralisation in unions was encouraged by the relatively low degree of capital concentration. Finally, and of major importance, British capitalism developed when the state itself was relatively weak, and its central objective (asserted through the doctrine of *laissez faire*) was to minimise the state's involvement in economic relations. Nineteenth-century judges and politicians, often derived from the old aristocracy, had no automatic sympathy for bourgeois industrialists; the preference of the latter for private arrangements with workers and their unions shaped the formation of modern labour law. Legal 'abstentionism', as it is often termed, mirrored an ideology of 'industrial self-government'.

Needless to say, the background has altered radically. Industrial obsolescence, sluggish productivity and the loss of imperial markets have all created a crisis of competitiveness, eliminating the scope for amicable bargaining relations. Since 1950 there has occurred a dramatic phase of concentration and centralisation of British capital; in many industries the bulk of production derives from two or three multi-plant (and often multinational) combines. Management organisation has become increasingly rationalised, new techniques of labour control have been elaborated, strategies for dealing with unions have become centralised and sophisticated. Finally, the state has become central to British industrial relations. Within an increasingly interventionist role in economic affairs (symbolised by the creation of the National Economic Development Council in 1962) there have been almost continuous attempts, overt or covert, to limit the rate of pay increases. The state has itself become a major employer: national and local government, the health service, nationalised industries and similar bodies account for roughly 40 per cent of total British employment and a half of all trade unionists; even in the absence of a formal 'incomes policy', the state determines the framework for pay negotiations. And since 1971 there has occurred a continuing process of legislation on industrial relations.

In this changed environment, British union traditions are an evident source of weakness. The lack of an overall vision of trade unions' role in society, the absence of strategic imagination which might inform day-to-day tactics, are profoundly disabling. Indeed, one consequence of a harsh material environment has been to accentuate parochialism and sectional divisions, and to overwhelm any possibility of longer-term perspectives though the intensity of short-term pressures.

DIMENSIONS OF THE CRISIS

The crisis confronting British unionism is certainly the most serious since 1926; some would say since the 1830s. Its sources are economic, political, and also ideological; and while these dimensions obviously interconnect, it is possible to analyse them separately.

In the course of a decade, the rate of unemployment in Britain has changed from one of the lowest in Europe to one of the highest. Since mid-1982 the official figure of registered unemployment has been over three million, equivalent to 13 per cent of the labour force. It is important to add that the official statistics have been increasingly manipulated and that the real numbers out of work are far higher; in the view of the TUC, well over four million. 'De-industrialisation', a process apparent since the mid-1960s,[3] has accelerated under the Thatcher government; roughly a quarter of all manufacturing jobs have disappeared since the 1979 election. At the same time, public sector employment – the growth of which until recently largely compensated for industrial contraction – has been curbed by a series of cuts and 'cash limits'[4] initiated under Labour but applied more stringently by the Conservatives. Thus the increase in unemployment is likely to continue, at least while monetarist policies dominate government strategy. Taking into account the implications of micro-processor technology, the labour market prospects are severe indeed. The impact on union membership is already considerable. The total, which in the ten years 1969–79 had increased by three million to 13½ million, fell by almost two million in the subsequent three years; and the decline continues. Individual organisations have suffered particularly badly; the largest, the Transport and General Workers' Union, has declined from 2.1 million to 1.6 million members. Trends in the structure as well as the aggregate level of employment accentuate the problem of organisation. Unionisation was traditionally strongest in the manufacturing and transport sectors which have been declining, while more recent growth has been particularly based in the public services which are now being cut back. The few areas of current employment expansion are in high technology establishments, often located away from the main trade union centres and employing few workers; and in financial and professional services which have proved resistant to unionism. Adverse membership trends have inevitable financial implications. British unions typically operate on tight budgets with low member-ship dues. The fall in subscription income has brought some organisations to the verge of bankruptcy.

Predictably, employers have taken advantage of union weakness. Real earnings, which rose by roughly 20 per cent during the 1970s, have stagnated in the 1980s and in some years have actually fallen. More significant, though, has been the determination with which many employers have pursued the reorganisation of production regardless of union opposition. Poor productivity and declining competitiveness have encouraged manufacturing firms to pursue radical programmes of rationalisation, involving more flexible use of labour, more intensive working, tighter disciplinary regulations, and hence a systematic assault on established 'custom and practice'. Rationalisation has also involved redundancies and plant closures, particularly in those companies which had acquired a diverse range of separate establishments during the merger wave of the 1960s and early 1970s. The threat of closure has itself provided employers with a powerful sanction in forcing through reorganisation and speed-up in the face of union (and particularly shop steward) resistance: workers have been offered the stark choice between co-operating with management or losing their jobs. The ability of employers to appeal to the workforce in this way, over the heads of union representatives, was most dramatically displayed in the case of British Leyland; here too it was also evident that a shop steward organisation rooted in the autonomy of each individual factory was extremely vulnerable to a centralised management seeking to play one plant off against another. The ruthlessness of management at British Leyland – or the British Steel Corporation, which cut employment by half in two years – is an extreme example. Ironically, the fact that these companies are state-owned has probably encouraged a hard-line strategy, in order to win continued financial backing from the Thatcher government. But 'macho management' has become a widespread feature of British industrial relations: an aggressive insistence on 'management's right to manage', a sharp restriction on the area of the negotiable. Associated with this refusal to negotiate on what are defined as 'management prerogatives' has been a remarkable growth in machinery of joint consultation, which a decade ago was regarded as virtually extinct in Britain.[5] Some commentators diagnose a trend towards the 'American model' or the 'Japanese model': the former involving the assertion of management rights to the exclusion of any significant role for unions, the latter based on new forms of workplace machinery for 'participation' and consultation (including the creation by some companies of 'quality circles'). In general, however, employer strategy has not entailed a frontal attack on union organisation or even on shop steward representation (though there has been a considerable restriction of the rights accorded to shop stewards, including a reduction in the number of stewards allowed to operate full-time at the employer's expense).[6] Yet it seems likely that most companies' continued acceptance of such representation is predicated on a high degree of union acquiescence in the broad direction of management strategy. It is clear that most union officials – including shop stewards – see little scope for effective resistance; unable (at least in the current economic climate) to sustain the traditional role of tough negotiators, most see participation in the feeble mechanisms of consultation as the only means to preserve their representative functions.

Acquiescence is apparent from the recent trends in strike activity. Officially recorded strikes averaged 2600 a year in the 1970s; in no year did the figure fall below 2000. In the 1980s, strike incidence has almost halved; the total for 1983 seems likely to be the lowest since 1940. The number of strikes lasting longer than a single day (shorter stoppages being normally token protests) has fallen even faster than the overall total. In the context of employer intransigence on pay and an offensive on working practices, this can only be understood as the erosion of the will to struggle. It is indeed possible to discern a 'demonstration effect' the reverse of that which operated a dozen years ago. Then, the successful struggles in which groups of workers with little or no tradition of militancy won substantial pay increases inspired others to follow their example. Today, the defeats inflicted even on strongly unionised sections of the working class (steel-workers, carworkers), and the limited achievements of the long and costly strikes of partially successful groups (the national engineering conflict of 1979, the health service dispute of 1982), have deterred others from following suit.

The political weakness of the unions is in part a reflection of their industrial weakness. From the early 1960s, with the elaboration of government economic planning and the associated policies for the control of incomes, traditional demarcations between 'politics' and 'industrial relations' have been undermined; the relationship between unions and the state became increasingly overt. The relatively high incidence of strikes in Britain, the restraints imposed by workplace unionism on management's control of production, and the cumulative effects of fragmented wage militancy, were all regarded within government as obstacles to national economic performance and competitiveness.[7] The preferred solution in the 1960s and 1970s (only briefly abandoned in the early years of the Heath government) was the co-option of union representatives in the formulation of policies to control incomes, increase productivity, and restructure collective bargaining procedures. Judicious attempts were made to strengthen the centralised authority of the TUC (traditionally one of the weakest union confederations in the world) and enhance the internal control of individual union leaderships; and as part of this process a whole array of tripartite institutions was created, involving representatives of state, unions and employers. Whether this process can best be understood as 'corporatism', as is often argued, is a contentious issue which need not be pursued here. What is clear, though, is that the attempts of governments (both Labour and Conservative) to involve unions in the administration of economic policy *did* enhance their political status. National union representatives were consulted by government ministers as never before, were allocated seats on a growing range of public bodies, and *appeared* to exert a significant influence on the direction of state policy even if their impact was in reality very slight.

What is also clear is that these developments rested, not on any corporatist ideology but on the pragmatic needs of governments to come to terms with the power of unions and their members to disrupt – however unintentionally – national economic policy. This disruptive potential has been considerably reduced by the unions' current economic weakness. Moreover, the process of industrial relations 'reform' in which British unions have co-operated – rationalised payment systems, productivity bargaining, formalised disciplinary and grievance procedures – has made British labour relations far more predictable and manageable than a decade ago. The erosion of members' identification with their unions – a problem discussed in detail below – has also reduced the value of the TUC leadership as mediators between state and working class. The material basis of 'corporatist' strategies has thus been eliminated, partly because of the very efficacy of such strategies in the past in advancing the economic objectives of the state.

This altered material context has favoured the Thatcher government with its commitment to 'free market' economics. Thatcherism is in principle against tripartism as an interference with the effective operation of the market. Its economic arguments also challenge the whole post-war consensus on which tripartite economic institutions have rested. Put simply,[8] these arguments are that the Keynesian commitment to full employment has removed the discipline of labour market competition, allowed trade unions to pursue inflationary wage claims, and frustrated the efficient management of labour; that unions' damaging power was further enhanced by a privileged legal status, and by the fact that many of them negotiated collusively with 'public sector monopolies'; and that labour market discipline was also weakened by state welfare provisions. While Thatcherite anti-unionism is embedded in a visceral ideological hostility, it thus also reflects an integrated economic analysis. The succession of anti-union laws, the attacks on public welfare, the 'privatisation' of state industries and services, the deliberate creation of mass unemployment, are all logical reflections of a passionate faith in the virtues of competitive capitalism.

Some would see the intention of this offensive as the 'de-unionisation' of British industrial relations on the American model: as has been seen, a more radical objective than that of most major employers. At the very least, the aim is to overturn the assumption in British public policy (dating at least from the Report of the Royal Commission on Labour in 1894) that collective representation and collective bargaining are inherently desirable. By consolidating definitions of worker interests opposed to those of capital and the state, trade unions necessarily contradict a politics which extols individual initiative in the market-place while also calling for universal sacrifice in the 'national interest'. Such a politics naturally addresses workers as individual citizens, not as members of collective organisations. The tradition of tripartism, of close consultative relationships with union leaders, is incompatible with such a politics. To attack the political legitimacy of unionism is thus to reinforce the politics of Thatcherism. At the same time, 'union-bashing' is regarded as electorally popular (for reasons which are examined below), as well as appealing to the shopkeepers and small businessmen who form Thatcherism's social base. This implies, then, that trade unions will be subject to a powerful and integrated political attack at least for the period of the present government's office.

The unions' political weakness is also closely linked to the present predicament of the Labour Party. Labour's share of the general election vote has fallen from 48 per cent in 1966 to 43 per cent in 1970, 39 per cent in 1974, 37 per cent in 1979 and 28 per cent in 1983. Only one-fifth of the total electorate voted Labour in June 1983. Among those trade unionists who voted, support was less than 40 per cent; half the trade unionists who are affiliated members of the Party did not vote, or else voted for other candidates. Thatcher's electoral triumph was based on little more than 40 per cent of the votes cast, but reflected the fact that Labour was almost displaced as second party by the SDP–Liberal alliance, the latter attracting uniform support from all social classes, including the unemployed.

Labour's collapse is damaging for the unions for three main reasons. Firstly, their official political perspectives have become increasingly identified with the Party during the past decade. In the aftermath of the Conservative victory in the 1970 election, a joint Liaison Committee was established linking Party and TUC leaderships; from this body emerged the elements of the 'social contract' between unions and government of the years 1974–79. Experience of Thatcher's first term of office intensified the bond, with leaders of most main unions not actually affiliated to the Party nevertheless encouraging their members to vote Labour. The 1983 result thus challenges their credibility as representatives. Secondly, the dominant response to the anti-union laws of 1980 and 1982 was the hope that a new Labour government (as in 1974) would repeal them. It is now clear that for most of the 1980s (at least) the unions will have to live with this legislation (and more to come); and the will to resist has crumbled (witness the September 1983 TUC decision to seek talks with the government on its current legislative proposals).[9] Thirdly, the TUC's 'alternative economic strategy' involving a return to Keynesian demand management, the restoration of welfare provisions cut since 1979, and increased state ownership and control in industry, clearly presupposed a Labour victory. Even if most union leaders really believed that neo-Keynesianism offered a solution to the crisis (which is doubtful) they evidently failed to persuade most workers that this represented an effective economic alternative to Thatcherism. The TUC's practice (initiated in 1968) of producing an annual economic assessment and programme in the hope of influencing government policy is now quite clearly futile.

There are at least four reasons for the political disaster which has struck the TUC–Labour alliance. The first is the record of recent Labour governments, which have proved unable to act as agents of even modest Keynesian social reform in a weak British economy overwhelmed by international crisis. In particular, the 'soft' monetarism which dominated policy after 1975 paved the way for Thatcherism, and its effects (a cut in real wages, attacks on the welfare state, and the beginning of the surge in unemployment) disillusioned many Labour supporters. The promise to do better next time was simply not believable.

The second reason was the inherent unattractiveness of the society with which Labour policies were identified: an expensive bureaucratic state socialism. Most British socialists and labour movement activists proudly proclaim the virtues of 'public enterprise' and the 'welfare state'; but their confidence does not match the attitudes and experiences of most members of the working class. In general, they do not regard it as *their* welfare state (with the important exception of the health service, which *is* highly valued). Most services are experienced as inadequate, hemmed in by bureaucratic regulations, and subject to inexplicable delays; while their administrators appear grudging, patronising, and eager to humiliate. Nationalised industries are likewise regarded by many customers and employees as slow, inefficient, unresponsive and expensive. In general, state officialdom is perceived as arrogant, incompetent and unaccountable; and the maintenance of this bureaucratic apparatus an unacceptable burden on ordinary people's incomes. Such perceptions, of course, are influenced by the propaganda of hostile politicians and media; but they also indicate the extent to which so much state activity is genuinely experienced as oppressive. Thatcher's rhetoric of personal choice, individual freedom and 'market democracy' clearly appealed (in however perverted a manner) to genuine grievances; Labour's tired formulae of more state intervention clearly repelled.

A third source of political decline stems from the nature of the Party–union relationship. Union-affiliated membership of the Labour Party is over six million, roughly ten times the number of individual members in the constituencies.[10] The unions provide the bulk of the Party's income, and they dominate conference decisions on policy and the election of the National Executive Committee. Since 1981 they have also held 40 per cent of the votes for Party leader (previously elected by the Parliamentary Labour Party alone). The deployment of a union's total vote (in the case of the largest, over one million) is traditionally determined by its conference delegation or executive committee, in either case strongly influenced by the general secretary. That the 'block vote' of major unions can be allocated to policies or candidates through the private decisions of small coteries in smoke-filled rooms has been a fact of life for a century or so; but this has suddenly become a matter of public controversy. This is partly because the trade union vote is now cast less overwhelmingly than in the past on the side of right-wing leadership (the central grievance of the SDP defectors from the Labour Party); partly because the new procedure for leadership elections (and the rather awkward attempts within some unions to permit greater membership involvement) has exposed the undemocratic aspects of customary arrangements to the glare of media publicity. The charge of Tammany Hall politics – however exaggerated – combined with the even more fanciful assertion that during the years of the 'social contract' the government was controlled by a handful of union bosses, was effective in discrediting Labour's claim to represent a force for democracy in British society.

The fourth point which deserves emphasis is the trend of internal Labour Party politics since the late 1960s. The Party has always represented a broad coalition: at first between socialists and Liberal trade unionists, later between 'left' and 'right', each professing to be socialist. The parliamentary leadership has traditionally been on the right, supported in policy controversies by the trade union block vote, yet also dependent on more radical grassroots activists to sustain constituency organisation and mobilise the vote at election time. To manage this tension, Labour has typically oscillated between radicalism in opposition and conservatism in office, combining the rhetoric of social transformation (notably the famous 'Clause 4' of the Party constitution) with the most limited and cautious reformism in practice. But from the time of the Wilson government (1964–70) the pattern has changed considerably. The government (which significantly contained far fewer members with a trade union background than had previous Labour cabinets) clashed with union leaders through its application of incomes policy and its proposals for industrial relations legislation. Within several major unions, concurrently, internal reforms resulted in more democratic forms of decision-making. Both developments entailed that Party leaders could no longer rely on the automatic support of the union vote. At the same time, the character of constituency politics altered, with a substantial decline in the participation of traditional activists rooted in established working-class communities and manual trade unionism. The vacuum has been increasingly filled by a more volatile and often leftist stratum of professional and non-manual workers, and has offered enhanced opportunities for take-over by organised left-wing groups. The overall result has been a growing left presence in the Party: a new salience for the 'traditional left' (exemplified by the election of Foot as leader in 1980 and of Kinnock as his successor in 1983); a substantial impact from the new 'hard left' (most notable in the case of Benn's near-election as deputy leader in 1981); and the advance in some localities of the 'far left' (particularly the Militant Tendency). The challenge to the traditional hegemony of the right explains, of course, the decision of some of its leaders to break away and form the SDP. What is crucial, though, is the *introspective* character of recent inner-party controversy: the left's victories (such as they are) have been fought and won within the dwindling ranks of committed party activists. Because the Labour left has so little base within the broader working class, its gains within the policy-making structures of the Party are always vulnerable; and they are moreover readily misrepresented by hostile commentators. Thus the widely cultivated image of Labour was a party torn apart by internal dissension, and the captive of a militant left able to dominate unrepresentative meetings by manipulative practices. However distorted, this view appears to have influenced many traditional Labour supporters.

These points connect directly with the problem of the *ideological* weakness of British trade unionism. For over a decade, opinion polls have regularly suggested that three-quarters of the population, including the majority of union members themselves, regard trade unions as 'too powerful'; only 5 per cent respond that they are not powerful enough. Surveys during the 1983 election indicated 72 per cent support for stricter laws to control union activities. While it may be wrong to place excessive credence on facile responses to pollsters' superficial questions – particularly when predicting how workers will react in the concrete circumstances of an attack on their material interests – such findings are deeply disturbing. Historically, trade unionism was deeply embedded in the culture and communal relationships of many sections of the working class: unions' strength rested primarily on a strong sense of collective identity expressed and reinforced by mass meetings, parades, banners, social activities. Today such manifestations of union commitment have withered, and workers' sense of class (or at least occupational or industrial solidarity) has been increasingly displaced by receptiveness to individualism and to notions of 'national interest' – which, as was indicated earlier, characterise the ideological appeal of Thatcherism.

These changes reflect in part far broader cultural transformations: the declining significance of traditional working-class communities with their tight-knit but often oppressive and introspective networks of social relationships; and the impact of new media of 'mass culture' owned and controlled by capitalists or those favourable to their interests. Also relevant are the shifts in the composition of employment and union membership which were noted previously. The work organisation and work culture of manual labour in mine and mill, dock and railway, shipyard and engineering factory, were relatively conducive to a 'spontaneous' sense of solidarity. Shops and offices, schools and hospitals are significantly different work milieux, with labour processes which are often fragmented and isolated. Clerks and typists, nurses and teachers, supervisors and technicians, typically respond to a complexity of interests and pressures; and their responses are rarely informed by a reflex commitment to the ethics and traditions of the labour movement.[11] Historically, 'making trade unionists' always depended on a deliberate effort of ideological struggle; this is even more necessary today.

But in large measure, British unions in recent decades have abdicated such a struggle. In effect, many have found it possible to boost membership without the need to win the active commitment of those recruited. It is a remarkable fact that the number of union members rose consistently and substantially throughout the 1970s, despite a particularly unfavourable economic environment and the climate of public hostility which has been noted. A major explanation is the growing extent to which union membership has become a condition of employment. In 1977–8 a survey of manufacturing industry showed 37 per cent of non-managerial employees covered by a 'closed shop'; a broader study in 1980 indicated that 27 per cent of the total workforce was so affected.[12] The 'closed shop' is a traditional feature of British industrial relations, but as a social institution reflecting the strong trade union commitment of the vast majority of the workers involved. Seeing collective organisation as a condition of their own standards and security, they refused to work with non-unionists, enforcing this principle often without the official recognition of either management or union. By contrast, the 1970s saw the elaboration of 'union membership agreements', often without reference to the workforce affected, and in areas of employment without strong union traditions. Many employers were happy to enforce such arrangements as a means of simplifying bargaining structure, preventing inter-union rivalry, and providing union officials with the disciplinary sanctions necessary to police agreements.

Recruitment through such mechanisms creates mere paper trade unionists.[13] Workers whose entry to the union is a routine corollary of commencing employment, and whose weekly subscription is automatically deducted from their wages by the employer, do not normally object to the fact of their membership. But they relate to the union passively, as atomised individuals and *not* as participants in a living collectivity. Not surprisingly, 'the union' represents a distant impersonal power, not an expression of their own identity and interests. The alienation of members from their own unions has almost certainly been accentuated by the 'reform' of industrial relations in the 1970s. A distinctive (though very far from universal) feature of British trade unionism in the 1960s was a vigorous pattern of decentralised bargaining over pay and work-related conditions, articulated by shop stewards in close and continuous relationship with those they represented. This situation was transformed by the formalisation of plant negotiating procedures designed to limit the scope for decentralised bargaining; by the growth of hierarchy within workplace union organisation; and by the increasing involvement of senior stewards in high-level consultative relations with employers. A more bureaucratised shop steward organisation often became dangerously isolated from the general membership: a situation which managements have proved quick to exploit.

Finally, unions' current ideological weakness must be seen in the context of the traditional sectionalism of British union practice. Though it would be wrong to dismiss the significance of appeals to a common movement in the language of British trade unionism, or to ignore the evidence of moments of wide-ranging solidarity, the typical constituency of collective identity and collective struggle is probably far narrower in Britain than in many other countries. Parochialism and sectionalism have clearly been reinforced, over the course of more than a generation, by the considerable *effectiveness* of fragmented militancy during the years of favourable labour market conditions. But not only is such fragmentation of struggle now often materially disabling, in the context of more co-ordinated and centralised strategies of capital and the state; its ideological effects are also damaging. Though there is little basis for an argument that sectionalism has significantly increased in recent years,[14] its implications have certainly altered as an extended social and detail division of labour has intensified the interdependence of disparate productive activities, and as an expanding area of people's everyday subsistence has come to depend upon the wage-labour of others within the framework of commodity production of 'services' or of state economic activity.

Sectional militancy (or even *defensive* action) now typically has disruptive consequences for workers not directly involved. Localised strikes commonly result in widespread lay-offs, often as a deliberate employer tactic of escalation. And disputes involving public service workers – an important feature of British industrial relations in the 1970s – have often had a particular impact on working-class households. The evident reaction of many workers (and indeed many trade unionists) is to regard themselves as *victims* of industrial disputes, and to express hostility to strikes – except their own. In a climate of strident press and television denunciation of strikers, it has been easy for the state to reinforce their ideological isolation in its role of defender of the 'public interest' and of the 'rights of consumers'. Lacking a persuasive and principled link between their parochial demands and struggles and a broader vision of the interests and projects of the class, trade unions in Britain today are largely defenceless in the face of ideological attack.

BEYOND THE CRISIS?

While the immediate causes of the crisis of British unionism have already been reviewed, it may also be regarded as a reflection of more general characteristics of the labour movement which have considerable theoretical importance. This concluding discussion outlines some of the issues involved.

The first is the problem of bureaucracy. Ever since the days of the Red International of Labour Unions, the term 'trade union bureaucracy' has been a popular condemnatory slogan of the left. Used to denote a particular stratum of officials, leaders or representatives, the term is virtually empty of theoretical content: not least in Britain, where so many of the 'bureaucratic' functions of trade unionism are performed by lay activists who are not on the union payroll.[15] There is value, however, in conceptualising bureaucracy as a *social relation* pervading trade union practice at every level: a social relation corrosive of the foundations of collective solidarity.

As Offe and Wiesenthal have persuasively argued,[16] the logic of collective action in working-class organisations involves a process of mobilisation and self-activity through which the dominant ideological mystifications of workers' interests can be transcended and the priorities of capital effectively challenged. Through struggle, perspectives are enlarged, aspirations heightened, distinctive collective interests defined. But collective bargaining undertaken by 'specialist' negotiators *on behalf of* the broader membership consolidates a representative hierarchy functionally oriented towards accommodation and compromise with capital and its agents; committed, in Gramsci's terms, to an 'industrial legality' which may signal an improvement in workers' conditions but simultaneously underwrites the legitimacy and the security of the employer.[17] Representation is detached from mobilisation; the preservation of the bargaining relationship with the employer bespeaks a containment of 'unofficial' exercises in class struggle. Without resorting to Michelsian 'iron laws' it is possible to identify a contradiction: workers' organisations which are defined and constituted through struggle tend also to contain and inhibit such struggle.

Bureaucracy as a social relation is manifest in a hierarchy not only of control (which may be partially mitigated by various norms and traditions of union democracy) but also of activism. In Britain, as has often been emphasised, the largely unremunerated activities of a substantial cadre of lay officers and representatives are vital for the operation of trade unionism. Because the relatively small staff of full-time officials is in many respects dependent on the work of such activists, a lively process of internal union democracy is facilitated. What is increasingly evident, however, is the disjuncture between this internal political process and the majority of union members. The routines of branch agenda, district committee meetings, conference procedure, of motions, amendments and resolutions, involve a minority of enthusiasts distinguished by interest and understanding from the broader membership. In this respect lay activists, who often regard themselves as the authentic voice of the rank and file, may be as far (or even further) removed from the sentiments of their constituents as are the full-time officials. It is precisely this hierarchy of activism and involvement, and the detachment of the formal mechanisms of policy and decision-making from the experience of most ordinary members, that has encouraged the present legislative proposals to displace traditional forms of union democracy by the application of obligatory ballots.[18]

It would be wrong to posit a crude dichotomy between 'active minority' and 'passive majority': there are many gradations of activism, and at certain moments or in certain contexts there may be a high degree of membership involvement in the collective relations which constitute trade union practice. Nevertheless, in most unions and at most times internal politics appear to operate as an esoteric pastime of exceptional enthusiasts. And it is not merely their activism which differentiates those so involved. Typically, activists and officials derive disproportionately from relatively advantaged sections of the workforce: male, white, higher-skilled, higher-paid, in more secure jobs. Such characteristics – commonly associated with greater self-confidence, familiarity with official procedure, standing with fellow workers, and identification with work and hence work-related institutions – may be seen as encouraging involvement in trade unionism and a successful 'career' as union activist. Hence hierarchy within the working class is replicated within trade union organisation. In identifying grievances, selecting demands, formulating strategies and determining priorities, the perspectives and interests of the dominant sections almost inevitably exert disproportionate influence. The consequential subordination (or even exclusion) of the concerns of women, immigrants, lower-skilled, lower-paid, less secure workers (not to mention the unemployed and casually employed) in the agenda of union action necessarily weakens their identification with 'the union'. In consequence, the bureaucratic-hierarchical tendencies of trade union organisational practice provide a material foundation for Conservative anti-union populism.

The problem of bureaucracy connects with that of the state, an arena in which the British labour movement's well-known 'contempt for theory' is particularly apparent. As indicated already, the conception of socialism dominant within the movement has always been identified with the state: state ownership of the 'commanding heights' of the economy, state provision of welfare, state redistribution of resources. Conflicts between left and right within the Labour Party have typically concerned the extent to which state intervention is desirable and the pace at which it is attainable, not the underlying model of state socialism. Yet it is clear that the application of this model has in practice (and many would add, necessarily) tended to replicate the hierarchical and authoritarian character of capitalist relations of production.[19] And these characteristics have rarely been coherently challenged on the left, precisely because they parallel the bureaucratic-hierarchical tendencies within the labour movement itself. The state functionary could be seen as analogue of the trade union representative: following the rulebook, applying specialised experience and expertise, acting beneficiently *on behalf* of the working class. If the reality was rather different, this was because of particular functionaries' lack of sympathy for the state socialist ideal and not because of any fundamental flaw in the model.

Hence the experience of Thatcherism has provoked little critical debate on the *qualitative* implications of bureaucratic state intervention as a strategy for socialists. The dominant responses have involved reassertions of traditional Labour politics: cutting unemployment through a return to Keynesian demand management (or through various 'Keynes plus' packages); fighting the cuts through a defence of the 'welfare state' as it exists. This virtual fetishism of the state has inhibited attention to alternative possibilities for collective control of social relations of production; and to the need for anti-capitalist struggle within and against existing state institutions to complement any resistance to cuts and privatisation.

Fetishism of the state reflects a more general vacuum of political imagination. British socialism is modest and banal in its long-term vision, even when superficially radical in its short-term programme. The attack on the unions puts in question the traditional forms of institutionalised accommodation between capital and labour, suggesting the need for a more explicitly anti-capitalist reaction; but the dominant response is the call to restore 'free collective bargaining'. Mounting unemployment puts in question the traditional conception of 'work' as a five-day-a-week subordination to the will of an employer, segregated from other spheres of social and domestic life; but the dominant response is the reiteration of the demand for a 'right to work'. The eclipse of Keynesianism and the brutalities and irrationalities of monetarism put in question the viability of any solution to the crisis, short of a fundamental restructuring of social and economic relations; but the dominant response is a blueprint for an 'alternative economic strategy'. Imagination is dangerous; in particular, it threatens to disrupt established bureaucratic routines. The official labour movement still has effective reflexes to contain such disturbing possibilities, even if it has no answer to the real crisis which envelops it: hence in autumn 1983 the TUC embraced the slogan of realism, the Labour Party that of unity. Both represent a reaffirmation of the politics of tradition.

There are indeed exceptions. The idea of workers' alternative plans has sought to link the defence and creation of jobs to the demand for socially useful production. Feminist critiques have stressed the need for an attack on women's subordination – inherent in the sexual division of labour and in the relationship of waged to domestic work – as part of any viable response to the crisis. Community-based action groups – occasionally with the support of left-wing Labour municipalities – have attempted to develop collective initiatives which transcend the division beween representatives and represented. And the revival of the peace movement has restored to the political agenda many of the forms of campaigning and mobilisation which have atrophied within the orthodox labour movement.

Any credible response to the crisis must build on such examples. The scale and complexity of the problems permit no easy solutions; the search for political short cuts, however popular on the left, is a futile exercise. Any cure for the sickness of British trade unionism requires major and difficult changes on at least three fronts. Firstly, the 'labour movement' – today a tired epithet rather than a lived reality – must be informed by workers' current experiences and aspirations, their hopes and fears, their grievances and enthusiasms. The right has shown, cynically and manipulatively, a frightening ability to communicate with the working class. Neither the trade unions nor the political left have displayed any parallel capacity – often assuming that they *are* the working class, or at least possess exclusive authority to speak on its behalf. The notions of humanity, of solidarity, of conscious collective determination of social existence, have become empty slogans which can be reinvigorated only when inspired by a social vision which connects with (even as it seeks to enlarge) people's own understanding of their current predicament.

Secondly, it follows that any strategy to unify existing disparate and fragmented struggles must proceed from the grassroots upwards. Sectionalism, it was suggested previously, is a source of both material and ideological weakness. Yet the decentralised character of British trade unionism, with its traditions of extensive lay involvement, provide a vital counterpoint to the bureaucratic tendencies which have been emphasised; thus centralisation at the *expense* of grassroots democracy is no solution to the problem, but would rather accentuate the alienation of the ordinary membership from the institutions of the labour movement. It is essential to co-ordinate activity; to avoid divisive demands and strategies; to relate particularistic interests to broader class interests; to show special concern for those sections of the class whose oppression by capital is matched by subordination within trade unionism itself. But such solidarity cannot be artificially imposed: it must derive from commitment and conviction, which in turn presuppose a process of internal education and argument of major extent and intensity. Such a process would represent a radical innovation: an initiative which can come only from the broad cadre of activists already indentified, many of them indeed anxious for new forms of response and receptive to new definitions of socialist trade unionism.

Thirdly, trade union activities must connect far more directly with wider social movements and social struggles. Trade unionists, and the majority of the socialist left, have traditionally accepted, by default if not through conviction, the capitalist fragmentation of social identity. 'Work' – identified with wage labour, and often also with the stereotype of a muscular male hammering metal – is separate from home, from community, from culture, and has priority over all of these. Accordingly, the trade union struggle is the organising centre of the class struggle; 'peripheral' activities are at best a reinforcement and at worst a distraction. Always disabling, such a conception is suicidal when so many workers – and so many who are at most marginally integrated within the realm of wage labour – place high priority on problems and commitments outside of employment, and are willing to act collectively in such contexts. More generally, the material and ideological dominance of capitalist production is not merely sustained and reproduced within the labour process and the labour market. The manifold but interconnected sources of hegemony and subordination will yield only to a no less integrated challenge.

What is at issue, then, is a radical redefinition of the collective identity of the labour movement and a no less radical alteration of strategy and structure. There are some elements in the movement's traditions which could inform such a response, and many today who appreciate the need for a drastic break with orthodox practices. Nevertheless, it would be remarkably naive to offer much optimism that these principles will be embraced by the sclerotic institutions of British labour. What is certain, however, is that minor and cosmetic adjustments will merely increase the improbability of any cure.

Notes

1. A recent survey covering a range of aspects – unions, employers and the state – is provided by G. S. Bain (ed.) *Industrial Relations in Britain*, Oxford, Blackwell, 1983.
2. See A. Kilpatrick and T. Lawson, 'On the Nature of Industrial Decline in the UK', *Cambridge Journal of Economics*, Vol. 4, 1980; and R. Hyman and T. Elger, 'Arbeitsplatzbezogene Schutzstrategien: Englische Gewerkschaften und "Restrictive Practices" ', in K. Dohse *et al.* (eds) *Statussicherung im Industriebetrieb*, Frankfurt, Campus, 1982.
3. See, for example, F. Blackaby (ed.), *De-Industrialisation*, London, Heinemann, 1978.
4. 'Cash limits' involve the imposition of rigid budgetary constraints on government departments and services, and the abolition of much of the traditional scope for 'supplementation' to compensate for cost increases or other contingencies. One corollary is that wage increases above the rate implied by the annual budget can be obtained only if the number of jobs is correspondingly reduced.
5. The most recent survey evidence on this trend can be found in W. W. Daniel and N. Millward, *Workplace Industrial Relations in Britain*, London, Heinemann, 1983.
6. See M. Terry, 'Shop Stewards Through Expansion and Recession', *Industrial Relations Journal*, Vol. 14, 1983.
7. See, for example, the *Report* of the Royal Commission on Trade Unions and Employers' Associations (the 'Donovan Report'), London, HMSO, 1968.
8. Thatcherism is of course more complex and contradictory, both in theory and in practice, than this summary implies. For a wide-ranging assessment see S. Hall and M. Jacques, *The Politics of Thatcherism*, London, Lawrence and Wishart, 1983.
9. At the time of writing (end 1983) the first major challenge to the new laws is being mounted by the print union, the National Graphical Association (NGA). Embarrassed by the alternatives of endorsing defiance of the 'rule of law' or disavowing the NGA, most union and Party leaders have reacted with equivocation.

10. The 1913 Trade Union Act requires unions to hold a ballot on the establishment of a 'political fund' (a prerequisite of affiliating to the Labour Party); most unions now affiliated balloted at that time. Draft legislation would now require new ballots, to be repeated every ten years. The law also provides that members objecting to their union's political activities should be enabled to 'contract out' of payment to the political fund; in practice, it is often difficult to do so. The government initially proposed that only members explicitly 'contracting in' should pay the levy, but seems to have dropped this proposal.

11. For a general discussion of this issue see R. Hyman and R. Price, *The New Working Class?*, London, Macmillan, 1983; and for a sensitive analysis of consciousness and organisation among hospital workers see J. Neale, *Memoirs of a Callous Picket*, London, Pluto, 1983.

12. W. Brown (ed.) *The Changing Contours of British Industrial Relations*, Oxford, Blackwell, 1981, p. 54; Daniel and Millward, p. 60.

13. This is one reason why the restrictions on the 'closed shop' in the 1980 and 1982 legislation may have far more impact than the parallel provisions in the 1971 Industrial Relations Act.

14. For an extensive debate on this score see E. J. Hobsbawm *et al.*, *The Forward March of Labour Halted?*, London, NLB/Verso, 1981.

15. See, for example, R. Hyman, 'British Trade Unionism', *International Socialism*, Vol. 2, No. 8, 1980.

16. C. Offe and H. Wiesenthal, 'Two Logics of Collective Action', *Political Power and Social Theory*, No. 1, 1980.

17. A. Gramsci, *Selections from Political Writings 1910–20*, London, Lawrence and Wishart, 1977.

18. Individual balloting is evidently calculated to undermine the principle of *collective* determination which is inherent in the traditional arrangements of British unions. At the same time, the fact that a majority of union members appear to support the Conservative initiative demonstrates that, *for them*, collective determination has not constituted a genuine reality.

19. For a powerful argument on this score see London-Edinburgh Weekend Return Group, *In and Against the State*, London, Pluto, 1980.

8 Dualism and Division in Labour Strategies*

INTRODUCTION: BRITISH LABOUR RELATIONS IN THE 1980s

The significance of the economic environment for the emergence and persistence of 'corporatist' political relations has long been a matter of some uncertainty. In the early post-war decades, many proponents of such arrangements viewed them as an element in a virtuous circle of union 'moderation'; high productivity, profitability and investment; and rapid economic growth. Within such a perspective, 'social partnership' could provide workers and their unions with the benefits of long-term improvements in real incomes and perhaps employment security as a reward for restraint in the exploitation of short-term bargaining advantages.

To this model of the 'corporatism of expansion' may be counterposed that of the 'corporatism of crisis'. British experience in the past quarter-century clearly falls within the latter rubric. The initial creation of tripartite machinery of economic planning – with wage restraint a key component – may have been conceived, optimistically, in terms of a strategy for rapid growth. Within both main parties in the early 1960s there were strong views that full employment, price stability and steady exchange rates were incompatible with 'free collective bargaining'; trade union self-discipline would allow government to abandon deflation as an instrument of economic policy, replacing the cycle of 'stop-go' by a sustained dash for growth.

Reality imposed a different scenario. The travails of the British economy, anticipating by some years the more general crises of the 1970s, transformed the agenda of tripartism from the benefits of growth to the costs of austerity. Given the experience of Labour's incomes policy in the late 1960s, and the 'social contract' of the 1970s, it is not surprising that the predominant interpretation of corporatism among writers on British industrial relations is of a mechanism to achieve workers' acquiescence in an erosion of their economic conditions.

*Originally delivered at a conference at the Institut für Sozialforschung, Frankfurt, December 1985.

188

For critics of trade union participation in such relations, these involved an unequal exchange of substantial material sacrifices by workers for symbolic political status for their representatives. Thus Panitch (1981, p. 38), for example, has argued that 'corporatist political structures became the vehicle for engineering, legitimating ("in the national interest") and administering the increase in exploitation which was necessary to sustain capital in the crisis'. Others (e.g. Crouch, 1982) replied that a more oppositional stance would have failed to protect workers' position, and by aggravating the crisis might have left them even worse off. On either view the presumption was that workers' ability to disrupt government economic policy inspired a strategy of enmeshing unions in its formulation and administration. Such a strategy, it might plausibly be argued, meets the requirements of state policy most directly when workers collectively are relatively strong but the overall economy is relatively weak; when there is a disjunction, in other words, between labour and product markets.

Such circumstances may well be both untypical and unstable. Beyond given limits, precarious product markets erode workers' collective strength. (*How* this has occurred in the British context is a major theme of the discussion that follows.) Yet if the will or the ability of workers to obstruct government priorities is undermined, the economic logic of corporatist strategies for the state evaporates. In seeking to banish the TUC (and, to a certain extent, the employers' counterpart) to the political periphery, the Thatcher government thus exhibits not simply dogmatism or vindictiveness but also a credible economic rationale. If workers' compliance is no longer problematic, why concede to unions a political status which – even if largely decorative – nevertheless implicitly legitimates the representation of distinctive working-class interests within the body politico-economic?

Parallel considerations apply at the micro level. In key sectors of manufacturing industry in the 1960s, the central problem of industrial relations for employers was the collective cohesion wielded by workers on the shop floor, independently of formal trade union organisation. Even if largely sectional and fragmented, shop-floor power represented a substantial obstacle to managerial efforts to plan and rationalise production. The strategy of industrial relations 'reform' embraced by governments as a complement to incomes policy proposed the formal absorption of trade unions within what Burawoy (1979), in a different context, terms the employer's 'internal state'. The proposition that 'managements . . . can only regain control by sharing it' (Flanders, 1967, p. 32) underlay initiatives in wide areas of employment during the 1970s which formalised and legitimised the role of workplace collective bargaining and the status and facilities of shop stewards. Management's explicit recognition – and in some cases, active sponsorship – of union representation in workplace policy-making may be viewed as a form of 'microcorporatism'; and the implications of this trend for workers' material interests engendered debates which replicated those provoked by developments at national level.

Even before the collapse of industrial employment under the Conservatives, there was evidence that the enhanced formal status of workplace trade unionism might accompany a more delimited role in the structure of interest representation. One of the most surprising findings of surveys of workplace industrial relations was the revival of machinery of joint consultation formally detached from trade union organisation (Brown, 1981; Daniel and Millward, 1983). The shift from the long-established management habit, in most strongly unionised workplaces, of communicating with employees *only* through the shop steward structure, has proceeded further during the 1980s. Some firms have experimented with Japanese-style 'quality circles'; others have introduced elaborate methods for informing and influencing employees as individuals. Fears of an American-type drive to *substitute* such in-house mechanisms for trade union (or at least shop steward) organisation were fuelled by an apparent upsurge of 'macho management' under the tutelage of the Thatcher government. Most notable was the experience at British Leyland, whose chairman saw the defeat of 'shop steward power' as one of his central objectives (Edwardes, 1983); the new regime brought the sacking of the chief convenor at the company's main plant, a considerable reduction in shop steward facilities and prerogatives, and the repeated use of employee newspapers and postal ballots to bypass trade union channels.

Yet at both national and workplace levels, it would be misleading to suggest that unions have been confronted with a simple strategy of exclusion. Certainly the Thatcher government, more brutally than any other this century, has denied the TUC the status of unquestioned representative of a distinct 'labour interest' and has challenged the whole philosophy of tripartism. Substantively, its approach to social and economic policy and to trade union legislation contradicts totally the aspirations of the trade union movement. Yet practice has not altogether matched the abrasive rhetoric: the promised massacre of the 'quangos' has been relatively modest; not all ministers and mandarins dismiss the ritual formalities of traditional consultative relations; and if real union influence within these channels is negligible, the same complaint could be heard even at the height of the 1970s social contract.

At workplace level, the evidence of continuity is far clearer. There have indeed been dramatic instances of an employers' offensive. But significantly, the most prominent cases have been in the public sector, involving managements confident that a strategy of confrontation would win political benefits (the goodwill of government paymasters) outweighing the economic costs of even large-scale and prolonged conflict. Private employers have by contrast had to apply a very different calculus. Stability in labour relations is normally a valued asset, particularly within an unstable market environment; *if* key company objectives can be achieved without directly challenging established institutions of worker representation, there is no obvious rationale in provoking gratuitous conflict. On the contrary, to the extent that shop stewards and their unions assent to managerial adaptations to the crisis – plant closures, work reorganisation, new technology and a variety of other forms of rationalisation – they provide an important channel of legitimation. And there is indeed much evidence of a tacit trade-off: shop stewards acquiescing in a drastic diminution of influence within a bargaining agenda which is itself severely circumscribed, but retaining their formal representative functions unscathed. 'Employers have regained significant job control,' argues Chadwick (1983, p. 9), 'but, unlike their counterparts in the States, it has been achieved while still protecting and maintaining the credibility as well as the existence of local trade union organisation.' Terry (1983, p. 57) has suggested the employers' rationale: they

> remain wedded to the principle of a 'collectivised' workforce, represented through trade union structures such as shop steward organisation, to facilitate the handling of relationships between managers and workers. A degree of managerial support for shop steward organisation therefore persists, if only because many managers fear that labour management would be more difficult without them, especially in the event of economic recovery strengthening the bargaining position of workers once again.

Facilities for shop stewards have not been substantially reduced;

some (notably Batstone, 1984) would even argue that they have increased. Closed shops have for the most part survived unscathed, despite the provisions of recent legislation. As the dust settles after the initial experience of Thatcherism, what is perhaps most striking is the persistence rather than the eclipse of established industrial relations institutions.

DUALISM AND DIVERGENCE

The confused and often contradictory character of recent developments suggests that there is little value in positing a *general* tendency either towards or away from corporatist relations. The evidence suggests that within societies, and indeed within the strategies of governments and individual employers, corporatist and anti-corporatist elements are increasingly intermingled. In short, economic crisis has engendered a new dialectic between strategies of inclusion and exclusion.

In a recent discussion, Goldthorpe has counterposed these as alternative responses to the problems of the 1980s. Corporatism is contrasted with the accentuation of dualist tendencies within the labour market, involving increased casualisation and marginalisation of employment. What is surprising is that while Goldthorpe (1984, pp. 336–7) concedes 'that corporatist and dualist tendencies can to some significant degree *co-exist* within the same society', he insists that this 'must give rise to increasing tension between them'; by implication, non-dualist corporatism or non-corporatist dualism should naturally emerge.

This appears to misconceive the *reciprocity* between contradictory modes of social control and interest mediation. Uneven development has been a constant feature of capitalist economies; and consequential differentiations within the working class ('dualism') have typically been associated with contrasting employer strategies and contrasting processes of collective representation. Friedman (1977, p. 105) has suggested as a general principle that 'the steady profits of large firms and the steady, high wages of privileged workers depend on the instability of profits and wages of small firms and unprivileged workers.' While an oversimplification (for example, there is not a straightforward link between company size and profitability) this correctly indicates that the segmentation of both product and labour markets can *redistribute* the uncertainty and insecurity which are inherent in anarchic social relations of production. 'Corporatist' relations may be viewed as one ideal-typical mode of labour control, in which workers and their unions may participate precisely because other, more abrasive models are available as an exemplary persuasive force.

One of the central themes of recent literature on labour market segmentation is the link between labour market situation and forms of worker subordination. For example, Friedman has counterposed the 'direct control' of peripheral workers to the 'responsible autonomy' conceded to central employees. Edwards (1979, pp. 177–83), in a more differentiated analysis, links 'simple control' to secondary, 'technical control' to subordinate primary, and 'bureaucratic control' to independent primary market segments. Such formulations share a common premise: that employers whose own market position permits are likely to seek stable, collaborative relations with employees whose skills, experience or strategic position make them relatively indispensable; that such strategies are the more likely to succeed where less favourable treatment is the norm for other groups of workers; and that this will indeed be so because many firms operate in marginal, insecure or highly competitive product markets. Analyses of this kind present, at the micro level, themes of co-operation and integration familiar in the corporatism literature; and where trade union representation is involved in the administration of the 'internal state' the parallels are even closer. Two questions then arise: what connections can be drawn between macro and micro levels; and in what ways is the pattern of strategic choice affected by the general transformation in labour market conditions?

A simple assumption would be that recession encourages a radical shift in the pattern of control strategies. If workers are vulnerable to competition from the 'reserve army of unemployed', and are unusually dependent on their current employer, there is less necessity for active measures to mobilise consent. At the same time, crisis management may require drastic initiatives in the organisation of production which do not permit positive-sum solutions and thus make consensual outcomes improbable. At the level of the state, parallel forces may be expected to strain co-operative relations to the limit.

Yet reality can be more complex. As Regini (1984, p. 141) has argued,

> prolonged recession ... will not necessarily bring concertation to an end. The weaker actors may well accept less favourable 'terms

of exchange' in order to preserve it. The stronger ones may come to think that, if new terms of exchange emerge which correspond to the new power relations, it may still be in their own interests to govern by agreement rather than by unilateral authority or by relying on unregulated market forces.

This thesis captures the essence of the 'new realism' in British industrial relations. The earlier discussion indicated that, in large measure, unions at workplace level have acquiesced in the terms of exchange which match the erosion of their power position. Often dependent on management goodwill in order to maintain membership and organisation, the preservation of a stable bargaining relationship has assumed overriding priority, even when bargaining yields negligible or indeed negative material outcomes. In such circumstances employers, for their part, have little need to transform the formal structure of industrial relations; indeed, as suggested earlier, union assent may represent a valuable legitimating factor when imposing uncongenial policies on the workforce.

At the macro level such continuity is more problematic. The public visibility and political symbolism of collaborating in government policies of austerity and sacrifice may force unions into a more oppositional posture, particularly since the fate of national tripartite institutions has little immediate impact on the course of routine bargaining relations with individual employers. Reciprocally, governments and national organisations of employers lack the same incentive as individual employers to sustain 'high-trust' relations (Fox, 1974) with workforce representatives, while political and ideological considerations may indeed encourage confrontational strategies.

LABOUR MARKETS AND PRODUCT MARKETS

There is an additional reason for the lack of any clear impact of recession on co-operative institutional relations at the level of individual employers: a major element in any pattern of labour market segmentation is a *differential association* between product and labour markets. The significance of this fact may be illustrated figuratively.

Dominant Mode of Employment Relations

		Individual	Collective
	High	A Independent	C Protected
Job *Security*			
	Low	B Exposed	D Endangered primary

The central theme of most segmentation literature is the relationship between cells B and C in this matrix. The contrast is commonly drawn between 'secondary' workers exposed to competitive labour market pressures, subject to management by hire-and-fire, and hence condemned to insecure (and typically inferior) employment and income; and 'primary' workers insulated from the external labour market, less exposed to arbitrary management action, and linked by ties of mutual dependence to their existing employer. The differentiation between exposed and protected segments of the workforce is explained partly in terms of the possession or lack of scarce skills, experience, or other valued traits; partly by the differing incidence and effectiveness of collective organisation and pressure through trade unions; partly by divergent managerial strategies, themselves associated to some degree with contrasting product market position and to secular variations in employer philosophies. The 'internalisation' of labour markets, it should be emphasised, does not *supplant* the individual employment contract. The initial search for employment may remain competitive and unstructured (though in some cases detailed regulation may apply), but relations *in* employment are collectively controlled. As a corollary, workers as individuals may still be subject to dismissal; but a framework of rules (e.g. seniority in the USA, co-determination rights in Germany) restricts the employer's ability to pick and choose.

It should be noted that individualised modes of employment relations cannot be simply equated with insecurity, and collectivised with security. Cell A represents those with particularly highly valued professional qualifications or managerial expertise and perhaps certain other scarce skills, who can 'play the market' to their own advantage. (This group is certainly smaller, outside periods of exceptional labour market tightness, than Edwards's 'independent primary' segment.) Conversely, collective regulation of employment relations does not necessarily render workers 'insulated from uncertainty and variability in demand' (Berger and Piore, 1980, p. 24). Though variability and uncertainty are to an important degree *displaced* on to more disadvantaged segments of the workforce, vulnerability to change in technology and work organisation, economic conditions or management policy is not eliminated; rather it assumes a more regulated form.

This contradictory phenomenon of *controlled uncertainty* is of central importance for any assessment of the industrial relations consequences of recession. 'De-industrialisation' has entailed the closure or contraction of many established fields of primary employment, and the emergence or expansion of areas of more insecure and marginal work – including the growth of temporary employment, part-time jobs, and forms of work without normal employment contracts. At times the process has involved an identifiable transfer of jobs from primary to secondary sectors, as with the privatisation of certain public services or the increased use of sub-contracting by major manufacturers. Despite understandable fears of a spate of 'runaway capital', however, the actual closure of operations based on a strongly organised labour force to re-open or expand elsewhere (whether nationally or internationally) does not appear to have been a widespread phenomenon. There is even less evidence of systematic attempts to draw on the secondary labour market as *direct substitutes* for an existing primary workforce.

In terms of the categories set out above, one may thus argue that economic crisis does not normally confront workers located in cell C with the prospect of relegation to cell B. Rather, they enter cell D as 'endangered primary' employees. In short, the main effect of the recession on primary workers is *not* through changed labour market conditions; the reserve army of unemployed does not act as a competitive force undermining established conditions. Rather, it is changed *product* markets (or their politically defined proxies in the public sector) which generate a (perceived) threat of job loss through closure or radical cont.action of operations. In such circumstances, 'new realism' represents an acceptance – or even, in some cases, an active pursuit – of forms of production (re)organisation which sustain the employer's market position. As Burawoy (1985, p. 150) has argued, this new pattern of relations may be viewed as a novel type of despotic regime:

The new despotism is the 'rational' tyranny of capital mobility over the *collective* worker. The reproduction of labour power is bound anew to the production process, but, rather than via the individual, the binding occurs at the level of the firm, region or even nation-state. The fear of being fired is replaced by the fear of capital flight, plant closure, transfer of operations, and plant disinvestment.

What many recent authors have identified by such terms as 'flexible specialisation' (Piore and Sabel, 1984) may be viewed, perhaps most notably in the British context, as an expression of the 'microcorporatism of crisis'. Even in Germany, where the established institutions of workplace representation are designedly non-conflictual, actual practice in the recession has often accentuated the collaborative bias. Streeck (1984, p. 297), for example, refers to 'the emerging "wildcat co-operation" of individual work-forces in workplace-based productivity alliances'. Kern and Schumann (1984, pp. 312–13) assess the motives of endangered primary workers and their representatives as follows:

We have identified a universally accommodative attitude towards rationalisation and innovation among workers and works councils in the core sectors of German industry. The fundamental source of this orientation is a judgment that the modernisation of their own workplace is the only safeguard against the abyss of unemployment. Or at least, those who work in these key sectors calculate that the risk of being made redundant as a consequence of rationalisation is not as great as the likelihood that, on the contrary, their co-operation will stabilise both the company and their own employment. Precisely because of the employment crisis 'out there', workers 'on the inside' feel with redoubled force their dependence on their own enterprise.

Conversely, in analysing the dynamics of employer strategy, Kelly (1985, p. 45) has argued that economic crisis has intensified the latent contradiction between the product market-labour process nexus on the one hand, and the labour market-labour process nexus on the other.

Product market competition has intensified in the recession, and should provide an even greater *incentive* for the use of job redesign as one way of resolving product market-labour process contradictions. Many firms who previously had an incentive to redesign jobs were prevented from doing so by trade union power, particularly when they tried to remove ancillary jobs and break down production-craft and inter-craft job barriers. One further consequence of the recession is that with the weakening of trade union power, some firms now have a greater *opportunity* to redesign jobs.

At the same time, though, this 'employers' offensive' may present a collaborative countenance. Moves away from Fordist mass production enlarge the employer's dependence on worker discretion, creating the need for 'high-trust' forms of organisation (Sabel, 1982, pp. 210–11). In order to sustain 'the sense of community among workers and employers ... the vital collaboration across different levels of the official hierarchy it may be necessary, for example, to *increase* guarantees of employment security for the core workforce' (Piore and Sabel, 1984, pp. 271–2).

What might be termed *segmented corporatism* is arguably a developing feature of macro-level relations. Even before the 1979 Thatcher election victory, Conservative leaders perceived the need to differentiate state policy according to the strategic importance of different trade unions. (See, for example, the notorious Ridley Report, summarised in the *Economist* of 27 May 1978.) At the level of specific industries, one may note the strategy of the National Coal Board (obviously in close consultation with appropriate ministers) in sustaining an obdurate posture towards the National Union of Mineworkers while encouraging the 'moderate' breakaway in the highly profitable central coalfields. Within government there would seem to be some enthusiasm for the much-discussed possibility of an 'alternative TUC' based *inter alia* on the breakaway miners and the electricians – the major beneficiaries of the spread of microelectronic technologies. Government sympathy for a fragmentation of national trade unionism contrasts radically with previous Conservative policy: it was the Macmillan government which on establishing the National Economic Development Council in 1962 insisted that the TUC should be the exclusive channel of employee representation, thus encouraging the adhesion to the TUC of all important non-affiliates. While governments in countries with divided trade union movements commonly discriminate in their relationships – typically adopting exclusionary policies towards left or communist organisations while offering inclusionary relations to more 'moderate' rivals – there are few recent examples of governments actively *initiating* such fission. Is Thatcherism incubating a new model?

SOME IMPLICATIONS

However tentative, this sketch of differentiating tendencies within strategies of and towards labour organisations indicates a number of key issues within contemporary industrial relations:
1. To the extent that stable trade unionism is predominantly rooted in primary segments of the workforce, unemployment does not constitute a direct and immediate problem. 'Business as usual' remains possible. And business unionism may well entail sectional solutions to the crisis based on new forms of co-operation – at micro and, perhaps, also at macro level.
2. Labour market segmentation parallels divisions of sex, race, age, education, etc. Racism and sexism may encourage indifference and even hostility towards the unemployed among those in work, particularly perhaps in the case of endangered primary workers. The process of exclusion within the politics of labour organisation – 'defining the unemployed outside the bounds of the solidaristic representation of collective interests' (Zoll, 1984a, p. 115) – may be reciprocated with alienation from the 'labour movement' on the part of the unemployed themselves.
3. A widely reported element in responses to economic crisis (see, for example, Zoll, 1984b) is a fatalistic assumption of the unmanageability of market forces; hence the search for piecemeal and parochial adaptations. Does this represent, in new and more pessimistic guise, the 'end of ideology' prematurely diagnosed a quarter-century ago? If so, arguments for working-class solidarity face even greater obstacles.

If these considerations point to a deepening process of acquiescence and division, there are nevertheless contradictory factors to be noted:
4. Historically, segmentation has owed much to active trade union intervention (Rubery, 1978). Today, the response of endangered primary workers is commonly to strengthen external barriers, exporting the problem of unemployment to other segments of the working class. Nevertheless, division and demarcation today seem to owe more than previously to deliberate strategies of employers and governments. If the role of trade unions in sustaining segmentation is more passive than in the past, does this offer greater possibility of broader solidarity?
5. The distinctive crisis of state employment (itself, it must be emphasised, internally differentiated) has created particularly

important concentrations of endangered primary workers. Here the scope for micro-corporatist solutions is often severely restricted; the political environment obstructs strategies for co-operative relations. Here is a potential source of more solidaristic, and necessarily macro-political, labour responses.

6. A fundamental issue which must be raised is the longer-term viability of co-operative solutions for the predicament of endangered primary workers. Is flexible specialisation, as some writers assume, a *generally* available model for contemporary capitalism? Or is the ability to create or sustain a specialised market niche necessarily the prerogative of an advantaged minority of firms and workers? If the latter, then the material basis for common action amongst excluded, marginalised and endangered workers may be more promising.

7. Much more speculatively one may pose the question: do the politics of work in the crisis erode the traditional boundaries of trade union economism? A local concentration of endangered employment makes closure or contraction a *community* issue for which collaborative restructuring at workplace level offers no solution. The passion and determination of the 1984–5 miners' strike demonstrate the possible results. In quite different fashion, recent inner-city conflicts indicate the explosive consequences which can stem from the redistribution of the impact of recession on to youth, and in particular young blacks. Or again, to the extent that co-operative relations based on flexible specialisation are methods of protecting advantaged *male* occupational groups, while changes in products and technologies are applied disproportionately to *women's* disadvantage (Faulkner and Arnold, 1985), industrial relations become unpredictably enmeshed with sexual politics. More broadly still, any restructuring of product and labour markets has inevitable repercussions in the sphere of consumption and the domestic division of labour (Gershuny, 1983). The stabilising function of traditional institutions of interest representation, whether at micro or macro level, surely becomes problematic.

These considerations necessitate caution in any assessment of the implications of recession for relations between organised interests. It is clear that economic crisis has not provoked the radical institutional breakdown which was widely anticipated a decade ago. It would be rash to conclude, however, that a new and functionally integrated system has now arisen.

References

Batstone, E. (1984) *Working Order*, Oxford, Blackwell.
Berger, S. and Piore, M. J. (1980) *Dualism and Discontinuity in Industrial Societies*, Cambridge, Cambridge University Press.
Brown, W. A. (ed.) (1981) *The Changing Contours of British Industrial Relations*, Oxford, Blackwell.
Burawoy, M. (1979) *Manufacturing Consent*, Chicago, Chicago University Press.
Burawoy, M. (1985) *The Politics of Production*, London, Verso.
Chadwick, M. G. (1983) 'The Recession and Industrial Relations', *Employee Relations*, Vol. 5.
Crouch, C. (1982) *Trade Unions*, London, Fontana.
Daniel, W. W. and Millward, N. (1983) *Workplace Industrial Relations in Britain*, London, Heinemann.
Edwardes, M. (1983) *Back From the Brink*, London, Pan.
Edwards, R. (1979) *Contested Terrain*, London, Heinemann.
Faulkner, W. and Arnold, E. (eds) (1985) *Smothered by Invention*, London, Pluto.
Flanders, A. (1967) *Collective Bargaining: Prescription for Change*, London, Faber.
Fox, A. (1974) *Beyond Contract*, London, Faber.
Friedman, A. L. (1977) *Industry and Labour*, London, Macmillan.
Gershuny, J. (1983) *Social Innovation and the Division of Labour*, Oxford, Oxford University Press.
Goldthorpe, J. H. (ed.) (1984) *Order and Conflict in Contemporary Capitalism*, Oxford, Clarendon Press.
Kelly, J. (1985) 'Management's Redesign of Work', in D. Knights *et al.* (eds) *Job Redesign*, Aldershot, Gower.
Kern, H. and Schumann, M. (1984) *Das Ende der Arbeitsteilung?*, Munich, Beck.
Panitch, L. (1981) 'Trade Unions and the Capitalist State', *New Left Review*, No. 125.
Piore, M. J. and Sabel, C. F. (1984) *The Second Industrial Divide*, New York, Basic Books.
Regini, M. (1984) 'The Conditions for Political Exchange', in Goldthorpe (1984).
Rubery, J. (1978) 'Structured Labour Markets, Worker Organisation and Low Pay', *Cambridge Journal of Economics*, Vol. 2.
Sabel, C. (1982) *Work and Politics*, Cambridge, Cambridge University Press.
Streeck, W. (1984) 'Neo-Corporatist Industrial Relations and the Economic Crisis in West Germany', in Goldthorpe (1984).
Terry, M. (1983) 'Shop Stewards Through Expansion and Recession', *Industrial Relations Journal*, Vol. 14.
Zoll, R. (ed.) (1984a) '*Hauptsache, ich habe meine Arbeit*', Frankfurt, Suhrkamp.
Zoll, R. (ed.) (1984b) *Die Arbeitslosen, die könnt ich alle erschießen!*, Cologne, Bund.

9 Trade Unionism and the State: Some Recent European Developments*

Most discussions of the relationship between trade unionism and the state – and in particular those analyses which employ the notions of corporatism or of political exchange – focus on the national linkages between unions and governments. Social relations within the workplace are, from this perspective, far removed from the domain of politics. Reciprocally, students of shop-floor industrial relations typically see little reason to consider the state as a relevant object of enquiry.

This compartmentalisation of analysis has been effectively challenged by Burawoy. If by politics we denote structured power relationships, then politics occur within every type of social institution, and any adequate political science (or should one say political economy?) should be able to illuminate the processes involved. Hence within economic organisations one may identify the politics of production. The 'political apparatuses of production', to use Burawoy's terminology (1985, p. 11), are directly or indirectly shaped and sustained by the state; for the latter 'is the apparatus that guarantees all other apparatuses. State politics include as their core the politics of politics' (p. 254).

In practice, Burawoy's explanatory model lacks subtlety. He classifies all capitalist production regimes as hegemonic or despotic forms, and does not seriously address the major differences which stem from distinctive national patterns of economic development and political history. The complexities of the institutional links between state and workplace regimes receive only superficial consideration. My aim in this chapter is to explore in more detail one aspect of the relationship between the politics of production and the politics of politics, namely the extent and significance of state intervention in the formation of institutions of employee representation within the workplace.

*Paper presented to a conference of the Association d'Economie Politique, Montreal, 23–24 October 1987, *Syndicalisme et Societé: Rapports Nouveaux.*

202

WORKPLACE UNION ORGANISATION

There is an evident ambiguity in the notion of workplace organisation. 'The Factory Council is the model of the proletarian state,' wrote Gramsci in 1919. Such a description scarcely applies to a German *Betriebsrat*; or, indeed, to a modern-day *consiglio di fabbrica*. Historically there have been phases of intense and largely spontaneous organisation on the shop floor – discussed systematically in an important study by Sturmthal (1964) – which appeared to pose a frontal challenge to capitalist work discipline and to the established routines of industrial relations. To many political militants of seventy years ago, workplace self-activism was the route to Soviet power (and a *soviet*, of course, is literally a workers' council); in more recent times, 'autonomists' have stressed the revolutionary potential of organisation at the point of production.

Yet historical experience surely indicates that only in exceptional circumstances does workplace organisation possess substantial autonomy from the constraining effects of managerial control, state regulation and the structures of collective bargaining. In Britain, a large volume of research has undermined any simple notion of shop steward militancy; in the much-quoted words of the Donovan Royal Commission (1968, p. 29), 'for the most part the steward is viewed by others, and views himself [*sic*], as an accepted, reasonable and even moderating influence; more of a lubricant than an irritant.' In the USA, certainly, the image of the militant shop steward of earlier generations has been displaced by that of the shop 'committeeman', a conservative functionary enjoying special privileges over fellow workers and locked into the bureaucratic routines of orderly collective bargaining. Or again, we may note the crucial distinction between the *workers'* council, often an explicit articulation of distinctive class interests, and the *works* council, a mechanism for integrating managements and their employees within the 'community' of the enterprise. The creation of *Betriebsräte* in Weimar Germany, and their reconstitution in 1952, can be seen as deliberate initiatives to displace potentially insurrectionary organs by the 'safe' machinery of employee representation: formally detached from the trade unions, and denied the right to mobilise opposition to the employer.

STATE AND WORKPLACE

In the USA, the taming of the early shop stewards' movement owed much to the intervention of the War Labor Board, and subsequent state initiatives to encourage the 'juridification' of industrial relations. In Germany, the functioning and indeed the very existence of works councils are legally prescribed; and the very title of the *Betriebsverfassungsgesetz* (Works Constitution Act) neatly exemplifies Burawoy's argument that the apparatus of production politics can derive immediately from the apparatus of the state.

Yet such *transparent* state construction of the framework of workplace relations is far from universal. One may consider, for example, the traditional British pattern of industrial relations institutions: workplace organisation has largely reflected 'voluntary' procedural agreement between unions and employers in a process sometimes explicitly characterised as 'industrial self-government'. How can such contrasts be comprehended? Sorge (1976, p. 290) has offered an interpretative model of the long-term evolution of workplace representation in nine European countries, in which he suggests that three broad developmental patterns can be identified. In the first (with Britain the exemplary case), the state at a relatively early stage adopted an 'abstentionist' approach to industrial relations, allowing unions to function and to negotiate with employers. Where representative structures were formed at workplace level, then typically they were either designed as a component of the machinery of collective bargaining, or else became absorbed within such machinery. In the second pattern, the state sought to repress trade unionism and strike activity (and perhaps also working-class political organisation). Industrial relations thus did not emerge as an institutional arena detached from state politics; the state was openly allied to capital, while unions were highly politicised – and often weakened by internal political divisions. In many such contexts, as in France and Italy, legal sanction was given to systems of workplace representation which possessed few significant powers and which were rooted in ideologies of social harmony. From similar origins, a third pattern could also develop – as in Germany – where the state intervened more radically to shape the factory regime, creating workplace machinery with altogether more force and substance. Such initiatives are explained by Sorge as responses to a social and political crisis, in which real modifications to the political institutions of production were essential if labour was to be pacified.

This represents an interesting taxonomy but only a sketchy and not altogether persuasive attempt at explanation. What is important, however, is Sorge's proposition that where labour *at national level* acquires the strength to exert significant influence on state policy, the outcome is likely to be the encouragement of forms of 'co-determination' within the apparatus of production at enterprise level. This thesis has relevance for recent debates on the potential influence of labour within the national political economy, and may be addressed by a brief examination of a more limited time-span than Sorge's: the period from the 'post-war settlement' to the present. In my discussion I will refer primarily to experience in five European countries: Britain, Sweden, West Germany, France and Italy.

VARIETIES OF POST-WAR SETTLEMENT

It is a familiar proposition that after the turmoil of war, the latter 1940s and the 1950s saw throughout Western Europe a stabilisation of class relations which displayed distinctive national characteristics. These 'post-war political-economic settlements' (Lange *et al.*, 1982, p. 209) generally reflected an enhanced influence of organised labour, the outcome of participation in wartime governments of national unity or in resistance struggles, or else of the discrediting of the pre-war political and economic elites. In some cases the old (im)balance of class relations was soon restored, in others a new class compromise was more firmly established.

Regini (1986, pp. 61–2) has classified the national settlements emerging in this period under three broad headings: *concertation* between unions and the state in the formulation of national economic policy; the *isolation* of unions from effective influence on state economic policy; and the *pluralistic separation* of 'politics' from 'industrial relations', whereby unions were external to policy formulation and exerted influence only indirectly as a result of their market power. I will sketch in general terms the relevance of these models to the five countries under examination, before turning specifically to their significance for workplace organisation.

Britain is conventionally regarded as the clearest case of pluralistic separation. Between the 1890s and the 1980s there was a broad consensus within 'public policy' that legal regulation and direct state intervention in the industrial relations arena should be kept to a minimum. Representatives of capital, confident of their own resources, were for the most part keen to keep the state at arm's length. Governments felt no necessity to intervene other than in exceptional circumstances; the state was both able and willing 'to hold itself aloof from the battles between capital and labour' (Edwards, 1986, p. 171). Unions themselves, conscious of the inherent anti-labour bias of the British judicial system, usually asked merely to be left alone to pursue their role as negotiators. 'Politics' was generally regarded as an activity to be delegated to the Labour Party, while unions themselves concentrated on 'free collective bargaining'. (The concept of voluntarism was in my view always misleading; the nature, limitations, preconditions and eventual erosion of this principle of 'collective *laissez-faire*' I have discussed at greater length elsewhere; for example, Hyman 1981, 1986, 1987.)

In the British case, the post-war settlement involved the consolidation of this traditional system in a manner favourable to unions' bargaining activities. Certain legal restrictions imposed after the General Strike of 1926 were removed. State welfare provision, notably in the fields of education, health and social insurance, was extended and systematised. A number of infrastructural industries were nationalised. And 'full employment' was embraced as an essential national objective. These features of the 1945–51 Labour government's policies were widely regarded as socialist advances, though they enjoyed bipartisan support. Certainly they strengthened unions' position in the labour market, though this power was deployed with customary 'responsibility', including acquiescing in an incomes policy in the late 1940s. Paradoxically, though, one effect of these developments was to undermine the foundations of 'voluntarism'. The deteriorating position of British manufacturing within world markets, and the growing contradictions between industrial and finance capital, certainly contributed substantially to this outcome. But equally significant was the expansion of public sector employment as an arena of industrial relations; the politics of production became inseparably linked to the fiscal crisis of the state. The record of the 1960s and 1970s was of a slow, tentative but cumulatively profound politicisation of industrial relations. For much of the period, this process involved half-hearted and precarious efforts at concertation. In the 1980s, labour has been brusquely excluded from the politics of politics.

In Germany, the immediate post-war strength of organised labour was rapidly contained. Employers and conservative politicians, 'although originally discredited and in disarray immediately after the

Second World War, managed in the context of the cold war to reassert their control and to impose on the workers' movement a settlement for the post-war economy that fell considerably short of the unions' vision' (Gourevitch *et al.*, 1984, p. 94). (In this process, the Harvard authors do not add, the German ruling class received more than a little help from their transatlantic friends.) For two decades, conservatives wielded uninterrupted control of the federal government. Their absurdly misnamed policy of the 'social market economy' ensured a high level of unemployment throughout the 1950s. The resulting weakness of trade unions in the labour market helped contain labour costs and consumption, facilitating the government in encouraging investment and manufacturing exports. In addition, the tradition of extensive legal regulation of industrial relations was reinforced.

The pattern of labour exclusion changed in the latter 1960s, by which time the reconstruction of German capitalism had been demonstrably accomplished. Following the admission of the social-democratic SPD to government in 1966 (initially as junior partner in the 'grand coalition', then as main governing party), the system known as *konzertierte Aktion* was initiated. Arguably this process of tripartite concertation served primarily to encourage union wage restraint within what had become a buoyant labour market. But given the high level of juridification of industrial relations, the unions for their part were encouraged to seek from the state a redefinition of key elements in the institutional structure of production politics, as will be discussed below. Reform of the 'works constitution' strained concertation, as too did the SPD government's conversion to monetarism and the rapid rise in unemployment from the late 1970s. Despite the return of the conservatives to government in 1983, however, the institutional pattern of 'social partnership' appears still relatively stable.

In Sweden – neutral during the 1939–45 war – the 'settlement' was already established in the 1930s. This 'Swedish model' involved three main elements: continuous social-democratic (SAP) government, sometimes within coalitions; 'Keynesian' policies of demand management and extensive public welfare provision; and tight central regulation of wage bargaining through the union and employer confederations, LO and SAF (specified under their 1938 Saltsjöbaden agreement). However, there is little public ownership or attempt by the state to influence the strategic decisions of private capital; and as a corollary, moderation in wage bargaining is not directly enforced by the state (though much indirect pressure may occur). Nor is legal regulation of industrial relations comparable in extent to the German model: indeed, the close institutional accommodation between central union and employer organisations reflects in part a mutual commitment to minimise legal interference.

The major post-war elaboration of this model was the result of trade union initiative: the introduction of an 'active labour market policy' to complement the principle of 'wage solidarity'. A tripartite board, the *Arbetsmarknadsstyrelsen*, was established in 1948 and accorded greatly enhanced powers in 1957. Its various functions – providing training and retraining programmes, administering unemployment insurance, arranging regional and temporary employment schemes – all cushion the effects of unemployment and thus facilitate the mobility of labour to profitable and 'efficient' firms, assisting the performance of a national economy highly dependent on export markets. Bearing as it did primarily on the external dimensions of the production regime, this institutional development was uncontentious. From the 1970s, the equilibrium of the Swedish model has seemed more precarious. Among the major challenges have been tendencies to decentralisation in wage bargaining; the expansion of white-collar unionism outside the control of LO; pressures for tax reductions and hence curbs on public expenditure; and the displacement of the SAP in government by bourgeois parties between 1976 and 1982 (for a more detailed discussion see Martin, 1986). But also of key importance have been LO's attempts to use the state to secure more radical alterations in the production regime: a response to the growing insecurity of employment (even though Swedish unemployment levels are among the lowest in the world) and to the ability of the most productive sectors of capital to reap the benefits of the unions' restraint in collective bargaining. These developments will be considered below.

In France there is a powerful tradition of a strong centralised state apparatus committed to the preservation of the established social and economic order, yet ready at times to engage in paternalistic reformism. The state has generally been suspicious of organised interest groupings (hence trade unions were long outlawed), yet occasionally has been obliged to make judicious concessions to episodes of mass mobilisation. The post-war settlement was shaped by the cold war, which shattered the initial attempts at national consensus government (one aspect of which was a substantial programme of nationalisation). An anti-communist minority split from the main trade union centre, the CGT; and divisions on the left have been a major source of weakness ever since. Under the fourth Republic, governmental instability helped concentrate effective state power within a technocratic elite, committed to close collaboration with large-scale capital (institutionalised in the *Commissariat du Plan*) in order to encourage industrialisation. During the Gaullist period, this characteristic was reinforced, providing 'a stable political formula for economic modernization under conservative auspices' (Pontusson, 1983, p. 62). Restraining wages and consumption was integral to this economic strategy (a statutory minimum wage introduced in 1950 was of limited effect). Legislation which affected the apparatus of production politics largely served to accentuate the weakness and fragmentation of labour.

After the *événements* of 1968, the unions were able to win significant legislative reforms, strengthening their status within the workplace, and also enhancing the minimum wage provisions. In the 1970s there were other minor advances. The most substantial changes, however, occurred after the election of the socialist government in 1981: first with a large increase in the minimum wage, then a major programme of legislation introduced by Auroux, the Minister of labour. Most notable were provisions requiring employers to negotiate with unions at enterprise level, and creating a new structure of workplace representation, the *groupe d'expression*. As will be seen in the discussion below, however, these initiatives were less radical than they appeared on the surface; and were indeed quite compatible with the rightward lurch in the government's whole economic strategy.

In Italy the nature of the post-war settlement was similar to that in France, and for analogous reasons. A labour movement dominated in both its political and trade union organisations by the communists (PCI, CGIL) was fractured and marginalised by the cold war. A Christian-democrat government (its power reinforced by extensive networks of clientelism within Italy's decentralised political system) pursued a strategy of export-based industrialisation through low wages and high productivity. The subordination and political exclusion of labour was made easier by the rapid influx to the industrial cities of rural workers, for the most part lacking collectivist traditions. As in France, labour legislation did not significantly affect the pattern of relations at the point of production between authoritarian managements and weakly organised workers.

Since the 1960s, however, Italian experience has diverged signi-

ment). Its members were prohibited from mobilising conflictual action, but could refer disputes to arbitration by the Labour Court. The union for its part had no standing within the workplace, collective bargaining taking place at multi-employer level. These restrictions were regarded by the unions as a serious defeat, as was the law on board level representation: employee representatives acquired notional parity on supervisory boards in coal and steel (*Montanmitbestimmung*) in 1951, but the provisions for other industries the following year involved only one-third of the seats.

The legal separation between mechanisms of co-determination and of union representation does not, however, fully indicate the reality. In practice, *Betriebsräte* in unionised establishments were elected from lists of union nominees; and in exercising their functions typically received advice and assistance from union officials. From the 1960s, in many large establishments, they became *de facto* negotiating bodies, bargaining over bonuses and a range of other workplace issues; nor was the 'peace obligation' always a total obstacle to pressure tactics. The relationship between unions and councils was reinforced by new legislation in 1972, which formalised some of the previous links and extended the rights of co-determination. In 1976, against strenuous employer resistance, board-level employee representation in all industries was brought close to parity.

Evaluation of the German system of production politics has always provoked controversy. As already indicated, the explicit purpose of the 'dual system' was to entrench a 'works constitution' obliging employees' collective representatives to collaborate with management, and excluding the potentially oppositional trade unions from the arena of production. There can be little doubt that the *offensive* potential of unionism was thereby seriously restricted. Yet conversely, the ability to defend established conditions during adverse circumstances may be increased. Certainly this is the appraisal made by Streeck (1986, p. 158) of recent German industrial relations: 'the legal institutions of co-determination protected trade unions from the potentially critical organizational impact of the changed balance of market power and foreclosed a return by management to unilateral decision-making.' Total union membership has barely altered in the past decade; unions have been able to mount major national struggles (though with limited success) for reduced working hours and protection against the adverse effects of technological innovation; but at shop-floor level they have been able to use the legal powers of the

Betriebsräte as an effective bargaining resource in responding to employer plans for rationalisation.

In the traditional Swedish model, the strong centralisation of collective bargaining left little scope for workplace organisation. In 1946 a national agreement did indeed permit the formation of works councils composed of union members, but their establishment was patchy and those which were created were largely inactive. As in Britain, there was no attempt to prescribe by law the machinery of production politics. To a modest degree, however, there emerged parallels to British shop steward organisation. Particularly in large establishments, the leaders of the workplace units of the local union branch could exercise considerable autonomy and negotiate with management over a range of issues which transcended their formal jurisdiction. Unofficial strikes, though illegal, were not uncommon. By the 1970s, this 'informal system' was sufficiently firmly established to induce the unions and employers nationally to give formal recognition to the shop steward role, and the rights of workplace representatives acquired some legal underpinning in 1974.

Far more radical in its implications, though, was the 1976 *Medbest-ämmandelagen*. This followed growing LO concern at the unions' inability to control the impact of technological change and the restructuring of employment. Following modest statutory initiatives in the early 1970s, the 1976 Act allowed workers to elect a minority of the members of company boards, and more importantly gave shop-floor representatives an effective right of veto (subject to the eventual determination of the Labour Court) over major managerial initiatives in work reorganisation. This initiative – proclaimed as a means to the 'democratisation of working life' – was followed by the intense controversy over the introduction of 'wage-earner funds'. In order to increase union influence over the investment decisions of private capital, and to redistribute the increased profits deriving from union bargaining restraint, LO developed in the mid-1970s a programme for a proportion of company profits to be allocated as shares to a union-controlled fund; eventually the funds might become majority shareholders in Swedish industry. The proposal was bitterly resisted by private capital and the bourgeois parties, failed to win the support of the non-LO unions, and was less than enthusiastically received by the SAP – which in any event lost the 1976 election. During the six years when the social democrats were in opposition they agreed with the LO a much diluted version of the scheme, and this became law in 1983. The direct material consequences of this legislation are probably slight; however, the *ideological* effects of the laws of 1976 and 1983 in questioning the prerogatives of capital ownership and management decision-making may have more far-reaching implications for the institutional structure of production politics.

In France, production politics have historically been founded on the authoritarian domination of the *patron*, tempered by the intermittent mobilisation of collective challenges (paralleling, and often intermeshing with, the trajectory of state politics). Formal union membership has always been low, though support is greater when measured by the ability to obtain workers' backing in conflicts with the employer. The main locus of bargaining is at national level (involving both single- and multi-industry negotiations). Within the workplace, rank-and-file activity often centres around campaigns over extra-plant demands; the whole process is moreover coloured by the ideological differences between union confederations, five of which possess legally sanctioned representative status.

In 1936 the popular front struggles resulted in a law prescribing the election within the workplace of *délégués du personnel*, chosen from union nominees, and with only minor consultative powers. A law of 1945, directed towards consensual economic reconstruction, provided for the election of *comités d'entreprise*; these have rights to information and consultation, but no real powers. In few cases do they seriously affect managerial control; and indeed their greatest influence often derives from their administration of employees' social facilities. More significant innovations occurred after the *événements* of 1968, with legal provision for election of *délégués* and *sections syndicales*. The evidence suggests, however, that while these institutions helped consolidate the role of unions where they were relatively strong, they had little impact elsewhere. In some ways more significant was the gradual and partial increase during the 1970s of individual companies' willingness to negotiate directly with unions, particularly over issues of work reorganisation.

This process was markedly accelerated by the Auroux reforms of the 1980s (Delamotte, 1986 and 1987; Erbès-Seguin, 1988). The new laws require employers to negotiate annually at workplace level over wages, hours and the organisation of working time; and create a wholly new institution, the *groupe d'expression*, which enables employees once a year to express directly to the employer their views on the organisation and content of work. These innovations have had limited practical effect. Employers are not obliged to reach agreement with workplace unions or even to bargain 'in good faith'; in many cases not even the formal letter of the law has been observed. *Groupes d'expression* possess few powers, have been only unevenly established, and are often dominated by management – functioning, in effect, as adjuncts or alternatives to 'quality circles'. It is significant that many of the labour law reforms of the 'government of the left' did not stem from union pressure – indeed, in some cases they provoked suspicion and opposition. Rather, they may be seen as cosmetic efforts to soften the traditional authoritarian style of French management in order to win employee assent to rationalisation and restructuring. Changes in the organisation of working time, and in the complex French system of job classification and training (Tallard, 1988), appear to require moves towards a workplace regime which could be termed 'micro-corporatist'. In this sense, the French state (and here there is a continuity between the 1981–86 government and its conservative successor) has in the 1980s encouraged a form of concertative workplace politics which does not alter the real distribution of power.

The background to Italian workplace politics was similar to that in France, with weak and divided unions forcefully resisted by most employers. The *commissione interna*, an institution dating from the first decade of the century, was reconstituted after the war under a national collective agreement, as a collaborative organ to aid productivity. The powers of the *commissioni* were few and their impact was normally equally small. Two developments in the 1960s, both linked to managerial pressure to increase productivity, helped transform the situation. The catholic trade union centre CISL – closely linked to the Christian democrats and widely regarded as a 'yellow' (i.e. employer-dominated) union – adopted a policy of workplace collective bargaining and asserted a more independent political stance. The communist-led CGIL, at first suspicious that decentralised bargaining would weaken class unity, eventually followed suit. Increased union attention to shop-floor issues coincided with an extensive upsurge of discontent in the major industrial centres. During the mass struggles of 1968 and 1969, workers in many factories irrespective of union membership elected section-level *delegati*, who combined in plant-wide *comitati unitarii di base* (joint rank-and-file committees).

These new institutions, and the dramatic actions with which they were associated, had three enduring consequences for the structure of factory regimes. The *Statuto dei Lavoratori* of 1970 established an extensive code of trade union rights within the workplace: protection for representatives, facilities to undertake union duties, provision to hold meetings in company time, restrictions on discipline and dismissals. The unions themselves, under shop-floor pressure, moved towards greater common action. And the new workplace mechanisms became institutionalised under the historically evocative title of *consigli di fabbrica*, in the process being shorn of their 'autonomist' qualities and subject to official union control; in some cases their existence and functions were recognised in collective agreements with employers.

Undoubtedly these changes represented the most radical alteration to the political institutions of production in any of the five countries. Their enhanced role within the workplace assisted the unions nationally in responding to the worsening economic environment as the 1970s unfolded. This entailed that in the process of concertation or 'political exchange', not all the concessions were made by the unions. While the latter agreed to curb wage claims, encourage work flexibility and control their workplace representatives, the state and employers agreed to such measures as tax benefits, price controls, employment-promotion measures, payment for redundancy (the *Cassa Integrazione Guadagni*), and a strengthening of the system of wage indexation (the *scala mobile*). In the 1980s there has been a weakening of trade unions' position in the workplace, symbolised by the traumatic defeat at Fiat in 1980; and with the further deterioration in the Italian economy, national 'political exchange' has involved surrendering many of the gains of the previous decade. Most recent developments have displayed some similarities to those in France, with moves through participative mechanisms at plant level to encourage greater flexibility in work organisation. In the Italian case, though, this has not involved legislation, though the state has exercised a significant influence: notably in a tripartite national agreement in 1983 sponsored by the Minister of labour (Scotti); and in a master agreement in 1984 signed between the three main union confederations and the IRI group of public enterprises (Negrelli, 1988). The significance of these developments is as yet unclear; but as Treu (1986, p. 178) has remarked, 'a common policy underlying these innovations is worthy of notice. While the need for greater flexibility of labour is recognized this does not mean simply that the employer is allowed wider discretion in the use of manpower. The implementation of flexibility is subject to collective control, usually coupled with public control.' This may help explain the otherwise puzzling readiness of the Italian unions to continue concertation with employers and the state.

STATE POWER AND PRODUCTION POLITICS: A CONCLUSION

What lessons can be derived from this varied experience? It provides a basis for addressing two questions which, though they derive from different problematics, are clearly related. Firstly, how can we refine Burawoy's model of how state intervention structures the politics of production in the workplace? Secondly, how far can labour achieve real gains – particularly in respect of production relations – through pressure on, or concertation with, the state in capitalist society?

Contrasts between national patterns owe much to historically consolidated traditions: the character of the state bureaucracy, the general extent of legalism within civil society. It is no accident, for example, that the notion of 'juridification' (*Verrechtlichung*) was coined in German (Simitis, 1986). The hostility provoked in Britain in 1977 by the Bullock Committee's proposals for employee representation on company boards probably reflected the challenge to the traditional *form* of institutional relations as much as the specific implications for the balance of power in production politics.

Thus in some national contexts, direct state intervention to define the factory regime is consistent with established practice; in others it appears radical even when the practical effects are modest. To rupture long-standing traditions typically requires a powerful motivating force: the manifest instability of existing production politics, or their manifest inefficiency. Just as a key function of the state in capitalist societies is to secure the often contradictory objectives of accumulation and legitimation, so must production regimes achieve the same goals. Thus it is significant that in all five countries surveyed, there occurred in the late 1960s and early 1970s a 'resurgence of class conflict' (Crouch and Pizzorno, 1978) which appeared to threaten both managerial legitimacy and economic performance. In Britain there was a sustained rise in reported strikes, reaching a peak of almost 4000 in 1970; in both Germany and Sweden, a wave of unofficial stoppages posed the first serious threat to the post-war record of industrial peace; France experienced the near-insurrectionary mass struggles of May 1968; in Italy there was the dramatic upsurge of the 'hot autumn' of 1969. If in some cases the significance of these episodes was exaggerated – often, it now seems, militancy was the outcome of narrow and short-lived material grievances rather than the climacteric then imagined – they nevertheless implied a new sense of instability in workplace industrial relations and hence a need, from the perspective of capital and the state, for institutional reconstruction.

A second key impetus to the restructuring of workplace regimes was the trend of the 1970s involving the collapse of old industries and the rise of new ones, the reorganisation of work and displacement of workers, the pursuit of more flexible methods of composing and applying collective labour. Institutional mechanisms which sustain managerial legitimacy when production relations are routine and stable may be seriously strained in circumstances of transformation and unpredictability. The growing managerial interest in mechanisms of 'employee participation', and the many instances of state intervention to further their establishment, must be seen against this background.

A third relevant consideration is the role of trade unions in national political-economic concertation. The argument of Sorge notwithstanding, there is no necessary link between 'corporatist' concertation at national level and co-determination in the workplace: for several decades, Sweden possessed the one but not the other. The relationship is rather more complex. The typical reason for union admission to economic policy formulation during the post-war years was the fear of the disruptive potential of workers' economic militancy. Unions' influence within the politics of politics thus derived from their members' confidence and cohesion within the politics of production. To the extent that mass unemployment and economic restructuring during the past decade have reduced or removed the power of organised labour on the shop floor, the union role in national political exchange is undermined. For unions themselves, then, the reconstruction of the institutions of workplace politics may well appear essential if their higher-level effectiveness is to be sustained or recovered.

This brings us to the second question: to what extent *can* trade unions achieve significant inroads into the power of capital at the workplace through intervention at the level of the state? Here, two arguments may be counterposed. One, a left-wing version of corporatist analysis (e.g. Panitch, 1981), insists that union involvement in state institutions is inevitably an unequal exchange: economically powerful movements are thereby integrated and domesticated, and their leaderships' organisational resources deployed to contain and discipline the rank and file, in return for largely token concessions by the state and capital. But recently there has been a growing counter-argument on the left, drawing primarily on Swedish experience, that through state action labour can significantly alter the balance of class forces. Thus Korpi (1983) suggests that there has been an incremental process in that country: labour has gained increasing influence within the state, the interventions of which in turn have strengthened labour in its struggles with capital, further enhancing the potential for political gains. In this analysis, the introduction of wage-earner funds represented a decisive step in labour's advance.

In a useful survey of this debate, Fulcher (1987) is sceptical of the claims that labour can restructure capital. Stressing the limitations of both the 1976 *Medbestämmandelagen* and the wage-earner funds as actually established in 1983, he argues that Swedish experience indeed fits the model of 'corporatist' integration of labour. Nevertheless, he suggests that this has not precluded real advances. The record of Swedish social democracy is of measures which 'benefit labour without endangering capitalism..., while employer power and market competitiveness are the heart of the capitalist economy and are not susceptible to marginal reform.... The Swedish labour movement may have produced radical surges, but these were to dash themselves against the rocks of the state's dependence on capital and the countervailing opposition of the employers' (Fulcher, 1987, pp. 248–9). Korpi's optimism, concludes Fulcher, is not well founded.

From a different starting point, Pontusson reaches similar conclusions. Swedish labour has indeed achieved important defensive gains during the crisis, but in no significant sense has it transformed the system. This is because 'private control of the investment process constitutes the principal obstacle to the extension of democratic control'; labour has failed to achieve more than marginal inroads into this control since 'the power exercised by labor within capitalism is not coterminous with nor directly translatable into the power to transform capitalism' (Pontusson, 1983, p. 68).

Nevertheless, most trade unionists would respond that even *defensive* control is of vital importance when faced by a crisis of policy and practice unprecedented in the post-war era. Without it, the very survival of unions as effective organisations is in question. From this viewpoint, a key question is whether legislation which sets limits to management's dominance within production politics is an effective route to such defensive control. Is it even possible to envisage a virtuous circle whereby such legislative supports, by strengthening labour economically, help restore its macropolitical influence? Such considerations certainly help explain the radical shift in orientation of the British TUC in the mid-1980s, when it abandoned its deep-rooted suspicion of legal intervention in industrial relations and endorsed an extensive programme of 'positive' law.

Certain propositions appear relatively uncontentious. A system of employee representation reinforced by law can indeed enhance unions' defensive effectiveness, as is shown by the German example, and even more dramatically by that of Italy. Without the statute of 1970, it seems likely that the traditional power of the *padrone* would have been quickly reasserted in the economic circumstances of the 1970s. If in most countries the corollary of positive rights for workers and their unions has been a set of restraints and restrictions on their operation, the price may appear more than justified in an economic climate when workers' position is so vulnerable.

Yet how can labour *achieve* a favourable framework of law? German unions appear to have gained from an unintended institutional lag: the mechanisms of *Mitbestimmung* now function very differently from the intention when they were instituted in material circumstances not comparable to those of today. Elsewhere, the successful pursuit of statutory support normally required a combination of economic and electoral strength. The latter is not always essential, as the Italian example shows: it was the explosion of workplace militancy which resulted in the *Statuto dei Lavoratori*. Conversely, the French experience of five years of left government without significant economic pressure from organised labour resulted in a legislative package clothed in the rhetoric of workers' rights but empty of content. It may be added that the law itself can scarcely generate organisation in a vacuum. It seems to serve labour best where it reinforces, stabilises and perhaps generalises the achievements of *prior* struggles within the politics of production. And where the material basis of workplace organisational strength is undermined, the law is unlikely to function indefinitely as an effective substitute. Again, the Italian case is exemplary.

This seems to suggest a pessimistic conclusion. State action to restructure the balance of power within production may indeed assist trade unions; but their ability to achieve such intervention is least, precisely when the need is greatest. One important qualification should be made, however. Therborn (1986, p. 111), in his analysis of the politics of unemployment, identifies in those countries which have maintained relatively full employment an institutionalised policy commitment to this end. This policy priority, he suggests, can derive *either* from 'the wish of strong labour movements for full employment as a class interest', *or* from 'the concern of certain bourgeoisies for social stability'.

Could a similar policy commitment towards the relative democratisation of production politics be identified? And if so, can labour influence the construction of such a commitment? Since the requirements of accumulation and legitimation can conflict, labour nationally may confront capitalists and state policy-makers who do not pursue consistent and coherent strategic projects. Such contradictions may create policy openings for labour to pursue a restructuring of production regimes which strengthens workers. The record, though, is not encouraging. There is indeed much evidence from Europe in the past two decades of relative consensus that industrial democracy is a worthy goal, and of legislative initiatives directed towards this aim. In practice, though, any consensus has rested on subordinating issues of workers' rights to those of workplace harmony and efficiency. The ideology of democracy has thus served – as, notably, in France – to oil the wheels of capitalist rationalisation. Could the outcome be different? Could unions recover the vocabulary of economic and industrial democracy to mobilise their actual and potential members? In the Swedish case, such attempts have provoked strenuous and seemingly effective resistance. Strategies for full employment are in the interests of at least significant fractions of capital, and may thus attract cross-class support. This is not the case with any serious challenge to capitalist dominance within relations of production; here, significant advance would seem to require the offensive mobilisation of working-class power.

To return to the broad general themes with which we began: the most successful of the union movements examined are those which have sustained a close articulation between the politics of production and the politics of politics. Those that have fared worst have failed, or have not attempted, to achieve an effective connection between strategies at these two levels. Unless this strategic linkage can be sustained, the future for trade unionism in an epoch of crisis is surely bleak.

222   *Problems of Contemporary Trade Unionism*

References

Burawoy, Michael (1985) *The Politics of Production*, London, Verso.

Crouch, Colin and Alessandro Pizzorno (1978) *The Resurgence of Class Conflict in Western Europe*, London, Macmillan.

Delamotte, Yves (1986) 'Industrial Relations in France in the Past Ten Years', *Proceedings of the Industrial Relations Research Association December 1985*, Madison, Wisconsin, IRRA.

Delamotte, Yves (1987) 'La loi et la négociation collective en France', *Relations Industrielles*, Vol. 42, No. 1.

Donovan, Lord (Chair, Royal Commission on Trade Unions and Employers' Associations) (1968) *Report*, London, HMSO.

Edwards, P. K. (1986) *Conflict at Work*, Oxford, Blackwell.

Erbès-Seguin, Sabine (1988) 'Industrial Relations and Workers' Representation at Workplace Level in France', in Richard Hyman and Wolfgang Streeck, *New Technology and Industrial Relations*, Oxford, Blackwell.

Fulcher, James (1987) 'Labour Movement Theory Versus Corporatism', *Sociology*, Vol. 21, No.2.

Gourevitch, Peter, Andrew Martin, George Ross, Stephen Bornstein, Andrei Markovits and Christopher Allen (1984) *Unions and Economic Crisis*, London, Allen and Unwin.

Hyman, Richard (1981) 'Green Means Danger?', *Politics and Power*, No. 4.

Hyman, Richard (1986) 'British Industrial Relations: The Limits of Corporatism', in Otto Jacobi, Bob Jessop, Hans Kastendiek and Marino Regini, *Economic Crisis, Trade Unions and the State*, London, Croom Helm.

Hyman, Richard (1987) 'Trade Unions and the Law', *Capital and Class*, No. 31.

Korpi, Walter (1983) *The Democratic Class Struggle*, London, Routledge and Kegan Paul.

Lange, Peter, George Ross and Maurizio Vannicelli (1982) *Unions, Change and Crisis*, London, Allen and Unwin.

Martin, A. (1986) 'The End of the "Swedish Model"?', *Proceedings of the Industrial Relations Research Association December 1985*, Madison, Wisconsin, IRRA.

Negrelli, Serafino (1988) 'Management Strategy: Towards New Forms of Regulation?', in Richard Hyman and Wolfgang Streeck, *New Technology and Industrial Relations*, Oxford, Blackwell.

Panitch, Leo (1981) 'Trade Unions and the Capitalist State', *New Left Review*, No. 125.

Pontusson, Jonas (1983) 'Comparative Political Economy of Advanced Capitalist States: Sweden and France', *Kapitalistate*, No. 10/11.

Regini, Marino (1986) 'Political Bargaining in Western Europe during the Economic Crisis of the 1980s', in Otto Jacobi, Bob Jessop, Hans Kastendiek and Marino Regini, *Economic Crisis, Trade Unions and the State*, London, Croom Helm.

Simitis, Spiros (1986) 'The Juridification of Industrial Relations', *Comparative Labor Law*, Vol. 7, No. 2.

Sorge, Arndt (1976) 'The Evolution of Industrial Democracy in the Countries of the European Community', *British Journal of Industrial Relations*, Vol. 14, No. 3.

Streeck, Wolfgang (1986) 'Industrial Relations in the Federal Republic of Germany, 1974–1985', *Proceedings of the Industrial Relations Research Association December 1985*, Madison, Wisconsin, IRRA.

Sturmthal, Adolf (1964) *Workers' Councils*, Cambridge, Mass., Harvard University Press.

Tallard, Michèle (1988) 'Bargaining Over New Technology', in Richard Hyman and Wolfgang Streeck, *New Technology and Industrial Relations*, Oxford, Blackwell.

Terry, Michael (1986) 'How Do We Know If Trade Unions Are Getting Weaker?' *British Journal of Industrial Relations*, Vol. 24, No. 2.

Therborn, Göran (1986) *Why Some Peoples Are More Unemployed Than Others*, London, Verso.

Treu, Tiziano (1986) 'Italian Industrial Relations in the Past Ten Years', *Proceedings of the Industrial Relations Research Association December 1985*, Madison, Wisconsin, IRRA.

10 Class Struggle and the Trade Union Movement*

In Britain today, two employees in five are union members: a lower percentage than in Scandinavia, where unionisation is almost complete, but higher than in most other European countries and more than double the rate in North America. Roughly one trade unionist in ten is likely to go on strike in any single year. In what sense, then, can unions be regarded as agencies of class struggle, of resistance to capitalism? There can be no straightforward answer to this question, for trade unionism itself is deeply ambiguous and contradictory. The aim of this brief survey is to illuminate some of the complexities of union organisation and action.

With very few exceptions, 'progressive' employers are happy to declare their support for 'responsible' trade unionism. The conclusion of the Royal Commission on Labour in 1894 was that strong organisations of workers and employers meeting regularly across the negotiating table were a source of order and stability in industry: strikes became less likely, and when they did occur were better disciplined and more easily settled than when unions were weak and unrecognised. For most of the present century, state policy has endorsed this view and has encouraged the development of collective bargaining. At times of crisis, the traditional response has been to seek to draw unions into a spirit of national unity in defence of the state and social order. During both world wars, union representatives participated in a multiplicity of committees at both national and local levels; the government's aim was that unions should encourage workers to support the war effort, prevent social unrest over the hardships involved, aid recruitment to the armed forces, and increase industrial productivity. In more recent times, as British capital has faced grave problems of international competitiveness, similar efforts have been made to win union support for policies of controlling labour costs and increasing management's control over the labour process. The National Economic Development Council (NEDC), set

*First published in Coates, D., Johnston, G. and Bush, R. (eds) *A Socialist Anatomy of Britain*, Cambridge, Polity Press, 1985.

up by a Tory government in 1962, is the most prominent of several hundred tripartite bodies currently functioning. The view of British unions as a sober and respectable component of national life was symbolised in 1968 by the issue of a special postage stamp to mark the centenary of the TUC.

Yet a totally contrary theme has always formed part of ruling-class opinion: that trade unions are dangerous, disruptive and subversive. Judges, hard-line employers and right-wing politicians and newspapers have always been hostile, and anti-unionism now dominates Tory party policy. Through the 1970s, 'trade union power' was increasingly defined as a central political issue: unions enjoyed legal privileges, restricted individual freedom, obstructed management efficiency, interfered with the working of the labour market, exerted undue political influence.[1] Keith Joseph set out this position in a pamphlet written shortly before the 1979 election entitled *Solving the Union Problem Is the Key to Britain's Recovery*, a position emphasised in the Tory manifesto. The philosophy of weakening the unions clearly inspired the Employment Acts of 1980 and 1982 as well as the subsequent legislation.

This contradictory mixture of ruling-class attitudes is mirrored on the left. When Engels first encountered the British labour movement at the height of the Chartist upsurge, he declared that 'these Unions contribute greatly to nourish the bitter hatred of the workers against the property-holding class. . . . As schools of war, the Unions are unexcelled.'[2] In the *Communist Manifesto*, Marx and Engels described the formation of trade unions as an important stage in the development of revolutionary consciousness within the working class. Yet they were soon to recognise that trade unions could serve merely as vehicles through which groups of workers who were relatively protected from the disruptive force of labour market competition could defend their own sectional interests through the routines of collective bargaining. 'Too exclusively bent upon the local and immediate struggles with capital, the trade unions have not yet fully understood their power of acting against the system of wage slavery itself', complained Marx in 1866.[3] 'They therefore kept too much aloof from general social and political movements.' Later, Engels recognised the limited import of even militant unionism in Britain: 'caught up in a narrow circle of strikes for higher wages and shorter hours without finding a solution'.[4] Reviewing his early impressions after the changes of forty years, he went on in 1885 to stress how ruling-class attitudes to unions had altered: they 'were now petted and patronised as perfectly legitimate institutions, and as useful means of spreading sound economical doctrines amongst the workers'. Most of the strongest unions represented an elite of skilled men: 'they form an aristocracy among the working-class; they have succeeded in enforcing for themselves a relatively comfortable position, and they accept it as final.'[5] And Marx himself complained that the emerging caste of full-time officials seemed to have been bought off by the ruling class: 'the leadership of the working class of England has wholly passed into the hands of the corrupted leaders of the trade unions and the professional agitators.'[6]

The approaches of the left in the twentieth century have reiterated the ambiguous character of trade unionism. Lenin's argument has been widely endorsed: that industrial struggle alone merely generates a 'trade union consciousness', reflected in sectional pressure for limited improvements. The notion that unions display inherent bureaucratic tendencies – as argued by Michels in his 'iron law of oligarchy' – underlies strategies built upon autonomous rank-and-file organisations and action. Yet does spontaneous grassroots initiative reinforce the tendencies to 'economism' – the preoccupation with narrow short-term gains which led some to call trade unionism 'the capitalism of the proletariat'? Socialists who identify production relations as the heart of capitalist exploitation normally treat industrial struggle as a key element in their political perspectives. Likewise, any attempt to win mass working-class support for a socialist programme must be conditioned by the fact of workers' current organised attachment to trade unions. So it is clear that an understanding of trade unionism must figure prominently in any conception of socialist transformation. But are unions part of the problems of capitalism, or part of the solution?

CAPITALISM AND THE LABOUR PROCESS

Trade unions are historical products of the relationship between wage labour and capital. Under capitalism, work is organised on the basis of a market relationship. Work is equated with employment, with 'earning a living' (and hence unpaid labour, such as the household tasks which are overwhelmingly performed by women outside the employment relationship, is not regarded as 'real work' either in popular perception or in official economic accounting). The prospective worker must find an employer willing to pay a wage or salary in return for the disposal of her or his skill, knowledge or physical strength. It is in the employer's interest to secure labour at the lowest possible cost, and to retain workers in employment only so long as they generate a profit. A fall in the price of the goods or services produced, or the development of new techniques allowing these to be produced more cheaply, may at any moment result in managerial decisions which throw men and women out of their jobs. Within private capitalism, the forces of competition sustain the pressure to economise on labour costs, to draw ever-increased production out of fewer workers, to undermine any basis of security and stability in the employment relationship. Socialists have often assumed that within state employment the situation must be very different; but it has become all too clear that within the framework of a capitalist economy, very similar pressures operate, and that the strategies and actions of managements differ very little between public and private sectors. Under Thatcher, indeed, state managers have often proved *more* ruthless than their private capitalist counterparts.

Under capitalism, labour is in one sense a commodity like any other; but in a different sense it is quite unique. The employment contract may lay down the wages which the worker receives, but does not define precisely what will be provided in return. The worker does not undertake to sell an exact quantity of labour; for work cannot be measured like potatoes, and in any case most employers cannot predict exactly their day-to-day labour requirements. They want to be able to make flexible use of their labour force as circumstances dictate; and the law supports their interests, since the employment contract imposes on workers an open-ended obligation. In return for their wages, employees surrender their *capacity to work*;[7] and it is the function of management, through its hierarchy of control, to transform this potential into profitably productive activity.

In two distinct respects, conflict is thus central to employment. The sale of labour power – the fixing of the worker's income, and hence the employer's labour costs – necessarily involves an opposition of interests. Some would say that this antagonism is resolved impersonally through the operation of market forces; but market relationships are never neutral. The superficial equality of buyer and seller conceals underlying inequalities of market power which underpin the terms of trade; markets are media of control just as much as they are media of exchange. This is particularly true of the labour market, where the employer represents the concentrated power of capital whereas workers participate in the employment contract as vulnerable individuals. Combination in trade unions is, most simply, a means of partially offsetting this built-in inequality. Conflict over the sale of labour power is discontinuous and intermittent. In unionised firms, annual wage and salary negotiations have become the norm. Non-union employers either follow agreements elsewhere, or else fix pay rates unilaterally and alter them infrequently, responding either to shortages of particular grades of labour or to the individual bargaining of particularly valued employees. Payment by results systems may offer scope for more frequent changes; a decade ago, some manufacturing firms in Britain were the scene of regular bargaining over individual piece-rates, often involving strike action. But management efforts to 'rationalise' payment systems have made such situations increasingly uncommon.

By contrast, the second main area of conflict – the control of the labour process – is often far more unstable. As Marx wrote, management control 'is rooted in the unavoidable antagonism between the exploiter and the living and labouring raw material that he exploits'.[8] To maintain profitability in the face of competition, employers must seek constantly to cut costs, intensify work pressure, introduce new techniques and technologies, make existing employees 'redundant'. An authoritarian structure of discipline and command – more smoothly and more usually known simply as 'management' – is necessary to sustain this drive for profit (or the analogous drive for economy within the public sector).

Conflict is therefore inherent in work under capitalism. Yet in most work situations it is remarkable how *rarely* this antagonism erupts to the surface of industrial relations. In part this is because the capitalist labour process is at one and the same time both conflictual and co-operative. The diverse activities which are fragmented by the capitalist division of labour must be integrated; different phases of the production cycle must be co-ordinated; machines appropriate for the various operations must be procured and maintained in working order; materials and components must be available at the correct time and place; finished products must be despatched. Because capitalism divides and confines workers' understanding of the overall process of production, management with all its disciplinary controls and material privileges nevertheless performs an indispensable production function. Management's role is thus necessarily contradictory, and workers' response no less so. And because people who work together – whether as equals or as superiors and subordinates – usually attempt (if only to make life easier for themselves) to avoid undue unpleasantness and antagonism, it is often management's function as co-ordinator of a complex and often baffling productive operation which is most clearly perceived.

There are, of course, strong ideological pressures to regard management as a neutral force performing functions which would be technically necessary with any social system, rather than as a vehicle of class oppression. There are also powerful traditional notions such as 'a fair day's wage for a fair day's work' which in practice have usually encouraged workers to accept low pay for hard effort. But there are other reasons why conflict is normally contained. In any situation, a dense network of unique and detailed relationships influences how far the conflictual or the co-operative aspects of management–worker relations predominate. A continuous process of experience and adaptation affects perceptions of management control as legitimate or illegitimate, reasonable or unreasonable, technically necessary or arbitrary. Some sociologists have talked about a universal tendency towards 'negotiation of order': whether or not a workplace is unionised, working relationships involve a large amount of give-and-take, of tacit and informal bargaining, which smooths some of the rough edges of management discipline and control. Even when there are some four million unemployed, few managers attempt to control simply by wielding the threat of the sack: the inevitable outcome would be bloody-minded resentment and active or passive sabotage. Sophisticated employers want to obtain at least some degree of 'voluntary' co-operation and self-discipline. By exercising control 'humanely' they hope to limit the degree of worker resistance.

Informal negotiation over the 'frontier of control' has been an important feature of British industry for over a century.[9] The 'custom and practice' which is so widely applied in shop-floor industrial relations may be viewed as the product of continuous trade-offs between first-line managers, themselves under pressure to achieve production targets, and workers conscious of their own ability to frustrate the employers' objectives in the day-to-day work process. Many factors influence the character and outcome of such bargaining: employer sophistication and determination, the vulnerability of production to workers' actions or omissions, workers' own collective cohesion and consciousness of their power. But in every situation where capital employs wage-labour, the terms of the relationship involve a constant process of negotiation with antagonistic implications which are often suppressed but at times erupt into open conflict.

Table 10.1 Aggregate union membership and density in the United Kingdom: selected years, 1892–1986 (*continued*)

1933	4392		19422		22.6	
1938	6053		19829		30.5	
1945	7875		20400		38.6	
1948	9363		20732		45.2	
1949	9318	−0.5	20782	+0.2	44.8	−0.9
1950	9289	−0.3	21055	+0.3	44.1	−1.6
1951	9530	+2.6	21177	+0.6	45.0	+2.0
1952	9588	+0.6	21252	+0.4	45.1	+0.2
1953	9527	−0.6	21352	+0.5	44.6	−1.1
1954	9566	+0.4	21658	+1.4	44.2	−0.9
1955	9741	+1.8	21913	+1.2	44.5	+0.7
1956	9778	+0.4	22180	+1.2	44.1	−0.9
1957	9829	+0.5	22334	+0.7	44.0	−0.2
1958	9639	−1.9	22290	−0.2	43.2	−1.8
1959	9623	−0.2	21866	−1.9	44.0	+1.9
1960	9835	+2.2	22229	+1.7	44.2	+0.5
1961	9916	+0.8	22527	+1.3	44.0	−0.5
1962	10014	+1.0	22879	+1.6	43.8	−0.5
1963	10067	+0.5	23021	+0.6	43.7	−0.2
1964	10218	+1.5	23166	+0.6	44.1	+0.9
1965	10325	+1.0	23385	+0.9	44.2	+0.2
1966	10259	−0.6	23545	+0.7	43.6	−1.4
1967	10194	−0.6	23347	−0.8	43.7	+0.2
1968	10200	+0.1	23203	−0.6	44.0	+0.7
1969	10479	+2.7	23153	−0.2	45.3	+3.0
1970	11187	+6.8	23050	−0.4	48.5	+7.1
1971	11135	−0.5	22884	−0.7	48.7	+0.4
1972	11359	+2.0	22961	+0.3	49.5	+1.6
1973	11456	+0.9	23244	+1.2	49.3	−0.4
1974	11764	+2.7	23229	+0.4	50.4	+2.2
1975	12026	+2.2	23587	+1.1	51.0	+1.2
1976	12386	+3.0	23871	+1.2	51.9	+1.8
1977	12846	+3.7	24069	+0.8	53.4	+2.9
1978	13112	+2.1	24203	+0.6	54.2	+1.5
1979	13447	+2.6	24264	+0.3	55.4	+2.2
1980	12947	−3.7	24632	+1.5	52.6	−5.1
1981	12106	−6.5	24551	−0.3	49.3	−6.3
1982	11593	−4.2	24170	−1.6	48.0	−2.7
1983	11337	−2.2	24032	−0.6	47.2	−1.7
1984	11086	−2.2	24194	+0.7	45.8	−3.0
1985	10716	−3.3	24698	+2.1	43.4	−5.3
1986	10333	−3.6	24822	+0.5	41.6	−4.1

Source: George Bain and Robert Price, 'Union Growth', in Bain, *Industrial Relations in Britain*, Oxford, Blackwell (updated). I am grateful to Bob Price for updating Tables 10.1, 10.2 and 10.4.

Table 10.2   Union membership and density by sex in Great Britain*

	Union membership (000s)	Male potential union membership (000s)	Union density (%)	Union membership (000s)	Female potential union membership (000s)	Union density (%)
1896	1356	9652	14.0	116	4230	2.7
1910	2330	11326	20.6	275	4935	5.6
1911	2799	11436	24.5	331	5002	6.6
1920	6937	11891	58.3	1316	5227	25.2
1933	3637	13040	27.9	713	5915	12.1
1948	7468	13485	55.4	1650	6785	24.3
1965	7610	14777	51.5	2132	8119	26.3
1968	7428	14452	51.4	2265	8251	27.5
1970	7994	14177	56.4	2634	8363	31.5
1973	8036	13945	57.6	2899	8790	33.0
1974	8151	13809	59.0	3062	9010	34.0
1975	8272	13920	59.4	3329	9122	36.5
1976	8492	14069	60.4	3462	9257	37.4
1977	8675	14085	61.6	3608	9431	38.3
1978	8940	14074	63.5	3639	9561	38.1
1979	8866	13979	63.4	3837	9708	39.5
1985	7458	14164	52.7	3258	10524	31.0

*i.e. excluding Northern Ireland (except for 1985, when the figures are for the whole UK)
Source: Bain and Price (updated).

thousand organisations officially recorded – but has become more rapid; the number has now fallen to 375. The average size of just under 30000 members represents a massive variation between different unions. As can be seen from Table 10.5, over half the unions have less than a thousand members; together they account for under half of one per cent of total membership. At the other extreme, the six largest unions account for half the total; while the twenty-four with over 100000 members together contain over 80 per cent of all trade unionists.[11]

This concentration of membership in a declining number of unions reflects a process of merger and amalgamation which has become particularly rapid in recent years: partly because the legal requirements have been eased, partly because of financial pressures encouraging rationalisation, partly because of empire building on the part of union leaders. Historically, the earliest amalgamations mainly involved the combination of local societies into national organisa-

Table 10.3   Manual and white-collar union membership and density in
Great Britain

	Manual			White-collar		
	Union membership (000s)	Potential union membership (000s)	Union density (%)	Union membership (000s)	Potential union membership (000s)	Union density (%)
1911	2730.9	13141	20.8	398.3	3297	12.1
1920	7124.1	13271	53.7	1129.2	3847	29.4
1931	3544.0	14157	25.0	1025.4	4639	22.1
1948	7055.7	14027	50.3	2062.1	6243	33.0
1968	6636.9	13322	49.8	3056.0	9381	32.6
1970	7095.0	12852	55.2	3533.0	9688	36.5
1973	6968.9	12468	55.9	3966.3	10266	38.6
1974	7082.3	12362	57.3	4130.8	10458	39.5
1975	7112.1	12327	57.7	4488.8	10715	41.9
1976	7321.6	12322	59.4	4632.3	11004	42.1
1977	7445.3	12265	60.7	4837.9	11251	43.0
1978	7549.7	12168	62.0	5029.1	11467	43.9
1979	7577.5	12035	63.0	5124.7	11652	44.0

Source: Bain and Price, 'Union Growth'.

tions. Then followed a series of mergers of unions catering for
cognate occupational groups, often within a single industry or sector.
Finally there have emerged a number of 'conglomerates' covering a
diverse array of industries and occupations.

It is common to distinguish between 'craft', 'industrial' and
'general' unions, but few of the largest organisations (see Tables 10.6
and 10.7) comfortably fit within these categories. A brief consideration of the 'top ten' demonstrates their complexity. Thus the TGWU
derives from an amalgamation in 1921 of some twenty unions of
dockers and road transport workers; but it subsequently acquired a
major base in manufacturing and recruited extensively in national
and local government services. In the past two decades it has
attracted many smaller unions into merger, including sizeable bodies
such as the Chemical Workers, the Plasterers, the Vehicle Builders
and the Agricultural Workers. The other main general union, the
GMB, was formed in 1924 from the merger of three unions with their
roots respectively among gasworkers, labourers in northern ship-
yards, and local authority manual workers: one of the component
bodies had previously merged with a separate union of women

Table 10.4 Union membership and density in Great Britain by sector

	1948			1968			1979			1985*		
	Union member-ship (000s)	Potential union member-ship (000s)	Union density (%)	Union member-ship (000s)	Potential union member-ship (000s)	Union density (%)	Union member-ship (000s)	Potential union member-ship (000s)	Union density (%)	Union member-ship (000s)	Potential union member-ship (000s)	Union density (%)
Public sector**	3278.5	4637.4	70.7	3661.0	5536.9	66.1	5189.9	6297.2	82.4	4989.2	6191.9	80.6
Manufacturing	3720.1	7290.4	51.0	4138.4	8285.9	49.9	5157.4	7385.8	69.8	3989.7	5478.0	72.8
Manual	3566.5	6123.9	58.2	3808.1	6139.9	62.0	4234.6	5273.5	80.3	n.a.		
White-collar	153.6	1166.5	13.2	330.3	2146.0	15.4	922.8	2112.3	43.7	n.a.		
Construction	611.2	1325.8	46.1	472.0	1570.7	30.1	519.7	1415.2	36.7	363.7	946.9	38.4
Agriculture, forestry and fishing	224.4	988.9	22.7	131.1	516.8	25.4	85.8	378.3	22.7	103.1	328.6	31.3
Private services†	664.8	4578.4	14.5	767.5	6042.0	12.7	1214.5	7283.6	16.7	1171.1	7945.6	14.7

Notes: Road transport and sea transport are not included in any of the sectors.
*Because of changes in official statistics, the figure of potential membership is calculated on a different basis in 1985, slightly deflating the figure and hence exaggerating density by comparison with previous years. Industries which suffered denationalisation are still included in the public sector.
**Comprises national government; local government and education; health services; post and telecommunications; air transport; port and inland water transport; railways; gas, electricity and water; and coalmining. The nationalised iron and steel industry is included in manufacturing.
†Comprises insurance, banking, and finance; entertainment; distribution; and miscellaneous services.
Source: Bain and Price, 'Union Growth'.

Table 10.5   Trade unions – numbers and membership, end 1985

Numbers of members	Number of unions	All membership (000s)	Percentage of Number of unions	Percentage of Membership of all unions
Under 100*	74	3	19.8	0.0
100–499	94	23	25.2	0.2
500–999	37	28	9.9	0.3
1,000–2,499	57	95	15.3	0.9
2,500–4,999	26	102	7.0	1.0
5,000–9,999	14	87	3.8	0.8
10,000–14,999	4	48	1.1	0.4
15,000–24,999	11	202	2.9	1.9
25,000–49,999	23	805	6.2	7.5
50,000–99,999	9	655	2.4	6.1
100,000–249,999	14	2,351	3.8	21.9
250,000 and more	10	6,317	2.7	58.9
All members	373	10,716	100.0	100.0

*Including newly formed unions whose membership is not reported. There were 12 such unions in 1985.
Source: *Employment Gazette*.

workers. Its membership also includes a large industrial component; recently it has amalgamated with the Water Workers and (in 1982) the Boilermakers. USDAW is to some extent a third general union: though primarily based among shopworkers it recruits also in food processing and manufacturing, particularly in the co-operative sector.

The AEU is an organisation which from craft origins has also developed into virtually a general union. Amalgamation in 1851 established it as a substantial national union and in 1920 as representative of all the main higher-skilled occupations in engineering. In the 1920s it opened its ranks to all male manual workers in the industry, and in 1943 admitted women. Today its membership extends through the broad complex of metal-based manufacturing to engineering maintenance workers throughout industry and the public services. In the 1960s it formed a loose federation, the Amalgamated Union of Engineering Workers (AUEW), with the Foundry Workers and the Constructional Engineers; and also with the Draughtsmen's Association, which became the Technical and Supervisory Section

Table 10.6   Major British unions, 1960

Transport & General Workers' Union (TGWU)	1 302 000
Amalgamated Engineering Union (AEU)	973 000
General & Municipal Workers' Union (GMWU)	796 000
National Union of Mineworkers (NUM)	586 000
Union of Shop Distributive & Allied Workers (USDAW)	355 000
National Union of Railwaymen (NUR)	334 000
National Association of Local Government Officers (NALGO)	274 000
National Union of Teachers (NUT)	245 000
Electrical Trades Union (ETU)	243 000
National Union of Public Employees (NUPE)	200 000
Amalgamated Society of Woodworkers (ASW)	192 000
Union of Post Office Workers (UPW)	166 000
National Union of Printing, Bookbinding & Paper Workers (NUPBPW)	158 000
Civil Service Clerical Association (CSCA)	140 000
National Union of Agricultural Workers (NUAW)	135 000
Iron and Steel Trades Confederation (ISTC)	117 000
National Union of Tailors & Garment Workers (NUTGW)	116 000

Source: *TUC Report 1961* or individual organisations.

(AUEW-TASS). During the 1980s there were protracted negotiations for a full amalgamation; eventually the two smaller bodies
agreed to merger terms, but discussions broke down with TASS.

The EEPTU has also diversified from a craft background to cover a
range of occupations in electricity supply, electrical installation and
maintenance, and electrical engineering, while its current form and
title derive from a merger with the Plumbers in 1968. UCATT,
created through a series of amalgamations in 1970, is successor to
many – but by no means all – of the traditional craft societies of
woodworkers and bricklayers, competes with the TGWU for many
other grades of construction workers, but also has a significant
membership among maintenance and production workers in other
industries.

Three of the largest British unions recruit solely among white-
collar occupations. NALGO covers the whole range of such occupations – from junior clerks to chief officers – within local government,
and also has members in gas, the health service, and universities.
ASTMS recruits in a wider range of industries and services but has a
narrow occupational base, mainly encompassing technical, supervisory and administrative groups. It has now, in 1988, amalgamated
with TASS to create a union of over half a million members with

Table 10.7   Major British unions, 1985

TGWU	1 434 005
AEU	974 904
GMB (previously GMWU)	826 920
NALGO	752 131
NUPE	663 776
Association of Scientific, Technical and Managerial Staffs (ASTMS)	390 000
USDAW	385 455
Electrical Electronic Telecommunication and Plumbing Union (EETPU)	384 577
NUT	253 672
Union of Construction Allied Trades and Technicians (UCATT)	248 693
NUM	248 456
Technical and Supervisory Staffs (TASS)	240 000
Confederation of Health Service Employees (COHSE)	212 980
Society of Graphical and Allied Trades 1982 (SOGAT)	206 898
Union of Communication Workers (UCW; previously UPW)	194 244
National Association of Schoolmasters and Union of Women Teachers (NAS/UWT)	169 839
National Communications Union (NCU)	161 315
Banking Insurance and Finance Union (BIFU)	157 468

Source: *Annual Report of the Certification Officer*, 1986. The Certification Officer lists one another organisation with over 150 000 members: the Royal College of Nursing, whose status as a trade union is questionable, claimed a membership of 251 127.

considerable potential for expansion, entitled Manufacturing, Science and Finance (MSF). The NUT recruits among all grades of teachers (and headteachers) in primary and secondary schools, but in competition with the NAS/UWT and with a number of non-TUC organisations. Finally, NUPE organises primarily in local government and the health service, mainly though not exclusively among manual workers, and often in competition with the general unions (and in the health service, with COHSE).

It is clear from this brief survey that British trade union structure is extremely complex and reflects a long process of historical evolution.[12] In another respect, however, the pattern is simpler than in most other countries: for all major unions are affiliated to a single central organisation, the TUC. By contrast, in such countries as France and Italy there exist rival federations based on different political or religious identities. In West Germany and Scandinavia

Table 10.8 British strike statistics: annual averages, 1900–86

	Number of strikes	Workers involved ('000)	Strike days ('000)
1900–10	529	240	4576
1911–13	1074	1034	20908
1914–18	844	632	5292
1919–21	1241	2108	49053
1922–5	629	503	11968
1926	323	2734	162233
1927–32	379	344	4740
1933–9	735	295	1694
1970	3943	1801	10980
1971	2263	1178	13551
1972	2530	1734	23909
1973	2902	1528	7197
1974	2946	1626	14750
1975	2332	809	6012
1976	2034	668	3284
1977	2737	1166	10142
1978	2498	1041	9405
1979	2125	4608	29474
1980	1348	834	11964
1981	1344	1513	4266
1982	1538	2103	5313
1983	1364	574	3754
1984	1221	1464	27135
1985	903	791	6402
1986	1074	720	1920

Source: *Employment Gazette.*

such divisions do not exist, but most white-collar unionists are not attached to the main central bodies. In the USA, major unions such as the Auto Workers are outside the AFL-CIO.

Ironically, the comprehensive scope of TUC membership owes as much to government policy as to the efforts of the TUC itself. In 1962 the Macmillan government set up the NEDC with the aim of winning union co-operation in its overall economic objectives, and in particular to obtain some form of acquiescence in wage restraint. As the price of its involvement the TUC gained the right to nominate, directly and exclusively, the six trade union members of NEDC. In consequence, non-TUC unions felt excluded from influence on government economic policy, a serious problem for those representing public sector groups. This encouraged NALGO to join the TUC, to be followed by the main civil service and teaching unions which had previously been outside.

In becoming fully representative of the main British unions, the TUC has inevitably altered significantly. Traditionally its membership was dominated by unions based on manual workers in private industry, or in such industries as mining and railways which were nationalised in the 1940s. The structure of the General Council, which oversees the main activities of the TUC in the period between each annual Congress, reflected the composition of the movement in 1920 when the system of representation by 'trade groups' was introduced. Unions were grouped according to the trade or industry in which they principally recruited, and each group was allocated a number of seats on the General Council roughly proportionate to its aggregate membership. This system had several anomalous consequences. Members of the General Council were elected by the votes of the whole of Congress; but where a trade group contained only one union, or where the various unions could agree amicably on the allocation of their trade group seats, there would be no contest. Where contests did occur there was a behind-the-scenes process of bargaining and trade-off, in which the largest unions could exert considerable patronage. The structure was slow to adapt to the changing composition of trade union – and TUC – membership. The trade groups for 'Public Employees' and 'Non-Manual Workers' – with the subsequent addition of 'Civil Service' and 'Technical Engineering and Scientific' groups – became the residual home of a multiplicity of the fastest-growing TUC affiliates. Conversely, the trade groups of declining sectors of employment retained General Council representation out of proportion to their dwindling membership.

This formed the background to the changes introduced in 1983. Unions with over 100 000 members are automatically represented on the General Council with a total of thirty-five seats, while the smaller bodies together elect a further eleven members. The number of additional seats for women unionists has been increased to six, elected by Congress as a whole. Debate on these contentious alterations was largely motivated by their expected effect in shifting the political balance of the General Council to the right; and certainly such predictions have been borne out in practice. But it should be noted that, historically, the power of patronage enjoyed by the largest unions under the old system normally buttressed right-wing control; and that the superficial 'left' majority during the 1970s was without practical effect, partly because it failed to reflect the real balance of commitment within the movement.

TRADE UNIONS ON THE DEFENSIVE

A decade ago, it was largely taken for granted on the left that trade unionism was both an expression and a vehicle of working-class advance. The experience of the Wilson government's attempts to curb trade union activity, and the more systematic attack on trade unionism by the Heath government, appeared to radicalise the movement. Traditionally, most of the largest unions had acted as bulwarks of the right within the Labour Party; now many were seen as forces for more progressive policies. Strike activity also seemed to demonstrate a rise in the temperature of struggle (see Table 10.8). Historically, the pattern of British strikes involved a relatively large number of small stoppages, but in addition a regular occurrence of major disputes which registered a high level of striker-days.[13] In the period of inter-war unemployment, the number of strikes fell substantially; and after the defeat of the 1926 General Strike, almost all that did occur were small-scale disputes. From the 1940s, the number of strikes rose again; but disputes remained small. For many years, indeed, the statistics were dominated by minor stoppages in coal-mining, typically concerning piece-rates or else working conditions which affected piece-work earnings. But in the 1960s, strikes became more widespread (though socialists might find it surprising how *few* there still were, given the number of workers who still did *not* strike against their exploitation by capital): in 1970 a record figure of almost 4000 strikes was recorded. Big, protracted strikes also became more common: notably the miners' dispute of 1972, the first national stoppage in the industry since the General Strike. And indeed, the number of striker-days in that year was the highest since 1926. The miners' strike – involving an open confrontation with the Tory government – symbolised the increasingly political character of many disputes, particularly in the public sector.

The period of the Social Contract after 1974 brought significant changes in the level and character of struggle. But trade union membership continued to increase. More importantly, perhaps, the pattern of shop steward organisation which for several decades had been a distinctive feature of trade unionism in British engineering spread far more widely, from manufacturing to the public sector, from manual to white-collar workers.

The situation has changed radically in the context of mass unemployment and a rabidly anti-union government. Thatcher's first term of office brought the destruction of a quarter of all jobs in manufacturing, the traditional stronghold of British unionism; while public employment, the more recent growth area, was hit by cuts and cash limits. Hence the decline in union membership, both in absolute terms and as a proportion of the labour force, which is revealed in Table 10.1. Some unions have fared particularly badly: the TGWU, for example, which claimed almost 2.1 million members at the end of 1979, has since lost a third of this total. Whatever happens to aggregate employment in the next decade – there are few grounds for optimism, given current economic, political and technological trends – its structural composition will almost inevitably continue to move away from concentrated workforces in the large industrial centres to smaller and more dispersed workplaces and to the private service sector which has traditionally proved resistant to unionism. Even maintaining current levels of membership will therefore involve an uphill struggle. Membership decline has had serious financial consequences, since British unions typically operate on tight budgets with membership dues which are low by overseas standards. Some organisations have been brought close to bankruptcy, a situation which will doubtless encourage further amalgamations.

Employers, themselves often faced by intense economic pressures, have taken predictable advantage of unions' current weakness. Real wages, which rose on average by about 20 per cent during the 1970s, stagnated and in some cases actually fell during the early 1980s. More serious, however, has been the challenge mounted on the frontier of control over the labour process. Capitalist rationalisation has involved major efforts to achieve more flexible use of labour, more intensive working, more elaborate supervision, tighter disciplinary regulations, and hence a systematic assault on established 'custom and practice'. Often integral to this attack has been the imposition of closures and redundancies, particularly in those companies which acquired a diverse range of separate plants during the merger wave of the 1960s and early 1970s. The attempt to reorganise production to enhance management's day-to-day control may be seen as a continuation of a trend widely proclaimed in the 1960s in the name of 'productivity bargaining'. Then, however, the underlying theme of sophisticated employers, government agencies and academic pundits was the need for 'management by agreement': transformation of the labour process had to be negotiated with union representatives in order to win workers' consent. It was this philosophy which encouraged many employers in the early 1970s to give full recognition and extensive facilities to shop stewards, in some cases stimulating their appointment where none had existed before.[14] Today the strategy is often very different: commercial pressures and the changed balance of labour market power have brought the unilateral imposition of reorganisation and speed-up, regardless of union (and particularly shop steward) resistance. The threat of closure has itself provided a potent sanction: workers have been offered the stark choice of co-operating with management or losing their jobs.

The altered material environment is reflected in a degree of defeatism and demoralisation reminiscent of the inter-war depression. As can be seen from Table 10.8, officially recorded strikes averaged 2600 a year in the 1970s; in no year did the figure fall below 2000. In the 1980s, the level has virtually halved, with the number in 1985 the lowest since the 1930s. The number of strikes lasting longer than a single day – indicating sustained resistance rather than token protest – has fallen even faster than the overall total. This seeming erosion of the will to struggle has been effectively exploited by many employers – most notably British Leyland (now Austin Rover) – in appealing over the heads of workplace union representatives to employees as individuals. Fatalism in the face of the employers' offensive is doubtless reinforced by the limited success – or in the case of such groups as the steelworkers, the unqualified defeat – of those trade unionists who *have* proved willing to fight.

'Macho management' characterised by a total repudiation of trade unionism is not yet typical of British employers. Three tendencies are, however, widespread. The first is a far greater strategic sophistication than in the past. Large multi-plant (and often transnational) firms pursue centrally co-ordinated objectives, often in the face of union organisation still committed to the autonomy of each workplace; the issues on which to risk or even provoke confrontation are often carefully chosen. Secondly, the area of the negotiable has been sharply restricted; managements increasingly insist on their 'right to manage', merely offering to 'consult' with union representatives over production-related questions. Third, piecemeal encroachments have been made on rights of collective organisation: notably, in many companies, a cutback in shop steward facilities. Often this is associated with the cultivation of alternative channels of management–worker relations: various forms of 'joint participation' at workplace level, and in some cases Japanese-style 'quality circles' designed to strengthen workers' commitment to the company's production goals.

To date, most large employers have proved less crudely anti-union than the government (often because their perspectives extend to a possible economic recovery and the prospect that union representatives might again constitute useful adjuncts to personnel management). At the level of the state, recession has exposed the fragile nature of the political status acquired by unions in the 1960s and 1970s.

As has already been indicated, the growing involvement of trade unions since the early 1960s in tripartite machinery of consultation and administration reflected government concern to co-opt them within the overall priorities of national economic strategy. The relatively high incidence of strikes in Britain, the restraints imposed by workplace unionism on management's control of production, and the cumulative effects of fragmented wage militancy, were all regarded within government as obstacles to national economic performance and competitiveness. The co-operation of union official-dom was viewed as essential in order to control incomes, increase productivity, and restructure collective bargaining procedures. Integration of union nominees within the elaborate if largely powerless mechanisms of national economic planning, and an extensive system of informal contacts and discussions, were viewed as an important means of encouraging union 'responsibility' and strengthening leadership controls over rank-and-file militancy.[15]

These developments rested, not – as some writers have argued – on a philosophy of 'corporatism', but on the pragmatic need of governments to come to terms with the ability of unions and their members to disrupt (however unintentionally) national economic policy. This disruptive potential has inevitably been much diminished by the unions' current economic weakness. Moreover the process of industrial relations 'reform' in which unions have co-operated since the 1960s – rationalised payment systems, productivity bargaining, formalised disciplinary and grievance procedures – has made labour relations far more predictable and manageable than a decade ago. It is plausible to argue that more bureaucratic procedures of collective bargaining have contributed to a growing alienation of ordinary members from their union representatives, both full-time officials and shop stewards. To the extent that workers' identification with their unions has been eroded, the value of union representatives as mediators between state and capital and the working class has been similarly reduced. Thus Thatcher's anti-union policies have an obvious material basis.

PROBLEMS OF A SOCIALIST STRATEGY

Trade unions are a product of capitalism, and are necessarily conditioned by their relationship with capital. Perry Anderson made this point neatly when he wrote that 'trade unions are dialectically both an opposition to capitalism and a component of it'. He went on to argue that 'as institutions, trade unions do not *challenge* the existence of society based on a division of classes, they merely *express* it. Thus trade unions can never be viable vehicles of advance towards socialism in themselves; by their nature they are tied to capitalism. They can bargain within the society, but not transform it.'[16]

Others would regard this as too mechanical a formulation. 'A trade union', declared Gramsci, 'is not a predetermined phenomenon. It *becomes* a determinate institution, i.e. it takes on a definite historical form, to the extent that the strength and will of the workers who are its members impress a policy and propose an aim that define it.'[17] Three questions immediately suggest themselves. In what circumstances, if any, are workers likely to conceive trade unionism as a vehicle for anti-capitalist class struggle? How far could a membership committed to such a goal impress their aspirations on official union policy? And is it possible for trade unions to challenge capitalism without provoking their own suppression? These questions will be pursued by exploring four familiar sets of antitheses: bureaucracy and democracy; compromise and struggle; class action and sectionalism; socialist politics and economism.

It is customary on the left to discuss internal relationships in unions in terms of a dichotomy between 'bureaucracy' and 'rank and file'. In their cruder versions, such arguments represent an inadequate analysis and a misleading basis for strategy.[18] The term 'rank and file' is a military metaphor without theoretical content; as employed on the left it has often involved a romantic and idealised conception of workplace action and shop steward militancy, an assumption that workers are held back from anti-capitalist struggle only by the machinations of a corrupt and reactionary leadership. The notion of 'trade union bureaucracy' – a familiar slogan since the foundation of Comintern – is itself theoretically flaccid. Where does the rank and file end and the bureaucracy begin? In British trade unions, the vast bulk of administrative and representative functions are performed by 'lay' branch and workplace officers rather than full-time officials; in general, the professional officialdom can exercise whatever influence and control they possess only with the assent and co-operation of large sections of this cadre of voluntary activists.[19]

Of course, there are occasions when militant union members are sold out by their leaders. But to make such instances the basis for a general theory of trade unionism is to treat officialdom as scapegoats for contradictions which are inherent in union practice as such. There is indeed a problem of bureaucracy within unions, but the problem is not primarily one of the machinations of a distinctive stratum of personnel; rather, it is a question of a corrosive pattern of *internal social relations*. In this sense, bureaucracy is manifest in a differential distribution of expertise and activism; in a dependence of the mass of union members on the initiative and experience of a relatively small group of leaders – both official *and* 'unofficial'. Such dependence *may* be deliberately fostered by leaders anxious to retain a monopoly of information, experience and negotiating opportunities, and to minimise and control the collective relations among the membership. But it can readily develop even in the absence of such manipulative strategies.

There can be little doubt that this occurred in British trade unionism, particularly in recent years. It is common for trade union activists to bemoan the 'apathy' of most members. Often this implies a somewhat idealised notion of the traditional, committed trade unionist; more importantly, the notion of apathy makes non-active unionists the scapegoats for unions' own failure to involve their membership. In a capitalist society in which notions, on the one hand of individualism, on the other of the common 'national interest' of employers and workers, form part of the 'common sense' of everyday life, unions cannot rely on a *spontaneous* mass identification with principles of working-class collectivism. 'Making trade unionists' has always required a deliberate effort of ideological struggle. But British unions have of late largely abdicated such an effort. This is partly because many have found it possible to boost membership numbers without winning workers' active commitment. Much union growth in the 1970s reflected the spread of closed shop arrangements, bureau-cratically administered by employers deducting subscriptions directly from workers' wages. 'Progressive' companies were happy to operate such 'union membership agreements' as a means of simplifying bargaining structures, preventing inter-union rivalry, and offering union officials the disciplinary sanctions needed to police agreements. Recruitment through such means creates no more than paper trade unionists. And the trend towards largely *passive* union membership has been reinforced by the 'reforms' of collective bargaining which have limited the scope for decentralised control of conditions and have generated more hierarchical shop steward organisations closely involved in high-level relations with senior management.

This helps explain the curious paradox of contemporary British unionism. There is a strong tradition of internal democratic life, of active debate and collective decision-making. Yet most union members regard 'the union' as an alien, bureaucratic and even hostile force. The routines of branch agenda, district committee meetings, conference procedure, of motions, amendments and resolutions, involve a minority distinguished by interest and understanding from the bulk of the membership. Lay activists – who often regard themselves as the authentic voice of the rank and file – may be as far (or even further) removed from the sentiments of their constituents as are full-time officials. Thus union democracy can be reduced to the esoteric pastime of exceptional enthusiasts. It is, of course, this alienation of the majority which provides the considerable working-class assent to current Tory attacks on trade unionism; in particular it explains support for proposals for compulsory introduction of secret individual ballots, an initiative designed to erode still further the collective basis of members' attachment to their unions.

Compromise and collaboration are often regarded as the special prerogatives of union officials; in Wright Mills's famous expression, 'the labor leader is a manager of discontent.'[20] This may in part reflect the material interests and personal ideologies of officialdom; at the very least, to persuade themselves and others of the significance of their role, officials are likely to stress their individual expertise and competence as professional negotiators acting *on behalf* of the members. This can in turn encourage an exaggeration of the importance of reasoned argument within the institutions of collective bargaining, and a depreciation of mass mobilisation and struggle as means of pursuing workers' interests. But compromise and collaboration also reflect the more general contradiction indicated at the outset of this chapter. On the one hand, trade union action can represent a threat to capitalism, an obstacle to the exploitation of workers which profitable production requires. For this reason, most employers in the past and many still today have fiercely resisted unionisation, and governments committed to sustaining capitalist production relations have sought to obstruct or suppress trade unionism. But on the other hand, trade union representation can assist employers and the state in containing the unrest which workers are always liable to express. Through collective bargaining, workers' grievances can be channelled and accommodated, can be made more manageable and predictable. Even strikes can often be anticipated, and their conduct is usually subject to such routines and regulations that their disruptive potential is minimised.

Collective bargaining creates what Gramsci called 'an industrial legality'.[21] Usually this involves some material concessions to workers, but against the continuing background of management domination and economic oppression these concessions are relatively marginal. Though this does not mean that they are made willingly by employers; and in a period of crisis even modest demands may be viewed as intolerable. At the same time, the 'rule of law' which collective bargaining institutes helps stabilise and legitimise the employer's control. The unspoken (or sometimes explicit) condition on which employers and governments are willing to recognise trade unions is that unions in turn should recognise the employer's right to exploit workers, and should restrict their demands and actions to those compatible with continuing profitability. Officials who are directly concerned with the institutional and financial security of their unions are particularly likely to favour a cautious approach to policy; and those who are constantly engaged in bargaining relationships with managers or state functionaries are particularly liable to take for granted the 'rules of the game' which such relationships presuppose. But such pressures are by no means peculiar to 'bureaucrats': they are evident to militant workplace activists as well. In essence, they reflect the problem of union survival in a hostile environment. Short of revolution, workers' representatives have to come to terms with the oppressor – or else they will be smashed. Compromise is unavoidable. The danger is that a truce or a pragmatic limitation of hostilities can become transformed into a permanent peace and collaboration.

Collaboration is encouraged by the traditional sectionalism of trade union practice. Where workers' struggles encompass only a narrow constituency of interest, the broader framework of class relations must normally remain unchallenged. The focus of action is what can realistically be conceded by a single employer or within a single industry; conceptions of possibility are bounded by the 'external coercive laws' of capitalist production which at this level confront management and workforce alike. Economic crisis has reinforced this lesson, as even militant sections of trade unionism have faced a stark choice between acquiescence in employer demands or wholesale closures and job loss. The sectional basis of union action is moreover ideologically as well as materially weakening. Given the widespread interdependence of modern capitalist production, and the extensive dependence of social life on 'services' provided by the state or private capital, disputes involving one group of workers typically have a disruptive impact on others as producers or consumers. Where struggles are not explicitly related to broader class demands and interests, workers rarely attract spontaneous support from fellow trade unionists, who are indeed likely to regard themselves as victims. Hence politicians and the media have little difficulty in mobilising hostility among workers to other workers' strikes.

Sectionalism has other damaging implications for trade unionism. Typically, union officials and activists alike derive disproportionately from relatively advantaged sections of the workforce: male, white, those higher-skilled, higher-paid, in more secure jobs. Holders of 'better' types of job commonly enjoy greater self-confidence, familiarity with official procedures, respect among fellow workers, and identification with work and hence work-related institutions: factors all of which tend to encourage involvement in trade unionism and often pave the way to a 'career' as a union activist. Hence hierarchy within the working class is replicated within trade union organisation. In identifying grievances, selecting demands, formulating strategies and determining priorities, the perspectives and interests of the dominant sections almost inevitably exert disproportionate influence. Correspondingly, the concerns of women, immigrants, lower-skilled, lower-paid, less secure workers (not to mention the unemployed and casually employed) are subordinated or excluded altogether in the agenda of union action.[22] This in turn is likely to weaken their identification with 'the union', creating a further disincentive to active involvement.

Such biases can occur 'spontaneously' even in unions formally committed to egalitarian principles. But they may also be deliberately built in to union policy. Historically, *exclusiveness* has often been a dominant theme of collective action. Craft unionism was founded on the preservation of restricted access to a monopolised area of work, resisting encroachments by other workers as much as by employers. In the present century, controlling entry to the job has often seemed the only means of mitigating the disruptive insecurity of the labour market. But as part of such control, the lines of demarcation have often been based upon criteria of sexism (quite openly, until recently at least) or racism (perhaps more usually, covertly). By such means, trade unionism can not only reflect but actually reinforce divisions and antagonisms within the working class.[23]

The tendencies towards bureaucratic practice, collaborative policy and sectional orientation are all associated with a segregation between union strategy and working-class politics. In Russia at the turn of the century, this 'economism' was denounced by Lenin. In the USA, such 'business unionism' is commonly applauded. In Britain, the majority of the larger unions are affiliated to the Labour Party, and professions of socialism are a familiar part of conference rhetoric. But traditionally there has been a sharp demarcation between 'political action' which is the party's responsibility, and 'industrial relations' where the unions concentrate their attention. Within this sphere, 'free collective bargaining' rather than any form of socialist politics provides the guiding principle. The slogan is in one sense absurd: collective bargaining, necessarily, is in large measure the outcome of the more general balance of class forces; and in recent years it has increasingly been conditioned by state intervention (thus dissolving the artificial boundary between 'industrial relations' and 'politics'). But the preoccupation with collective bargaining has tended to exclude any meaningful attention to the possibilities of social transformation; has entailed fundamental commitment to the parochial interests of each discrete 'bargaining unit'; and has increased the dependence of the ordinary membership on those who display the appropriate 'negotiating skills'. The subordination of politics to collective bargaining has meant that even radical trade union strategies are normally essentially *national* in focus (as, for example, in the case of most demands for import controls); the principles of international class solidarity, of common interests in resisting transnational capital, rarely intrude upon the agenda.

What is to be done? The central argument of this chapter is that trade unions operate within an environment of hostile forces which condition and distort their character and dynamics. Bureaucracy, collaboration, sectionalism and economism are all reflections of those potent external forces. Bureaucracy, collaboration, sectionalism and economism are powerful and often overwhelming tendencies; but they are not uncontradictory and irresistible 'iron laws'. The contradictions inherent in trade unionism – as in the experience and consciousness of workers within capitalist society – create space for socialists. The malleability of unions is doubtless limited: many appear rigid and ossified institutions. But in any union there is some scope for members to fight for more democratic patterns of internal relations; for more radical aims and imaginative forms of struggle; for strategies which broaden solidarity among different groups of workers; for policies informed by socialist politics.

Trade unions are *at one and the same time* part of the problem and part of the solution, a form of resistance to capitalism and a form of integration within capitalism. Trade unions can never become fully anti-capitalist organisations, but socialists can help strengthen their anti-capitalist tendencies. They can never be more than one element in a multiplicity of forms of resistance to capitalism, a resistance which must encompass action in every arena of oppression (and not simply the sphere of wage-labour); but they can form an important and indeed essential element in such a wider movement. In recent years, many socialists have rejected the 'workerism' which for so long dominated the British left: the identification of the working class with a muscular male hewing coal or hammering metal, and the assumption that the trade union militancy associated with such stereotypes was the only valid expression of class struggle. Today it is obvious that we need a broader, more varied conception of the working class; and a far more sensitive appreciation of the range of collective experience and action in which socialist imagination and commitment can be forged. But any credible movement for socialism must still recognise the key importance for analysis and strategy of struggles 'at the point of production'. The collective mobilisation inherent in trade unionism remains the most significant example which we have of sustained working-class challenge to the underlying principles of capitalist society; the struggle for socialism must build, though critically, upon this tradition.

Notes

1. For a critical discussion of such arguments see David Coates, 'The Question of Trade Union Power', in David Coates and Gordon Johnston, *Socialist Arguments*, Oxford, Martin Robertson, 1983.
2. Friedrich Engels, *The Condition of the Working Class in England in 1844*, London, Allen and Unwin, 1968 (reprint of 1892 English edition), pp. 219, 224.
3. Karl Marx, *The First International and After* (ed. David Fernbach), Harmondsworth, Penguin, 1974, p. 91.
4. Letter to Bernstein, 17 June 1879.
5. 'England in 1845 and in 1885', *Commonweal*, 1 March 1885.
6. Letter to Liebknecht, 11 February 1878.
7. Central to Marx's contribution to the analysis of capitalism was his distinction between labour as a process and *labour power* as the commodity exchanged by the worker for wages. On the basis of this distinction it was possible to illuminate the exploitation at the heart of capitalism: the value of the typical worker's contribution to production was typically greater than the value of the commodity, labour power, purchased by the capitalist – who was able to pocket the surplus.
8. Karl Marx, *Capital*, Vol. 1, London, Lawrence and Wishart, 1959, p. 331.
9. This notion was first used in the classic study by Carter Goodrich, *The Frontier of Control*, London, Pluto Press, 1975 (originally published in 1920).
10. For a discussion of official labour statistics see Richard Hyman and Bob Price, 'Labour Statistics', in John Irvine, Ian Miles and Jeff Evans, *Demystifying Social Statistics*, London, Pluto Press, 1979.
11. There is a discrepancy between the analysis of large unions in Table 10.5 and the list given in Table 10.7. It would appear that the Department of Employment figures for NUM and NUT include retired and student members respectively, bringing the totals to over 250 000; that the Royal College of Nursing (a non-TUC body claiming some 214 000 members) is included in the total; and that neither TASS nor the Boilermakers are counted as separate organisations.
12. A far more detailed survey of the main unions, from a somewhat right-wing perspective, is provided by Robert Taylor, *The Fifth Estate*, London, Pan, 1980. Information on the TUC and every affiliated union is given at length in Jack Eaton and Colin Gill, *The Trade Union Directory* (2nd edition), London, Pluto Press, 1983.
13. For a discussion of the various dimensions of strike statistics see Richard Hyman, *Strikes*, London, Macmillan, 1988; and for a historical analysis see James Cronin, *Industrial Conflict in Modern Britain*, London, Croom Helm, 1979.
14. For an interesting case study of such strategies see Theo Nichols and Huw Beynon, *Living with Capitalism*, London, Routledge and Kegan Paul, 1977.
15. By the late 1970s the TUC was able to nominate members to an array of positions (some at substantial salaries) on public bodies; many

members of the General Council occupied multiple positions (see Ken Coates and Tony Topham, *Trade Unions in Britain*, Nottingham, Spokesman, 1980, ch. 4). The Thatcher government has cut back on this 'quango' system and in particular on the number of trade union appointments.

16. Perry Anderson, 'The Limits and Possibilities of Trade Union Action', in Robin Blackburn and Alexander Cockburn (eds), *The Incompatibles*, Harmondsworth, Penguin, 1967, pp. 264–5.
17. Antonio Gramsci, *Selections from Political Writings 1910–20* (ed. Quintin Hoare), London, Lawrence and Wishart, 1977, p. 265.
18. I have made this point more fully in 'The Politics of Workplace Trade Unionism', *Capital and Class*, No. 8, Summer 1979.
19. The British situation with its tradition of lay involvement contrasts sharply with the context in which Michels developed his notion of an 'iron law of oligarchy' at the beginning of the century: a German labour movement top-heavy with full-time officials.
20. C. Wright Mills, *The New Men of Power*, New York, Harcourt Brace, 1948, p. 9.
21. Gramsci, *Selections from Political Writings*.
22. The most detailed analysis of such tendencies has focused on sexism in trade unions; see, for example, Jenny Beale, *Getting It Together*, London, Pluto Press, 1983 and Anne Phillips, *Hidden Hands*, London, Pluto Press, 1983.
23. See, for example, Jill Rubery, 'Structured Labour Markets, Worker Organisation and Low Pay', *Cambridge Journal of Economics*, Vol. 2, No. 1, March 1978.

Index

AEU 234
Allen, S. 144
Allen, V. L. 44, 47, 52, 94, 100, 118, 140
Anderson, P. 245, 253
Arnold, E. 200f
ASTMS 237

Bain, G. S. 186, 232ff
Baldamus, W. 31, 52
Balfour Committee 4
Barbash, J. 103, 118
Barker, C. 161, 164
Barker, D. L. 144
Batstone, E. V. 112, 118, 163f, 192, 201
Beale, J. 253
Bean, R. 117f
Becker, H. S. 31, 52
Beechey, V. 145
Belgium 36
Bendix, R. 30, 51f
Bentham, J. 56
Bentley, A. F. 58
Berger, S. 196, 201
Bergmann, J. 145
Betriebsrat Ch. 9 passim
Beynon, H. 33, 35, 40, 52, 127, 158, 162ff, 252
Blackaby, F. 186
Blackburn, R. 142
Bloom, G. C. 91
Booth, C. 4
Boraston, I. 112, 118, 142, 163f
Braverman, H. 129, 142f
Brecher, J. 109, 118
Brough, I. 25, 50, 52, 95
Brown, R. 145
Brown, W. A. 25f, 52, 162, 164, 187, 190, 201
Bullock Committee 94, 217
Burawoy, M. 189, 196, 201f, 204, 217, 222

Canada 105
Carchedi, G. 23, 52, 131, 142, 144
Carpenter, L. P. 88
Carpenter, M. 163
cash limits 169, 186, 242
Chadwick, M. 191, 201
Chamberlain, N. W. 70, 77f, 91, 94, 122
Chile 44
Clack, G. 165
Clegg, H. A. 8, Ch. 3 passim, 140, 142, 164
Cliff, T. 50, 52, 142, 161, 164
closed shop 37, 178f, 192, 246f
coal-mining 37, 43, 143, 198, 231, 240f
Coates, D. 252
Coates, K. 253
COHSE 238
Cole, G. D. H 6, 63, 88f
comité d'entreprise Ch. 9 passim
commissione interna Ch. 9 passim
Commission on Industrial Relations (USA) 4, 138
Commons, J. R. 136
Comte, A. 141
consiglio di fabbrica Ch. 9 passim
corporatism 97, 107f, 136, 145, 151, 154, 157, 172f, Ch. 8 passim, 218, 244
Coser, L. A. 102, 118, 122, 139
Craig, A. W. J. 139f
Crick, B. 88
Cronin, J. E. 109, 111, 116, 118, 252
Crouch, C. 115, 118, 145, 189, 201, 217, 222
Cutler, T. 142

Dahl, R. A. 60, 82f, 88, 122
Dahrendorf, R. 60, 89, 122
Daniel, W. W. 186f, 190, 201
Davidson, R. 18
Delamotte, Y. 214, 222

Doeringer, P. B. 131, 144
Donovan Commission 8ff, 18, 39,
    52, 65, 68, 71, 76, 85f, 93, 151ff,
    163f, 186, 203, 222
Dubin, R. 98, 102, 118f, 122, 139
Dubois, P. 103f, 118
Duguit, L. 57, 88
Duhm, R. 142
Dunlop, J. T. 84, 91, 95, 121f, 138
Durand, C. 103f, 118
Durkheim, E. 57, 70f, 88, 93, 95,
    122, 141

Eaton, J. 252
economism 45f, 51, 136, 226, 245,
    250
Edwardes, M. 190, 201
Edwards, P. K. 116, 118, 206, 222
Edwards, R. C. 144, 193, 196, 201
EEPTU 237
Eldridge, J. E. T. 61, 85, 89
Elger, T. 142, 186
Employment Acts 225
Engels, F. 49f, 52, 125, 140, 225,
    252
Erbès-Seguin, S. 214, 222

'fair day's work' 21, 30, 49, 229
Faulkner, W. 200f
Feuille, P. 139
Figgis, J. N. 57
Fine, B. 142
Flanders, A. 9, 18, 41, 52, Ch. 3
    passim, 140, 190, 201
Fox, A. 18, 29, 31, 34, 39, 44, 52,
    Ch. 3 *passim*, 194, 201
France 106, 113, 127, Ch. 9 *passim*,
    238
Frenkel, S. 112, 118, 164
Friedman, A. L. 142ff, 163f, 192f,
    201
frontier of control 32f, 38, 47f, 229,
    242
Fryer, R. H. 87, 138, 163
Fulcher, J. 219, 222
Furnivall, J. S. 89

Galbraith, J. K. 64, 91
Germany 116, 127, 143, 195, 197,

Ch. 9 *passim*, 238, 253
Gershuny, J. 200f
Giddens, A. 143
Gierke, O. 56f, 88
Gill, C. 252
Glaberman, M. 114, 118
Glass, S. T. 88
Glyn, A. 50, 52, 142
GMB 234
Goldthorpe, J. H. 85f, 91f, 141,
    192, 201
Goodrich, C. L. 33, 36, 52, 252
Gorz, A. 144
Gouldner, A. W. 16, 19, 52, 93
Gourevitch, P. 207, 222
Gramsci, A. 40, 52, 114, 118, 141,
    161, 163, 165, 181, 187, 203,
    245, 248, 253
Griffin, J. I. 102, 118
groupe d'expression 209
guild socialism 59, 63, 88

Hall, S. 186
Harris, L. 142
Hartman, P. T. 104, 106, 119, 122,
    139
Herding, R. G. 40f, 52, 115, 118,
    144
Hibbs, D. 105f, 117f
Hill, J. M. 98, 118
Hill, S. 33, 52
Hirsch, F. 16, 19
Hobsbawm, E. J. 187
Hoxie, R. F. 136

Industrial Relations Act 48, 187,
    211
Italy 106, 114f, 127, 142, Ch. 9
    passim, 238

Jackson, D. 50, 53
Jacobi, O. 143
Jacques, M. 186
James, W. 56f, 87f
Johnson, T. 143
Joseph, K. 225

Kahn-Freund, O. 83
Karsh, B. 102, 109, 111, 118

Kelly, J. 197, 201
Kerr, C. 60ff, 67, 84, 89, 91, 95, 98, 119, 122, 138f
Kern, H. 127, 142, 197, 201
Kilpatrick, A. 186
Kornhauser, A. 98, 139
Korpi, W. 107, 117ff, 219, 222
Korsch, K. 126, 140

Labour Party 44f, 167f, 174f, 206, 241, 250
laissez-faire 10f, 46f, 168, 206
Lane, T. 162, 165
Lange, P. 205, 222
Laski, H. 56ff, 88
Lawson, T. 186
Lenin, V. I. 45, 51, 136, 164, 226, 250
Lipset, S. M. 82, 94
Lockwood, D. 143
Lukács, G. 141
Lukes, S. 89
Luxemburg, R. 126, 140

McCarthy, W. E. J. 18, 39, 53, 163, 165
McKersie, R. B. 102, 119, 139
Macpherson, C. B. 55, 88
Mallet, S. 144
Mandel, E. 143
Mann, M. 45f, 53
Marcuse, H. 17, 19, 89
Marglin, S. 50, 53
Martin, A. 208, 222
Martin, K. 56, 88
Marx, K. 21f, 28f, 43, 49ff, 53, 100, 117, 119, Ch. 5 *passim*, 225f, 228, 252
Merton, R. K. 14, 19
Michels, R. 113, 156, 181, 226, 253
Miliband, R. 45, 53, 89, 124, 133, 140, 145
Millward, N. 186f, 190, 201
Milne-Bailey, W. 89f
Mills, C. W. 13f, 18, 40, 53, 89, 117, 119, 124, 140, 162, 165, 247, 253
Miners' Next Step 158
Montgomery, D. 115f, 119

Moore, W. E. 63, 91
MSF 238
Mückenberger, U. 144
Müller-Jentsch, W. 146

NALGO 232, 240
NAS/UWT 238
National Board for Prices and Incomes 50
National Economic Development Council 169, 198, 224, 239
Neale, J. 187
negotiation of order 32, 34f
Negrelli, S. 216, 222
new unionism 4
NGA 186
Nicholls, D. 56, 58f, 88
Nichols, T. 50, 53, 142, 163, 165, 252
Nicolaus, M. 143
Northrup, H. R. 91
NUM 252
NUPE 163, 238
NUT 238, 252

O'Connor, J. 145
Offe, C. 110, 114, 119, 145, 181, 187

Paci, M. 144
Panitch, L. 117, 119, 189, 201, 218, 222
Parker, S. R. 39, 163, 165
Parsons, T. 71, 92, 121f
Pateman, C. 88
Perlman, S. 136
Phillips, A. 253
Piore, M. J. 131, 143, 196ff, 201
Pizzorno, A. 115, 117ff, 145, 217, 222
Pontusson, J. 209, 219, 222
Poulantzas, N. 145
Price, R. J. 187, 232ff, 252

quality circles 171, 190, 211, 215, 244

racism 35, 132, 199, 250
rank and file 42, 48, Ch. 6 *passim*, 219, 244ff

Red International of Labour
    Unions 136, 162, 181
Regini, M. 193, 201, 205, 222
Rimmer, M. 164
Roberts, G. 162, 165
Ross, A. M. 98, 104, 106, 119, 122,
    139
Ross, N. 65ff, 92
Rousseau, J.-J. 30
Rubery, J. 144, 199, 201, 253
Ruskin, J. 17
Russell, B. 15, 19

Sabel, C. 197f, 201
Schelling, T. C. 102, 119
Schumann, M. 127, 142, 197, 201
Schumpeter, J. 58f, 72, 82, 88,
    122
Scott, W. H. 117, 119
sectionalism 27f, 43, 130ff, 151,
    169, 179f, 199, 226, 245, 248f
Selekman, B. M. 64, 91
sexism 34f, 132, 199, 250
Shalev, M. 106f, 117ff
shop stewards 9, 39, 41f, 86, 108,
    112, 115, Ch. 6 *passim*, 171,
    179, 190f, Ch. 9 *passim*, 241,
    243, 245, 247
Shorter, E. 105, 111, 113, 119
Simitis, S. 217, 222
Simmel, G. 60, 122
skill 33, 192, 195, 226
Slichter, S. H. 63f, 91
Smelser, N. 138
Snyder, D. 105, 119
Sorge, A. 204f, 218, 222
South Africa 111
soviets 203
Stearns, P. N. 117, 119
Strauss, A. 32, 53
Strauss, G. 139
Streeck, W. 108, 119, 197, 201,
    212, 223
strikes 44, Ch. 4 *passim*, 171f, 180,
    217, 224, 226, 241, 243f, 248
    General Strike 1926 76f, 206,
        241
    London Docks 1889 4
    miners 1972 241

miners 1974 76f
miners 1984–5 200
Sturmthal, A. 203, 223
Sutcliffe, B. 50, 52, 142
Sweden 36, 107
Sykes, A. J. M. 33, 51, 53

Taft-Hartley Act (USA) 64, 91
Tallard, M. 215, 223
TASS 237, 252
Taylor, R. 252
technology 32, 35, 129, 170, 196,
    198, 213, 228
Terry, M. 162, 164, 186, 191, 201,
    211, 223
TGWU 170, 234, 242
Thatcher, M. 169, 171, 173ff, 178,
    183, 186, 189ff, 198, 211, 227,
    242, 245, 253
Therborn, G. 221, 223
Thompson, E. P. 141
Tilly, C. 105, 111, 113, 119
Tocqueville, A. de 59
Trades Union Congress 44, 154,
    167, 169, 172ff, 189f, 198, 220,
    238ff, 252
Treu, T. 216, 223
Trist, E. L. 98, 118
Turner, H. A. 53, 91, 163, 165

UCATT 237
unemployment 5, 8, 14, 30, 37, 48,
    169, 173, 183, 193, 196f, 199,
    207f, 218, 221, 229, 231, 241f
USA 18, 24, 36f, 41, 56, 58f, 61,
    105, 115f, 120ff, 131, 139, 142,
    144, 195, 203f, 239, 250
USDAW 236
USSR 58

Wagner Act (USA) 63, 91
Walton, P. 143
Walton, R. E. 102, 119, 139
War Labor Board (USA) 204
Webb, B. 5ff, 10, 15, 18, 53, 62f,
    70, 84, 89, 94, 136, 139, 162, 165
Webb, S. 5ff, 10, 14f, 53, 62f, 70,
    84, 89, 94, 136, 139, 165
Weber, M. 130, 141, 143, 145, 162

Wiesenthal, H.   110, 114, 119, 181, 187
Whitley Committee   4, 138
Wilkinson, F.   53
Wolff, C. von   56

Wolff, R. P.   82, 89
Wood, S. J.   138
Worsley, P.   141

Zoll, R.   146, 199, 201